P9-BYK-169

THERE IS A DREADFUL HELL,
AND EVERLASTING PAINS;
THERE SINNERS MUST WITH DEVILS DWELL
IN DARKNESS, FIRE, AND CHAINS.

Isaac Watts (1674-1748) *from Divine and Moral Songs for Children. 1720.*

YOU DON'T HAVE TO STAY ANYWHERE FOREVER.

Edwin Paine (1901-1914), *in conversation, December 1990.*

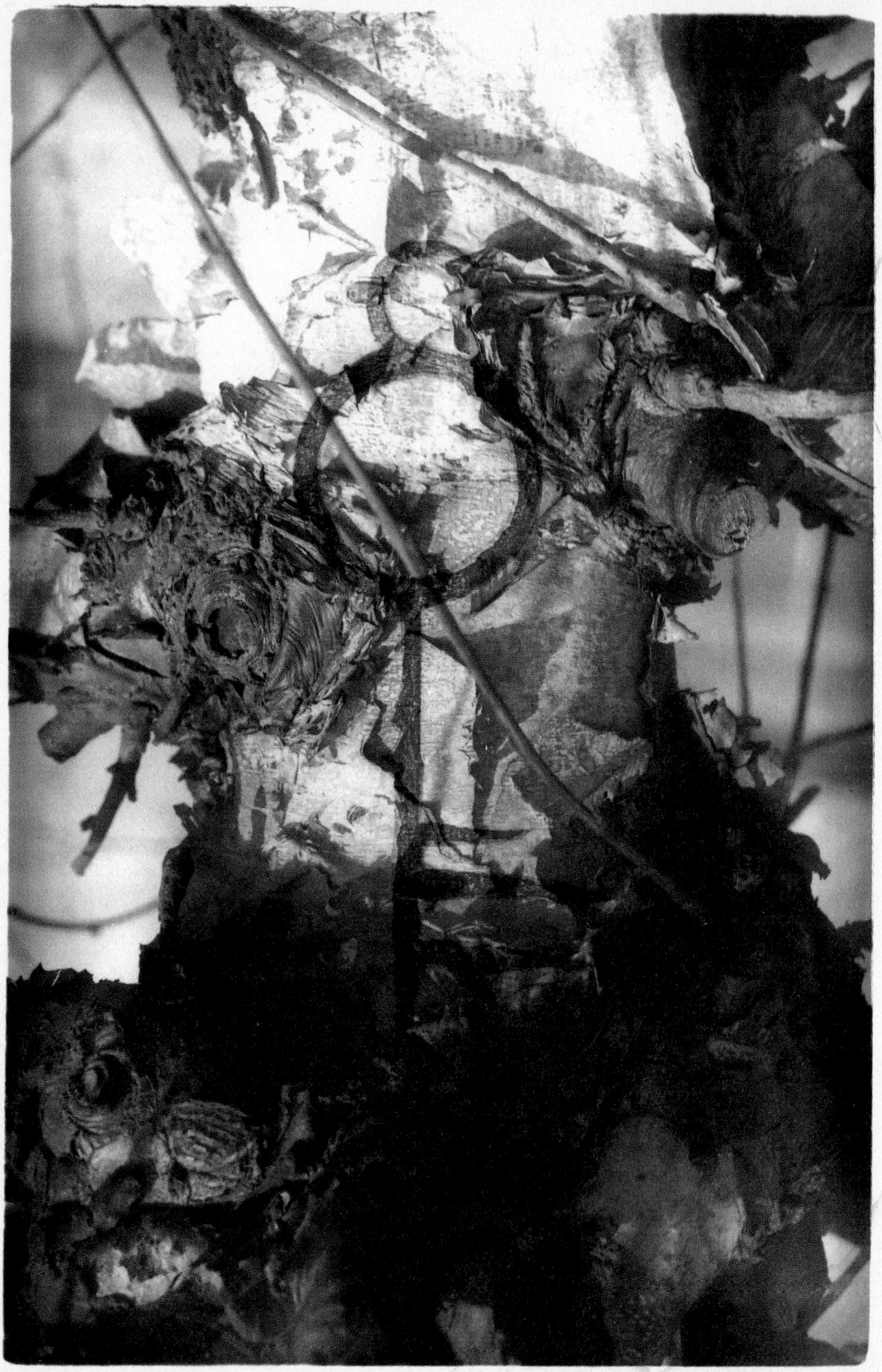

the SANDMAN

SEASON OF MISTS

writer   **NEIL GAIMAN**

artists   **KELLEY JONES**
              MIKE DRINGENBERG
              MALCOLM JONES III
              MATT WAGNER
              DICK GIORDANO
              GEORGE PRATT
              P. CRAIG RUSSELL

letterer   **TODD KLEIN**

colorists   **STEVE OLIFF**
              DANIEL VOZZO

covers   **DAVE McKEAN**

Introduction by
HARLAN ELLISON

Featuring characters created by
NEIL GAIMAN, SAM KIETH, MIKE DRINGENBERG

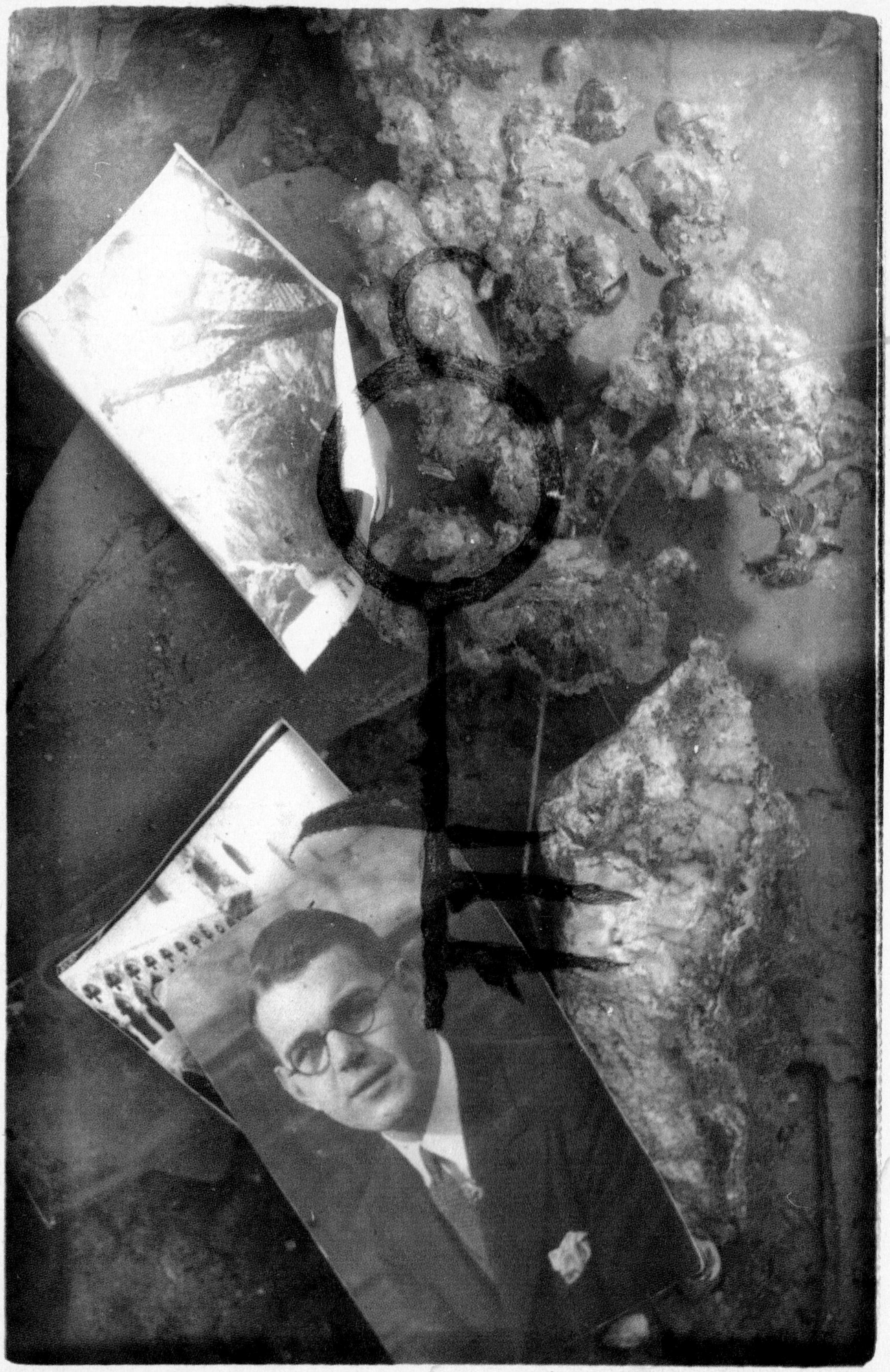

the SANDMAN: SEASON OF MISTS

Published by DC Comics.
Cover and compilation
copyright © 1992 DC Comics.
All Rights Reserved.

Originally published in single
magazine form as THE SANDMAN
21-28. Copyright © 1990, 1991
DC Comics. All Rights Reserved.

Introduction copyright © 1992
Kilimanjaro Corp.

All characters, their distinctive
likenesses and related elements
featured in this publication are
trademarks of DC Comics.
The stories, characters and
incidents featured in this
publication are entirely fictional.
DC Comics does not read or
accept unsolicited submissions
of ideas, stories or artwork.

Cover and publication design
by DAVE McKEAN.

DC Comics
1700 Broadway
New York, NY 10019

A Warner Bros.
Entertainment Company.
Printed in Canada.
Twelfth printing

ISBN: 1-56389-041-0
ISBN 13: 978-1-56389-041-3

DC Comics

*vp-executive editor
& editor-original series*
KAREN BERGER

editor-collected edition
BOB KAHAN

senior art director
ROBBIN BROSTERMAN

president & publisher
PAUL LEVITZ

vp-design & dc direct creative
GEORG BREWER

senior vp-creative director
RICHARD BRUNING

senior vp-finance & operations
PATRICK CALDON

vp-finance
CHRIS CARAMALIS

vp-managing editor
TERRI CUNNINGHAM

senior vp-sales & marketing
STEPHANIE FIERMAN

vp-manufacturing
ALISON GILL

vp-book trade sales
RICH JOHNSON

vp-general manager-wildstorm
HANK KANALZ

senior vp & general counsel
LILLIAN LASERSON

editorial director-wildstorm
JIM LEE

senior vp-business & legal affairs
PAULA LOWITT

vp-advertising & custom publishing
DAVID MCKILLIPS

vp-business development
JOHN NEE

senior vp-creative affairs
GREGORY NOVECK

senior vp-brand management
CHERYL RUBIN

vp-business development, dc direct
JEFF TROJAN

vp-sales
BOB WAYNE

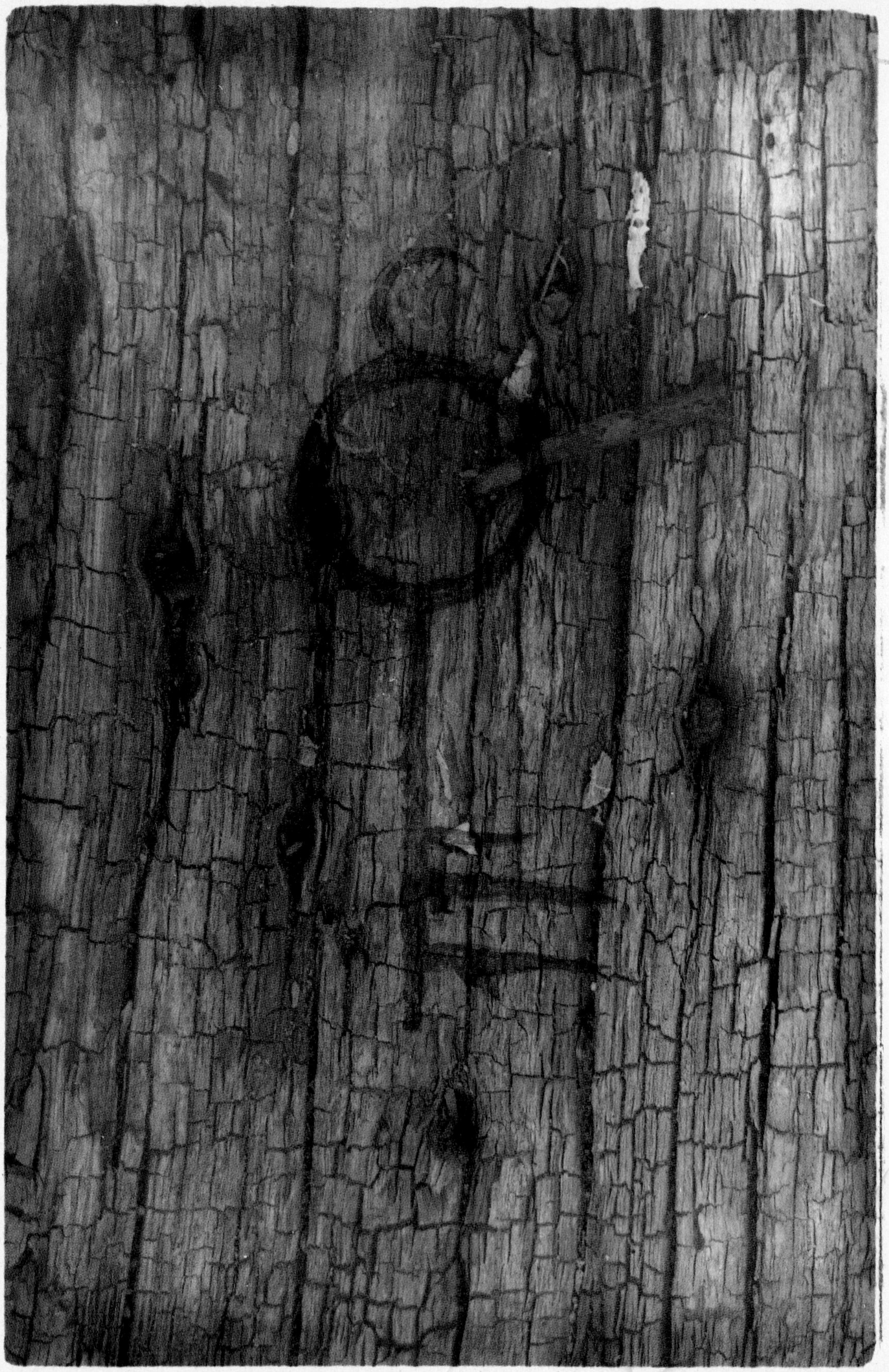

introduction

by HARLAN ELLISON

Possibly the only dismaying aspect of excellence is that it makes living in a world of mediocrity an ongoing prospect of living hell. The subtle distressing perturbation.

Michelangelo wrote: "Trifles make perfection and perfection is no trifle." Hardly a sentiment for our times, for a world of assembly lines and buck-passing and litterbugs.

Perfection. Excellence. What a passionate lover. But once having tasted the lips of excellence, once having given oneself to its perfection, how dreary and burdensome and filled with anomie are the remainder of one's waking hours trapped in the shackled lock-step of the merely ordinary, the barely acceptable, the just okay and not a stroke better.

Sadly, most lives are fashioned on that pattern. Settling for what is possible; buying into the cliché because the towering dream is out of stock; learning how to avoid taking the risk of the dizzying leap. Miguel de Unamuno (1864–1936) wrote: "In order to attain the impossible one must attempt the absurd." So the paradigm becomes all the Salieri shadows unable to touch the Mozart reality, all the respectably-talented but not awesomely-endowed Antonios fulminating with frustration at the occasional Amadeus. Excellence in the untalented and ordinary produces pleasure and awe; but in the minimally-talented it produces hatred and envy that boils like sheep fat.

Excellence is its own master, owes no allegiance, bows its head to no regimen. It exists pure and whole like the silver face of the moon. Untouchable, unreachable, exquisite. But frustrating because it reminds us of how much mediocrity we put up with, just to get through the week.

The point being: Neil Gaiman's work on *The Sandman*.

In any field of endeavor, in any medium of the arts or sciences, an occasional talent will manifest itself and, through bare existence, we perceive how mundane has been the effort in that field or genre, that medium or category. Until Monteverdi, was there higher achievement than that of Palestrina, Wm. Byrd, Andrea Gabrieli? Before Mark Twain, what were the names of the writers at the pinnacle: Sir Walter Scott, R.D. Blackmore, James Fenimore Cooper? Prior to John L. Sullivan, can anyone make a rational comparison of excellence with any of the nameless bare-knuckle champions who spilled their blood in sawdust arenas? There was only one Machiavelli, only one Chaka Zulu, only one Alexander of Macedon. Name the highest and brightest and most accomplished till you get to Fellini or Billie Holiday or George Bernard Shaw; and compare; and recognize how much higher thereafter is the high water mark. Suddenly, there is more sunlight in the world.

The point being: Neil Gaiman's work on *The Sandman*.

This is remarkable work. Perhaps you know that already. Nonetheless, I tell you. A fact: do with it what you will.

It is not merely that Mr. Gaiman (who is midway between being a frequent acquaintance and a close friend of mine, something more than a pal but less than an intimate, and thus available to me as "Neil" rather than "Mr. Gaiman") has committed with these Sandman stories what is usually known as *macrography*, "huge writing," work that is to be examined with

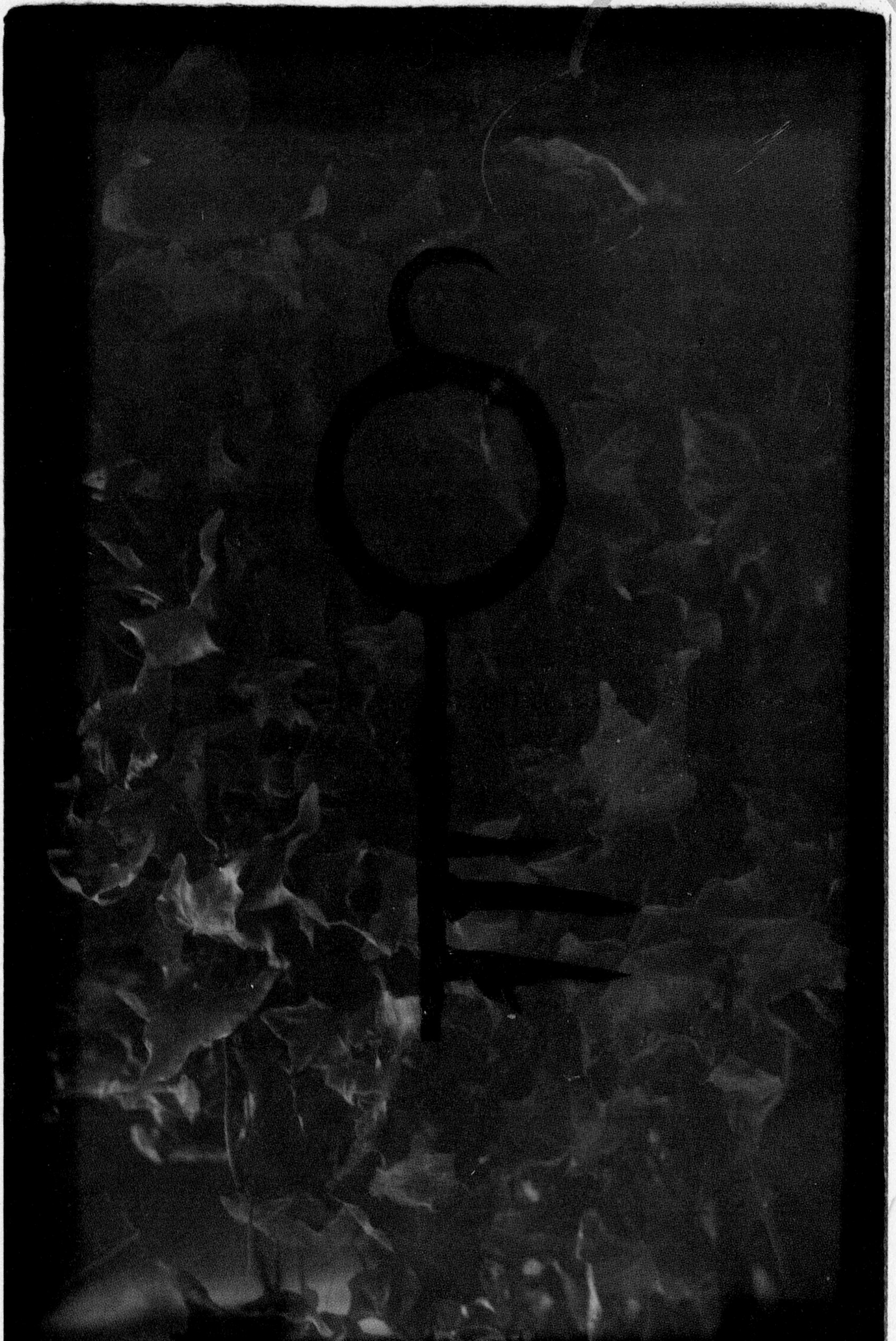

the naked eye, the opposite of *micrography*. Nor is it unique that Neil has created a compelling internally-consistent universe for these stories: a fully-realized cosmology with a pantheon of beings and godlike non-beings, a non-Aristotelian superimposed pre-continuum, a freshly-minted polytheism as compelling as it is revisionist. Hardly unique, because *every* fantasist builds a new universe each time s/he creates a new story. It's the way the game of "what-if?" is played. Some people do it better than others; and most people can't do it at all (which is why there are folks who believe actors make up their own lines, that truth is stranger than fiction, that one picture is worth a thousand words, and that we are regularly visited by far-traveling malevolent incredibly intelligent aliens in revolving crockery, who have nothing better to do with their time than snag couch potato humans so they can have unfulfilling sex with them and just for laughs give these lousy sex partners rectal examinations with mechanical appendages the size of oil pipeline caissons); and every once in a while a person does it so splendidly that it raises the high water mark and puts more sunlight into the world.

The point being: Neil Gaiman's work on *The Sandman*.

Notwithstanding the macrography and the new cosmology, the runaway excellence of what Neil has done with this character is wrapped up in the sense one gets, as one reads *The Sandman*, that what one is reading is *new*, is of consequence, and isn't as transitory (however entertaining) as most of what is done day-in-and-day-out in comics. If you have been following the progression of Neil as guiding intelligence on *The Sandman* —

(Available for the aficionado in three previous graphic novels — PRELUDES & NOCTURNES, THE DOLL'S HOUSE and DREAM COUNTRY — and even as a boxed set of the trio as THE WORLD OF THE SANDMAN.)

— you will have been snared by an outstanding intellect given to esoteric amusements and surreal re-viewings of the Natural Order. You will certainly (if you're one of the few surviving atavists who still read for the pure pleasure of intellectual invigoration) have been mesmerized by the sneaky wit and puckish nastiness of the Gaiman reformation of the received universe. I would praise his erudition, his frequent seeding of the stories with arcane facts and literary glyphs, but as it is a truism that it takes a *very* good con artist to con a very good con artist, so it is possible that Neil "Scam Man" Gaiman is no more widely-read and filled with erudition than the con artist who writes these words of introduction. And, knowing what a fraud *I* am, quoting here and there in Latin and colloquial French just to seem clever, *ignorantia legis neminem excusat*, like *n'est-ce pas*, I have my suspicions that Neil has as diverse and bellyful a library of references as I maintain just to drop in something obscure to remind the groundlings what a smart cookie I am.

Not to be diverted too long on that preceding point, but let me give you a f'rinstance:

Early on in the story of SEASON OF MISTS, when Morpheus sends Cain to deliver the message of his imminent visit to the nether regions, the emissary tells Lucifer what is about to transpire, and the fallen angel goes off into one of those wonderful rhapsodic panegyrics all mad scientists, despots, nitwit super-villains and televangelists indulge in for many odd-shaped panels. He culminates his paralogical blather by ranting, "Better to reign in hell, than serve in heav'n."

And just in case the reader hasn't seen the 1941 Warner Bros. adaptation of Jack London's THE SEA WOLF, in which Edward G. Robinson as the tyrannical freighter skipper Wolf Larsen quotes that quotation repeatedly, Neil bangs us over the head with the information that the aphorism comes from Milton's PARADISE LOST (1667). Leaf ahead to that page and take a look at it.

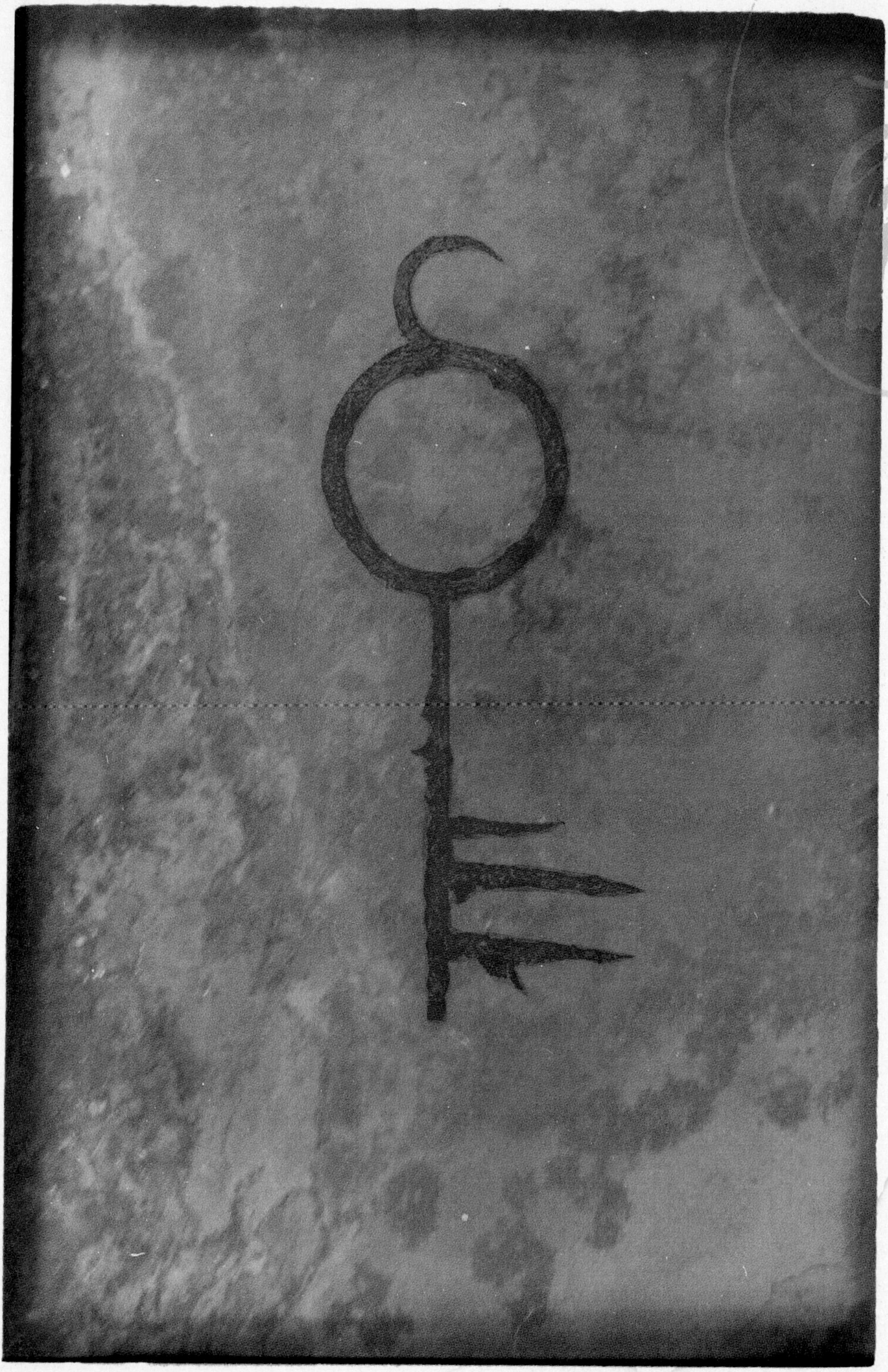

See what I mean? A *really* intellectual guy, secure in his own voluminous erudition, wouldn't have bothered making sure we know how goddam sharp he is. Now, I'm not saying Neil *isn't* as sharp as he wants us to believe he is, I'm merely suggesting that he is so intent on building all the buttressing into his fictional structure that he makes certain we perceive of what excellent granite is made the basement slab.

So excellent that one might quote yet again from Milton: "The mind is its own place, and in itself can make a Heav'n of Hell, a Hell of Heav'n."

The point being: Neil Gaiman's work on *The Sandman* is so excellent, so much a presentation of the new high water mark, that we realize as we read, that it is *about something*, that it is not merely an amusing entertainment. (Though it is *that*, of course.)

I'll not reconnoiter the story in this graphic novel … what originally appeared in monthly comic book format as sections 0 through 7, December 1990–July 1991. The story lies before you, and I wasn't engaged to restate the obvious. (As critic John Simon wrote in 1981: "… there is no point in saying less than your predecessors have said." Which is good advice that should be taken by all those who write Sherlock Holmes or Sam Spade pastiches.) Nor will I play the role of the carping bluejay, shrieking that Neil says in the earliest section of the story that Destiny casts no shadow, but Dringenberg has repeatedly scumbled in shadows only pages earlier. That sort of petty bitching is beneath me, a guy as clever as I am.

I will only repeat the theme of this preamble by reporting that excellence, as contained in the work of Gaiman's *Sandman*, has made the awareness of the mediocre world extremely painful for a great many people. I know this to be true, for I sat there at the 13th annual World Fantasy Convention in Tucson in 1991 and watched with devilish pleasure as Neil won the highly-prized FantasyCon "Howard Philips Lovecraft" trophy for the Year's Best Short Story … an issue of *The Sandman* "comic book." Devilish pleasure, I tell you, because all those artsy-fartsy writers and artists and critics sitting there expecting a standard-print short story to win, choked on their little almond cups as this renegade funnybook guy carted off the Diamond as Big as the Ritz. Much snorting through the nose. Much umbrage taken. Many dudgeons raised to new heights. And screams and cries of foul play at the polls. So infuriated were the Faithful at such a choice having been made by a blue ribbon panel of experts who couldn't be suborned or shamed into overlooking excellence, that the Great Gray Eminences who run the FantasyCon from behind their nightshadow veil of secrecy, have rewritten the rules so that, heaven forfend, no "comic book" will ever again be nominated, much less have an opportunity to kick serious artistic butt.

The point being: Neil Gaiman's work on *The Sandman* brings that perennial DC Comics character, whom I first loved in 1940 in the 96-page 15¢ *New York World's Fair Comics*, with his green business suit, his orange-colored snapbrim fedora, his fuchsia cape, his World War I doughboy gas mask and his deadly gas gun, into a refurbished state of rebirth, transmogrified for our angst-festooned era, not merely as a marvelous and entertaining myth-figure, but as the symbol of excellence in a world where mediocrity is our normal prison.

And how do we know that what Gaiman has done is excellence?

We know it because of something critic Susan Sontag wrote. She said, "Real Art has the capacity to make us nervous."

Nervous. You should've been there at the awards ceremony. Those suckers like as almost laid square bricks.

The point being: isn't this Gaiman just too cute for words!

In which a family reunion occasions certain personal recriminations; assorted events are set in motion; and a relationship thought long done with proves to have much relevance today.

Episode 0

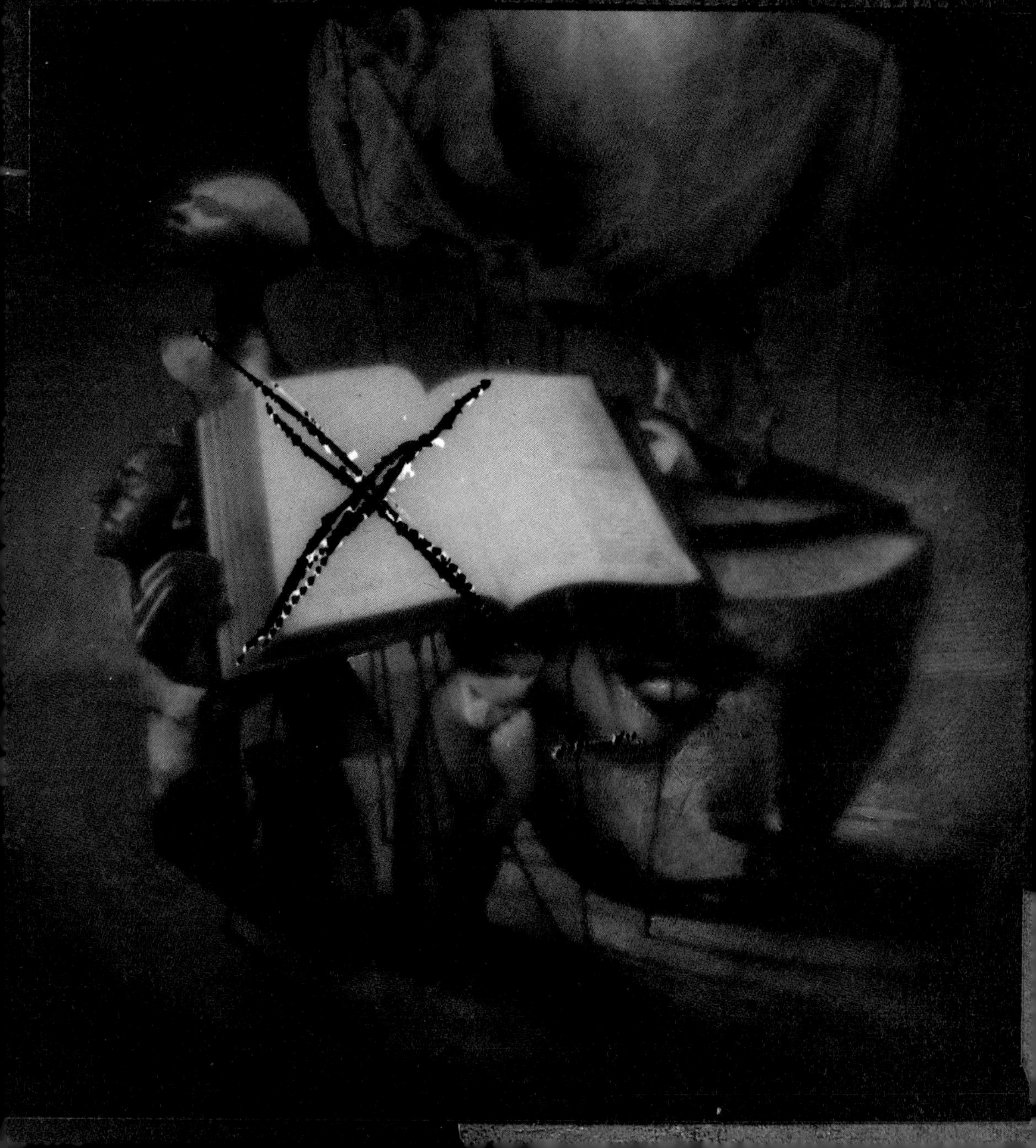

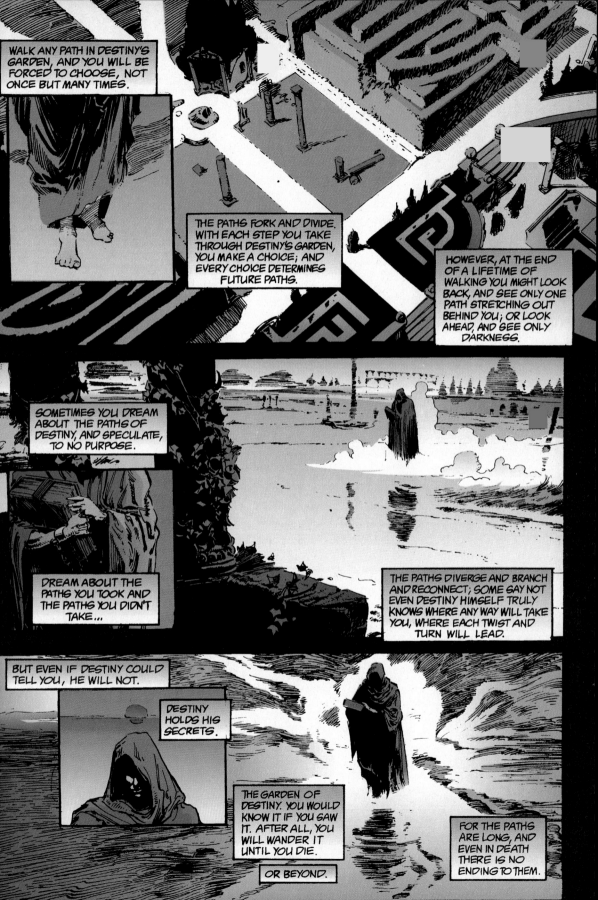

WALK ANY PATH IN DESTINY'S GARDEN, AND YOU WILL BE FORCED TO CHOOSE, NOT ONCE BUT MANY TIMES.

THE PATHS FORK AND DIVIDE. WITH EACH STEP YOU TAKE THROUGH DESTINY'S GARDEN, YOU MAKE A CHOICE; AND EVERY CHOICE DETERMINES FUTURE PATHS.

HOWEVER, AT THE END OF A LIFETIME OF WALKING YOU MIGHT LOOK BACK, AND SEE ONLY ONE PATH STRETCHING OUT BEHIND YOU; OR LOOK AHEAD, AND SEE ONLY DARKNESS.

SOMETIMES YOU DREAM ABOUT THE PATHS OF DESTINY, AND SPECULATE, TO NO PURPOSE.

DREAM ABOUT THE PATHS YOU TOOK AND THE PATHS YOU DIDN'T TAKE...

THE PATHS DIVERGE AND BRANCH AND RECONNECT; SOME SAY NOT EVEN DESTINY HIMSELF TRULY KNOWS WHERE ANY WAY WILL TAKE YOU, WHERE EACH TWIST AND TURN WILL LEAD.

BUT EVEN IF DESTINY COULD TELL YOU, HE WILL NOT.

DESTINY HOLDS HIS SECRETS.

THE GARDEN OF DESTINY. YOU WOULD KNOW IT IF YOU SAW IT. AFTER ALL, YOU WILL WANDER IT UNTIL YOU DIE.

OR BEYOND.

FOR THE PATHS ARE LONG, AND EVEN IN DEATH THERE IS NO ENDING TO THEM.

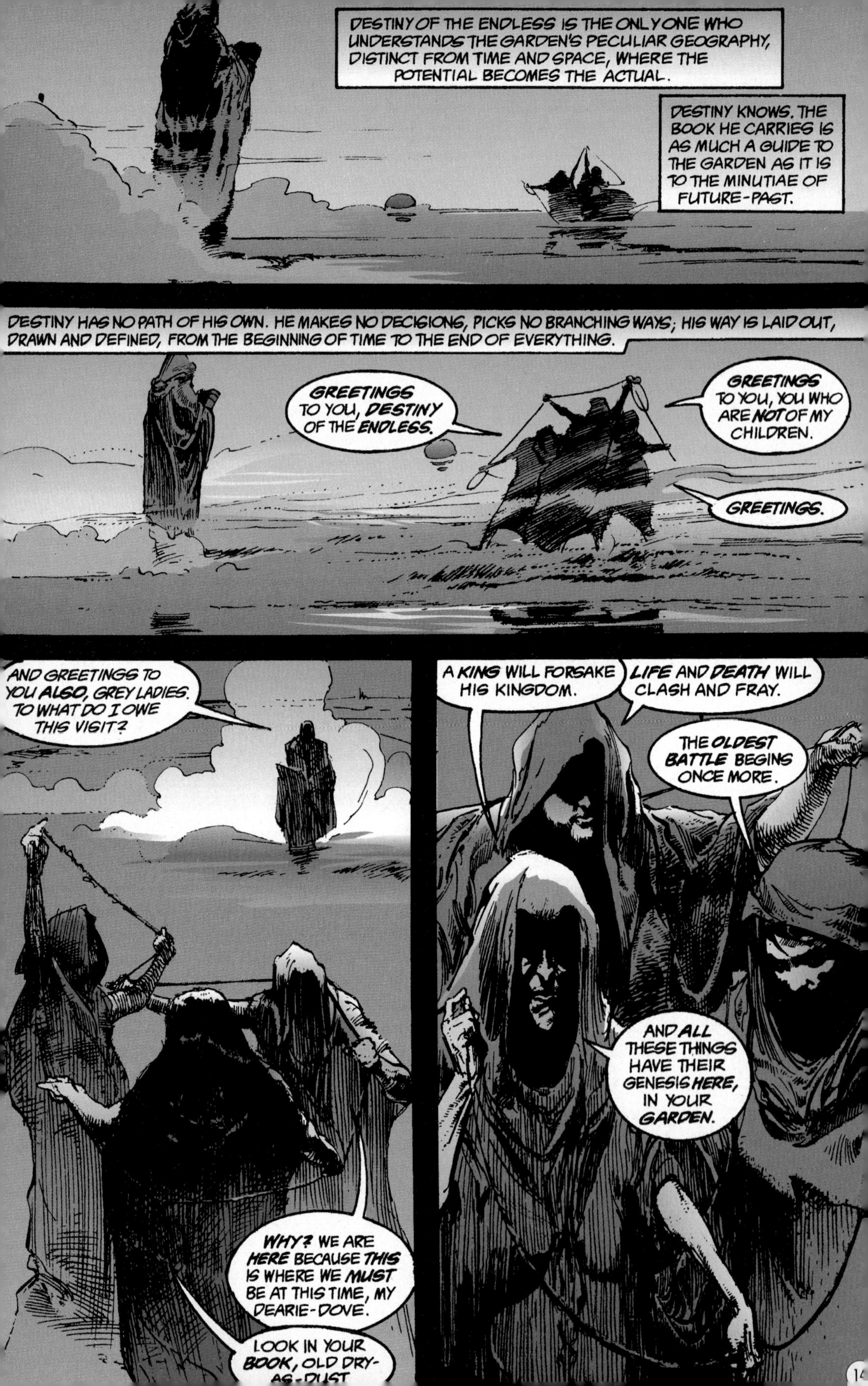
DESTINY OF THE ENDLESS IS THE ONLY ONE WHO UNDERSTANDS THE GARDEN'S PECULIAR GEOGRAPHY, DISTINCT FROM TIME AND SPACE, WHERE THE POTENTIAL BECOMES THE ACTUAL.
DESTINY KNOWS. THE BOOK HE CARRIES IS AS MUCH A GUIDE TO THE GARDEN AS IT IS TO THE MINUTIAE OF FUTURE-PAST.
DESTINY HAS NO PATH OF HIS OWN. HE MAKES NO DECISIONS, PICKS NO BRANCHING WAYS; HIS WAY IS LAID OUT, DRAWN AND DEFINED, FROM THE BEGINNING OF TIME TO THE END OF EVERYTHING.
GREETINGS TO YOU, DESTINY OF THE ENDLESS.
GREETINGS TO YOU, YOU WHO ARE NOT OF MY CHILDREN.
GREETINGS.
AND GREETINGS TO YOU ALSO, GREY LADIES. TO WHAT DO I OWE THIS VISIT?
WHY? WE ARE HERE BECAUSE THIS IS WHERE WE MUST BE AT THIS TIME, MY DEARIE-DOVE.
LOOK IN YOUR BOOK, OLD DRY-
A KING WILL FORSAKE HIS KINGDOM.
LIFE AND DEATH WILL CLASH AND FRAY.
THE OLDEST BATTLE BEGINS ONCE MORE.
AND ALL THESE THINGS HAVE THEIR GENESIS HERE, IN YOUR GARDEN.

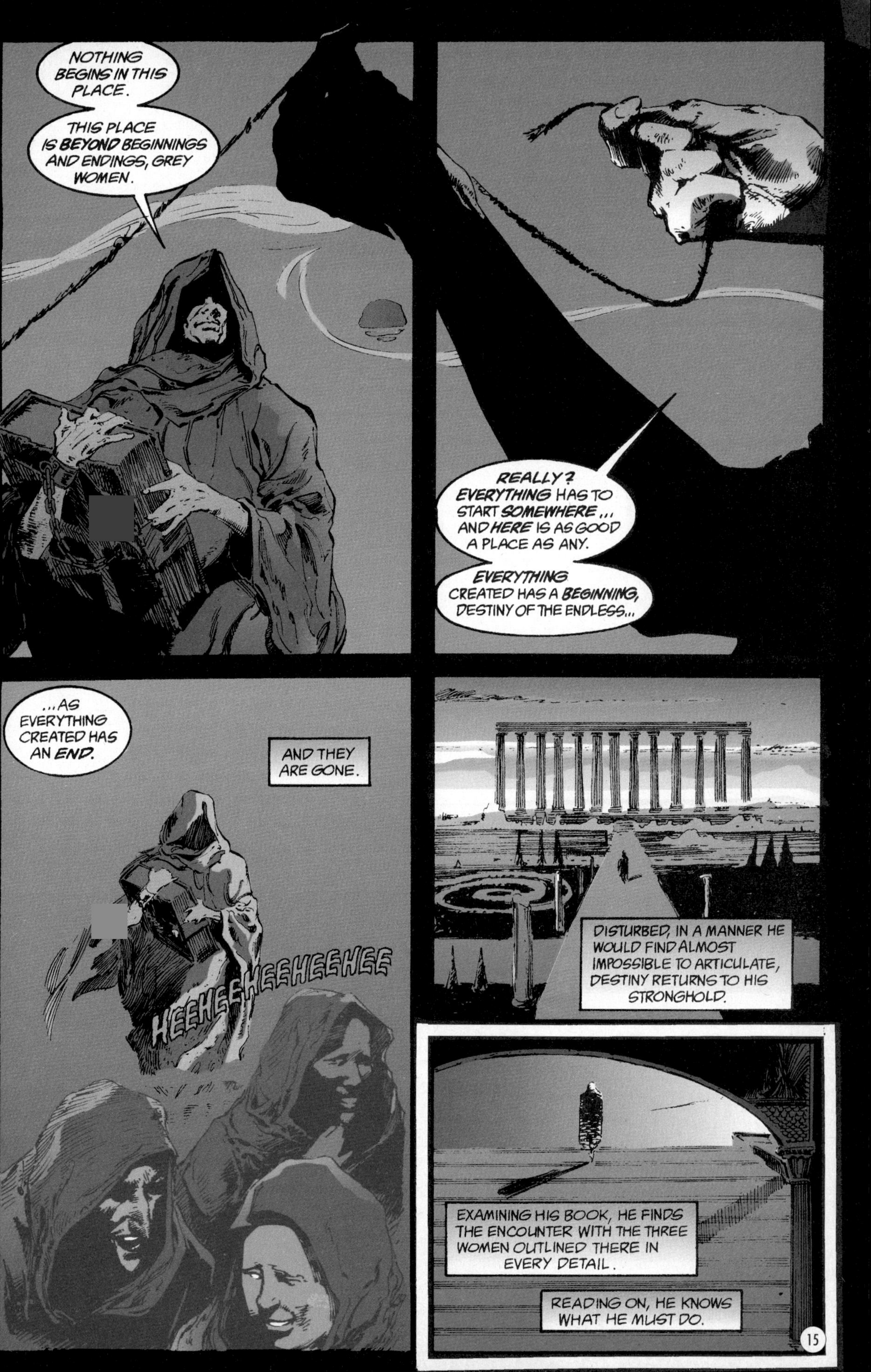
NOTHING BEGINS IN THIS PLACE.
THIS PLACE IS BEYOND BEGINNINGS AND ENDINGS, GREY WOMEN.
REALLY? EVERYTHING HAS TO START SOMEWHERE... AND HERE IS AS GOOD A PLACE AS ANY.
EVERYTHING CREATED HAS A BEGINNING, DESTINY OF THE ENDLESS...
...AS EVERYTHING CREATED HAS AN END.
AND THEY ARE GONE.
HEEHEEHEEHEEHEEHEE
DISTURBED, IN A MANNER HE WOULD FIND ALMOST IMPOSSIBLE TO ARTICULATE, DESTINY RETURNS TO HIS STRONGHOLD.
EXAMINING HIS BOOK, HE FINDS THE ENCOUNTER WITH THE THREE WOMEN OUTLINED THERE IN EVERY DETAIL.
READING ON, HE KNOWS WHAT HE MUST DO.

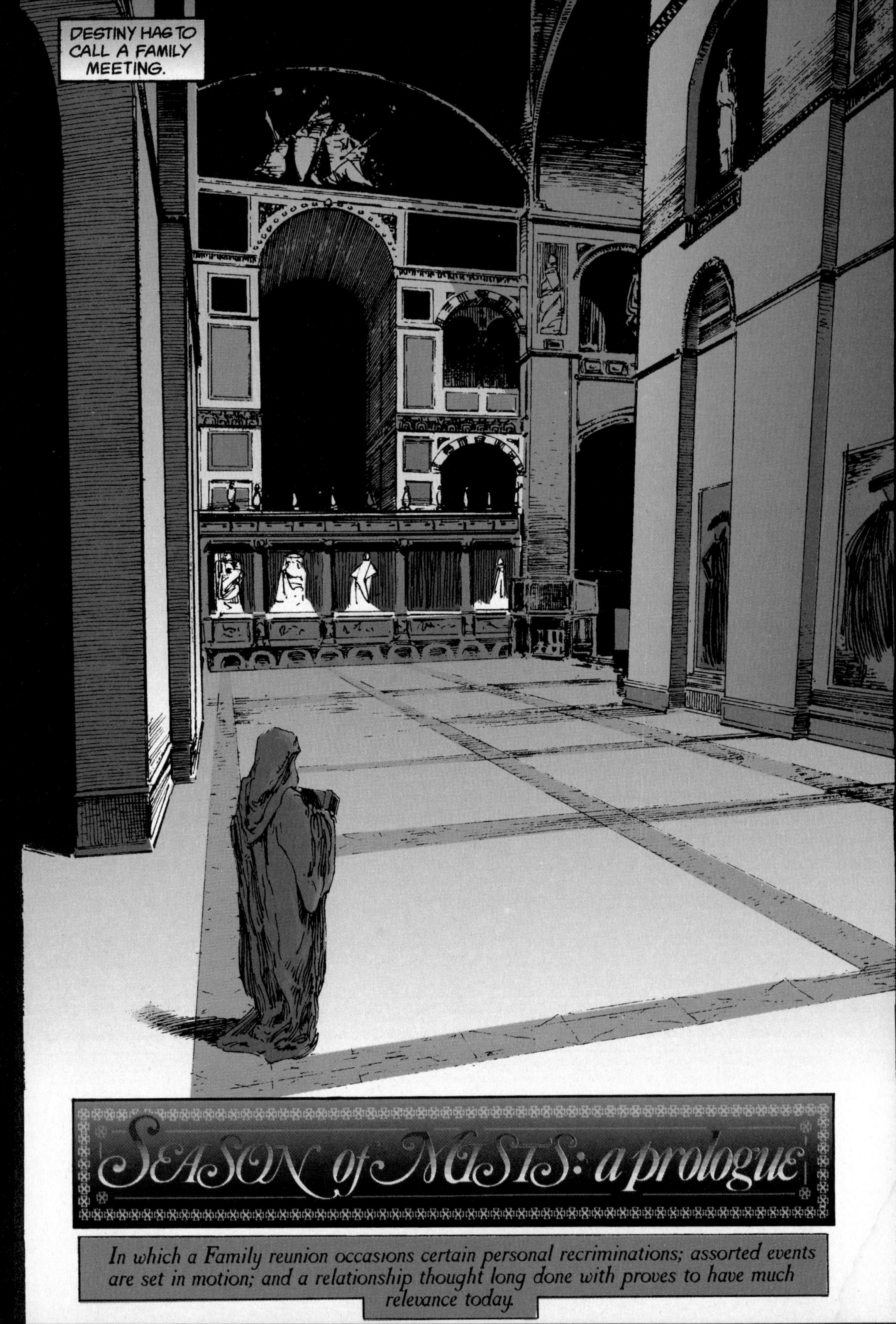
DESTINY HAS TO CALL A FAMILY MEETING.
SEASON of MISTS: a prologue
In which a Family reunion occasions certain personal recriminations; assorted events are set in motion; and a relationship thought long done with proves to have much relevance today.

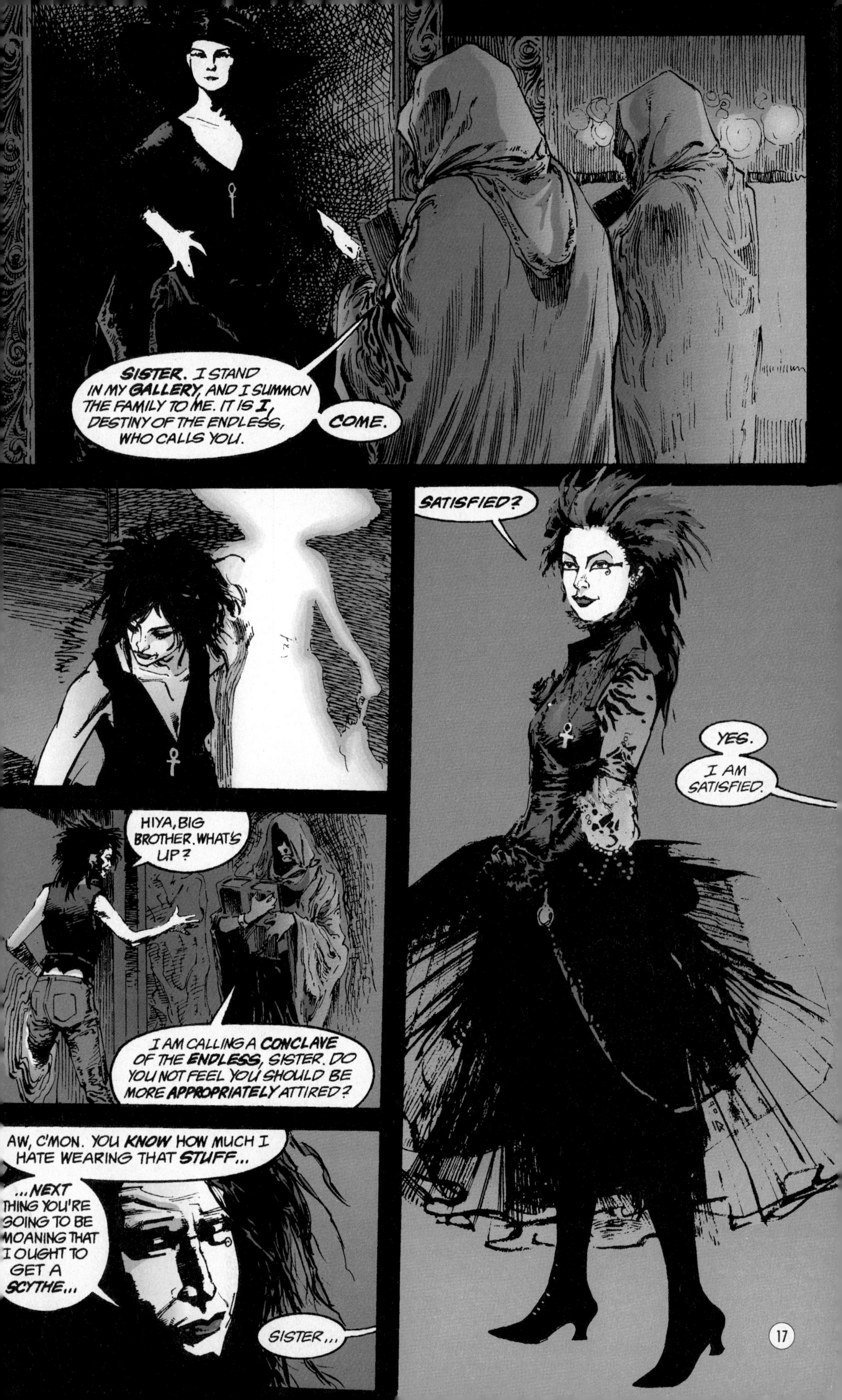
SISTER. I STAND IN MY GALLERY, AND I SUMMON THE FAMILY TO ME. IT IS I, DESTINY OF THE ENDLESS, WHO CALLS YOU.
COME.
HIYA, BIG BROTHER. WHAT'S UP?
I AM CALLING A CONCLAVE OF THE ENDLESS, SISTER. DO YOU NOT FEEL YOU SHOULD BE MORE APPROPRIATELY ATTIRED?
AW, C'MON. YOU KNOW HOW MUCH I HATE WEARING THAT STUFF...
...NEXT THING YOU'RE GOING TO BE MOANING THAT I OUGHT TO GET A SCYTHE...
SISTER...
SATISFIED?
YES.
I AM SATISFIED.

BROTHER DREAM. IT IS I, DESTINY OF THE ENDLESS WHO CALLS YOU. THE FAMILY MUST MEET.

COME TO ME.

Hmm. Well met, my brother.

INTERESTING? PERHAPS. FOR YOU MORE THAN ANY OF US, MY BROTHER.

BUT IN GOOD TIME. THERE ARE THREE MORE OF US STILL TO COME.

So: a family meeting... the first since the prodigal announced his intention to leave us.

Well, well. It will be interesting to find out why you have called us here.

Well-met, sister.

You have dressed formally also, I see. My compliments.

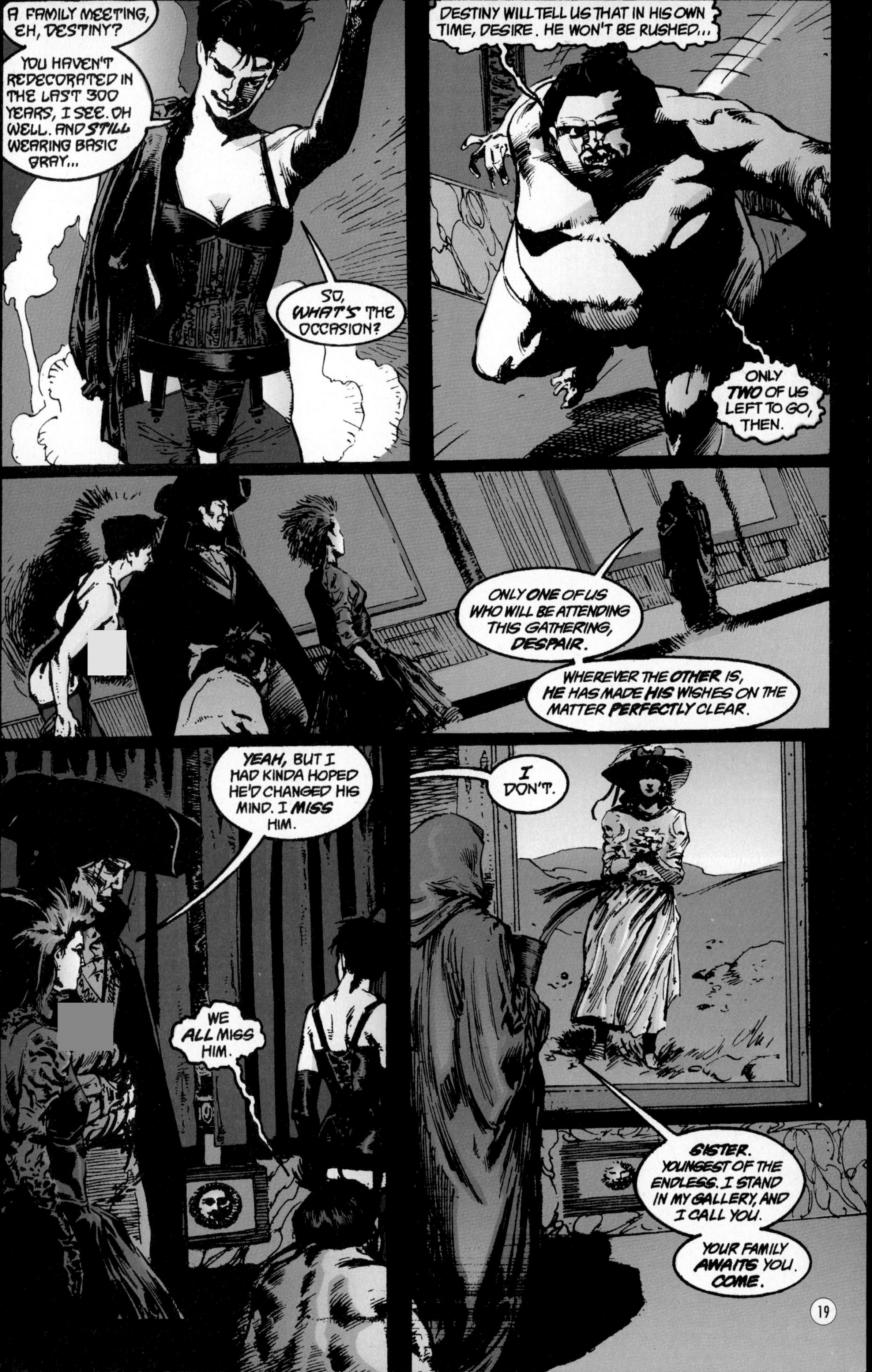
A FAMILY MEETING, EH, DESTINY?
YOU HAVEN'T REDECORATED IN THE LAST 300 YEARS, I SEE. OH WELL. AND STILL WEARING BASIC GRAY...
SO, WHAT'S THE OCCASION?
DESTINY WILL TELL US THAT IN HIS OWN TIME, DESIRE. HE WON'T BE RUSHED...
ONLY TWO OF US LEFT TO GO, THEN.
ONLY ONE OF US WHO WILL BE ATTENDING THIS GATHERING, DESPAIR.
WHEREVER THE OTHER IS, HE HAS MADE HIS WISHES ON THE MATTER PERFECTLY CLEAR.
YEAH, BUT I HAD KINDA HOPED HE'D CHANGED HIS MIND. I MISS HIM.
WE ALL MISS HIM.
I DON'T.
SISTER. YOUNGEST OF THE ENDLESS. I STAND IN MY GALLERY, AND I CALL YOU.
YOUR FAMILY AWAITS YOU. COME.

Despair, Desire's sister and twin, is queen of her own bleak bourne. It is said that scattered through Despair's domain are a multitude of tiny windows, hanging in the void. Each window looks out onto a different scene, being, in our world, a mirror. Sometimes you will look into a mirror and feel the eyes of Despair upon you, feel her hook catch and snag on your heart.

Her skin is cold, and clammy; her eyes are the colour of sky, on the grey, wet days that leach the world of colour and meaning; her voice is little more than a whisper; and while she has no odour, her shadow smells musky, and pungent, like the skin of a snake.

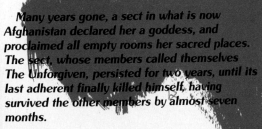

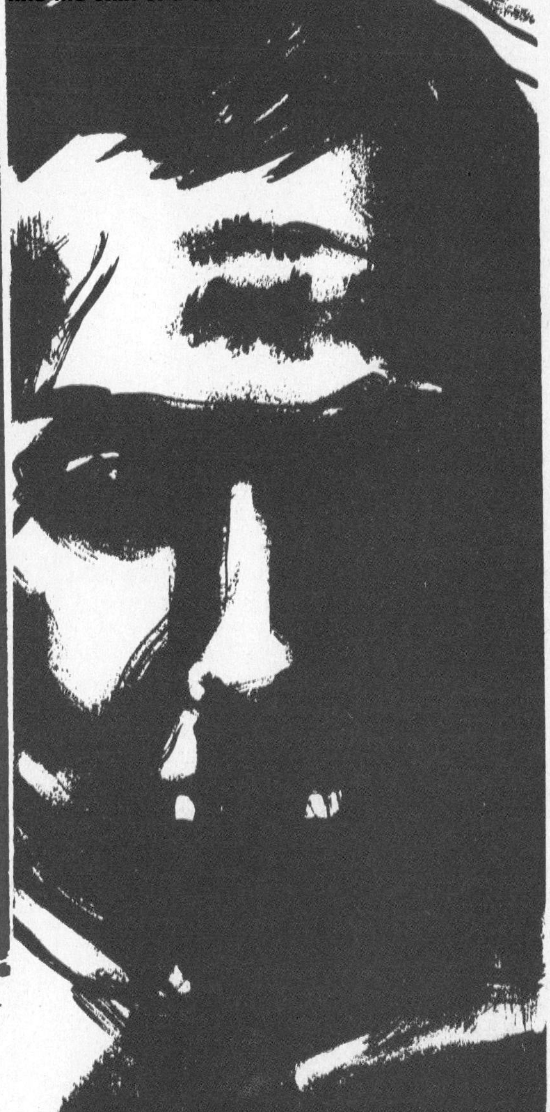

Let us pause for a moment, as they descend the grey steps toward Destiny's banqueting hall, to consider the Endless.

Desire is of medium height. It is unlikely that any portrait will ever do Desire justice, since to see her (or him) is to love him (or her),—passionately, painfully, to the exclusion of all else.

Desire smells almost subliminally of summer peaches, and casts two shadows: one black and sharp-edged, the other translucent and forever wavering, like heat haze.

Desire smiles in brief flashes, like sunlight glinting from a knife-edge. And there is much else that is knife-like about Desire.

Never a possession, always the possessor, with skin as pale as smoke, and eyes tawny and sharp as yellow wine: Desire is everything you have ever wanted. Whoever you are. Whatever you are.

Everything.

Many years gone, a sect in what is now Afghanistan declared her a goddess, and proclaimed all empty rooms her sacred places. The sect, whose members called themselves The Unforgiven, persisted for two years, until its last adherent finally killed himself, having survived the other members by almost seven months.

Despair says little, and is patient.

Destiny is the oldest of the Endless; in the Beginning was the Word, and it was traced by hand on the first page of his book, before ever it was spoken aloud.

Destiny is also the tallest of the Endless, to mortal eyes.

There are some who believe him to be blind; whilst others, perhaps with more reason, claim that he has travelled far beyond blindness, that indeed, he can do nothing but see: that he sees the fine traceries the galaxies make as they spiral through the void, that he watches the intricate patterns living things make on their journey through time.

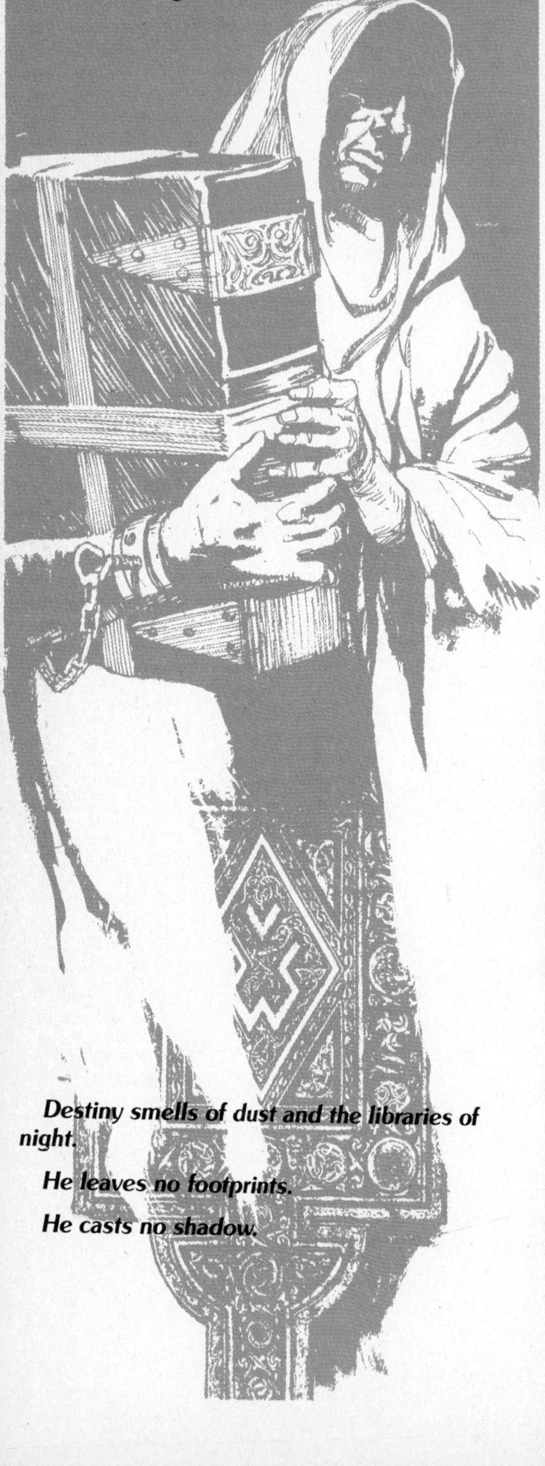

Destiny smells of dust and the libraries of night.

He leaves no footprints.

He casts no shadow.

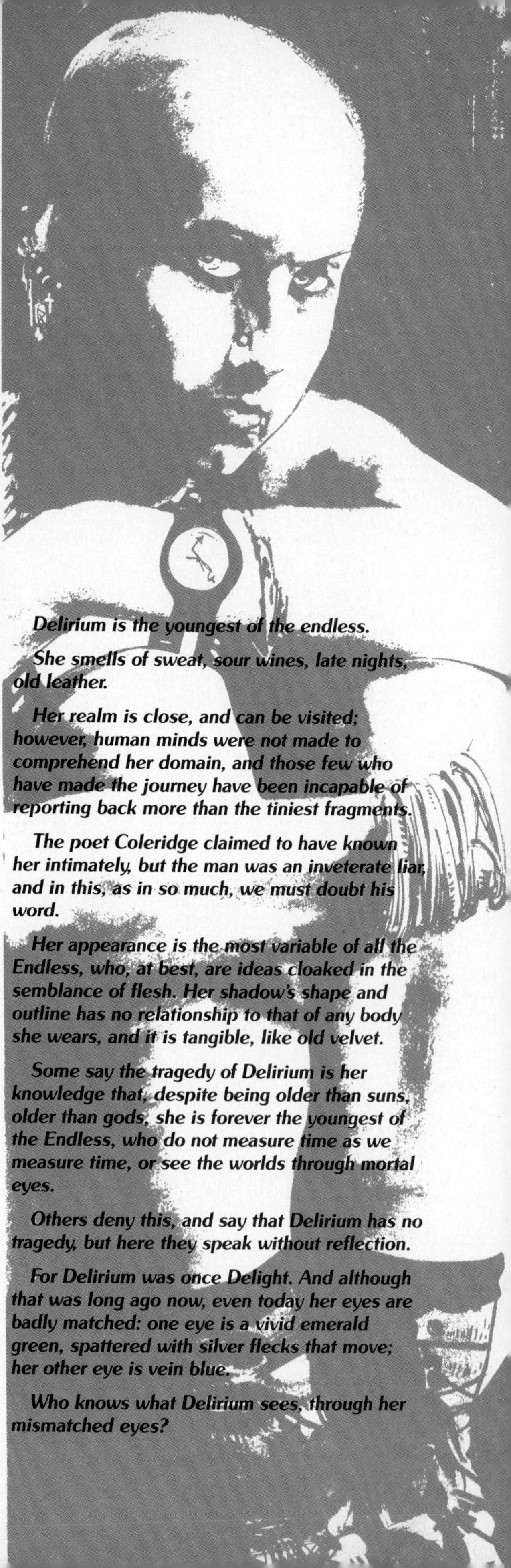

Delirium is the youngest of the endless.

She smells of sweat, sour wines, late nights, old leather.

Her realm is close, and can be visited; however, human minds were not made to comprehend her domain, and those few who have made the journey have been incapable of reporting back more than the tiniest fragments.

The poet Coleridge claimed to have known her intimately, but the man was an inveterate liar, and in this, as in so much, we must doubt his word.

Her appearance is the most variable of all the Endless, who, at best, are ideas cloaked in the semblance of flesh. Her shadow's shape and outline has no relationship to that of any body she wears, and it is tangible, like old velvet.

Some say the tragedy of Delirium is her knowledge that, despite being older than suns, older than gods, she is forever the youngest of the Endless, who do not measure time as we measure time, or see the worlds through mortal eyes.

Others deny this, and say that Delirium has no tragedy, but here they speak without reflection.

For Delirium was once Delight. And although that was long ago now, even today her eyes are badly matched: one eye is a vivid emerald green, spattered with silver flecks that move; her other eye is vein blue.

Who knows what Delirium sees, through her mismatched eyes?

Dream of the Endless: ah, there's a conundrum.

In this aspect (and we perceive but aspects of the Endless, as we see the light glinting from one tiny facet of some huge and flawlessly cut precious stone), he is rake-thin, with skin the color of falling snow.

Dream accumulates names to himself like others make friends; but he permits himself few friends.

If he is closest to anyone, it is to his elder sister, whom he sees but rarely.

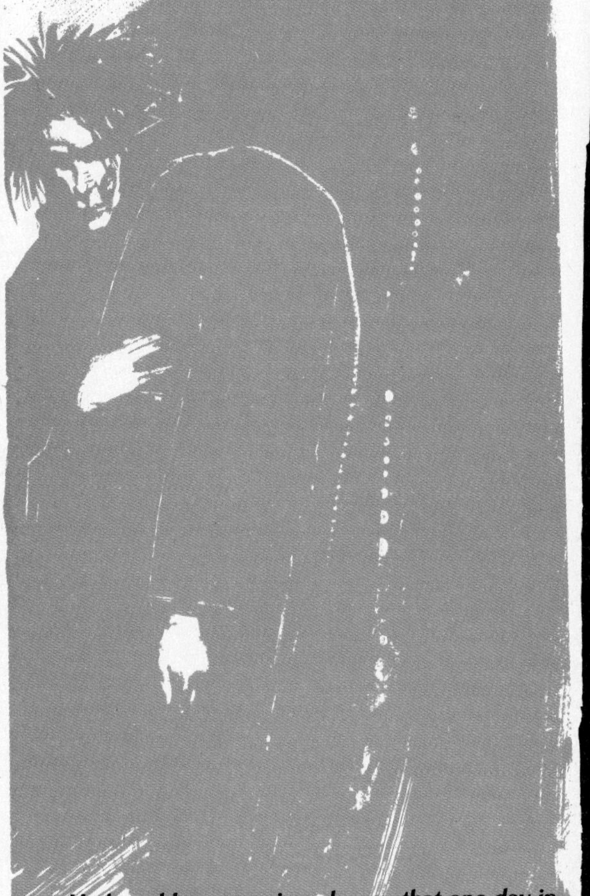

He heard long ago, in a dream, that one day in every century Death takes on mortal flesh, better to comprehend what the lives she takes must feel like, to taste the bitter tang of mortality: that this is the price she must pay for being the divider of the living from all that has gone before, all that must come after.

He broods on this tale, but has never questioned her about its truth. Perhaps he fears that she would answer him.

Of all the Endless, save perhaps Destiny, he is most conscious of his responsibilities, the most meticulous in their execution.

Dream casts a human shadow, when it occurs to him to do so.

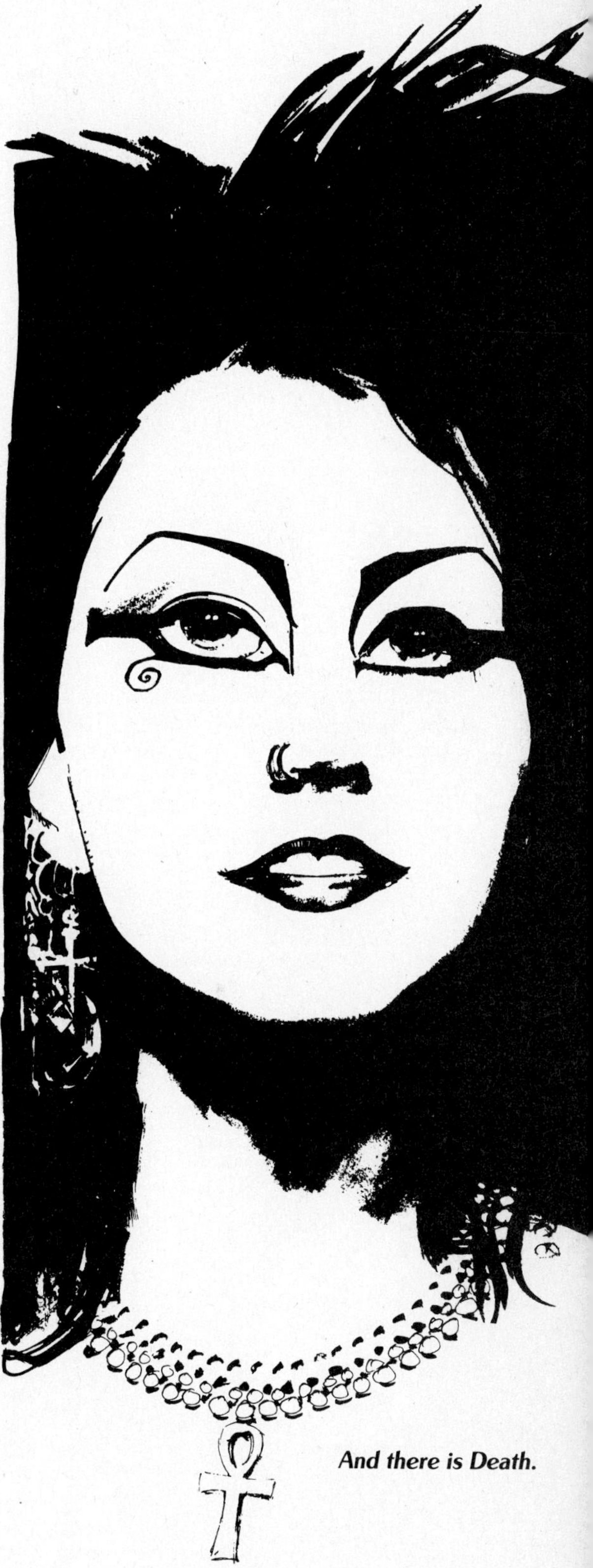

And there is Death.

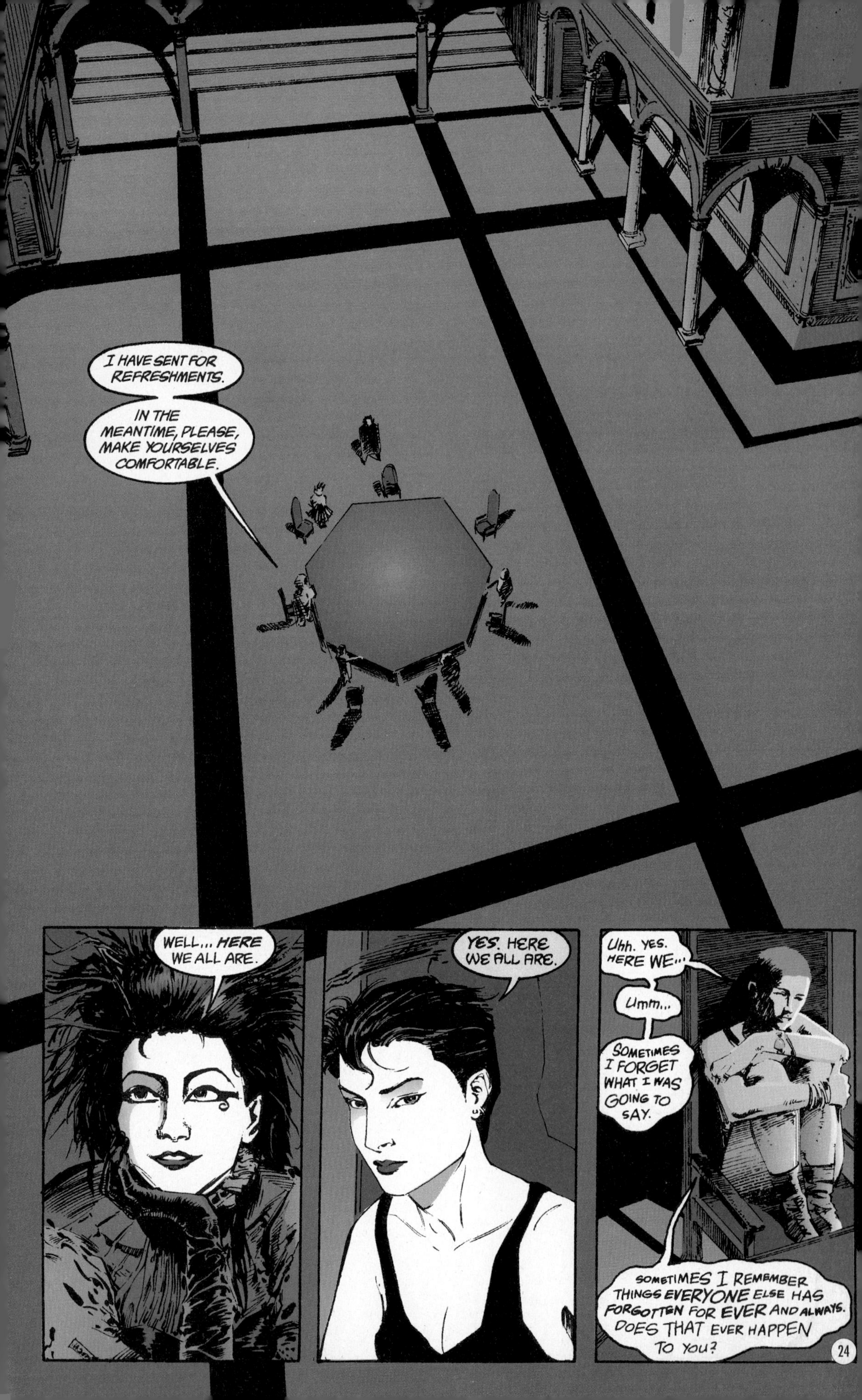
I HAVE SENT FOR REFRESHMENTS.
IN THE MEANTIME, PLEASE, MAKE YOURSELVES COMFORTABLE.
WELL... HERE WE ALL ARE.
YES. HERE WE ALL ARE.
Uhh. YES. HERE WE...
Umm...
SOMETIMES I FORGET WHAT I WAS GOING TO SAY.
SOMETIMES I REMEMBER THINGS EVERYONE ELSE HAS FORGOTTEN FOR EVER AND ALWAYS. DOES THAT EVER HAPPEN TO YOU?

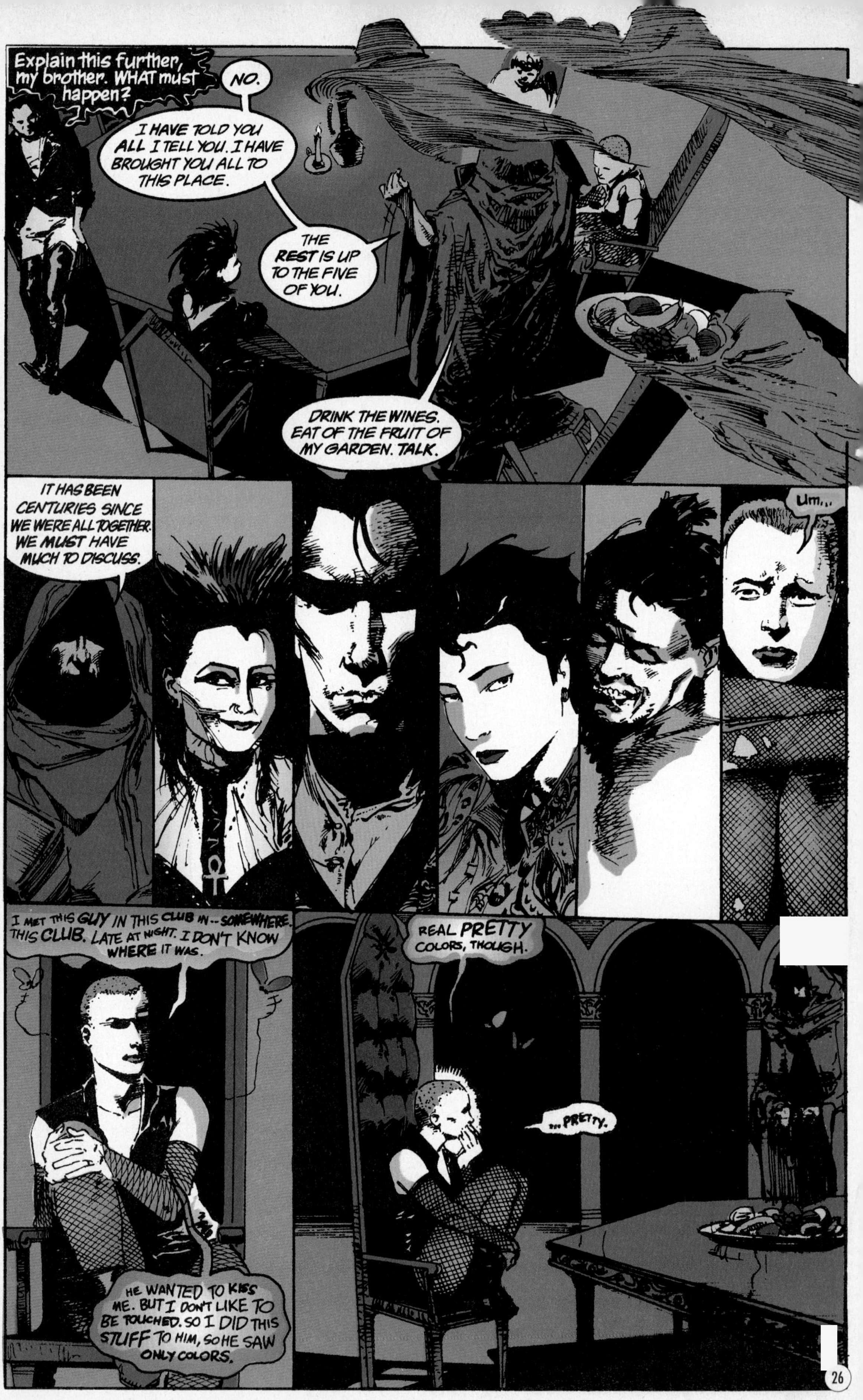
Explain this further, my brother. WHAT must happen?
NO.
I HAVE TOLD YOU ALL I TELL YOU. I HAVE BROUGHT YOU ALL TO THIS PLACE.
THE REST IS UP TO THE FIVE OF YOU.
DRINK THE WINES. EAT OF THE FRUIT OF MY GARDEN. TALK.
IT HAS BEEN CENTURIES SINCE WE WERE ALL TOGETHER. WE MUST HAVE MUCH TO DISCUSS.
Um...
I MET THIS GUY IN THIS CLUB IN... SOMEWHERE. THIS CLUB. LATE AT NIGHT. I DON'T KNOW WHERE IT WAS.
HE WANTED TO KISS ME. BUT I DON'T LIKE TO BE TOUCHED. SO I DID THIS STUFF TO HIM, SO HE SAW ONLY COLORS.
REAL PRETTY COLORS, THOUGH.
...PRETTY.

You are saying that you summoned us here because it is necessary for us to be here at this time.

EXACTLY.

This is foolish. I am currently rebuilding my kingdom. I have duties to attend to, and there is much that must be done.

THAT WILL NOT HAPPEN, YET.

I will leave now.

AW, C'MON. HANG AROUND FOR A LITTLE. WHAT'S SOME LOST TIME? WE'VE GOT ALL THE TIME THERE IS.

HAVE A GRAPE.

I LOST SOME TIME ONCE. IT'S ALWAYS IN THE LAST PLACE YOU LOOK FOR IT.

I do not want a grape.

I COULD MAKE YOU WANT ONE.

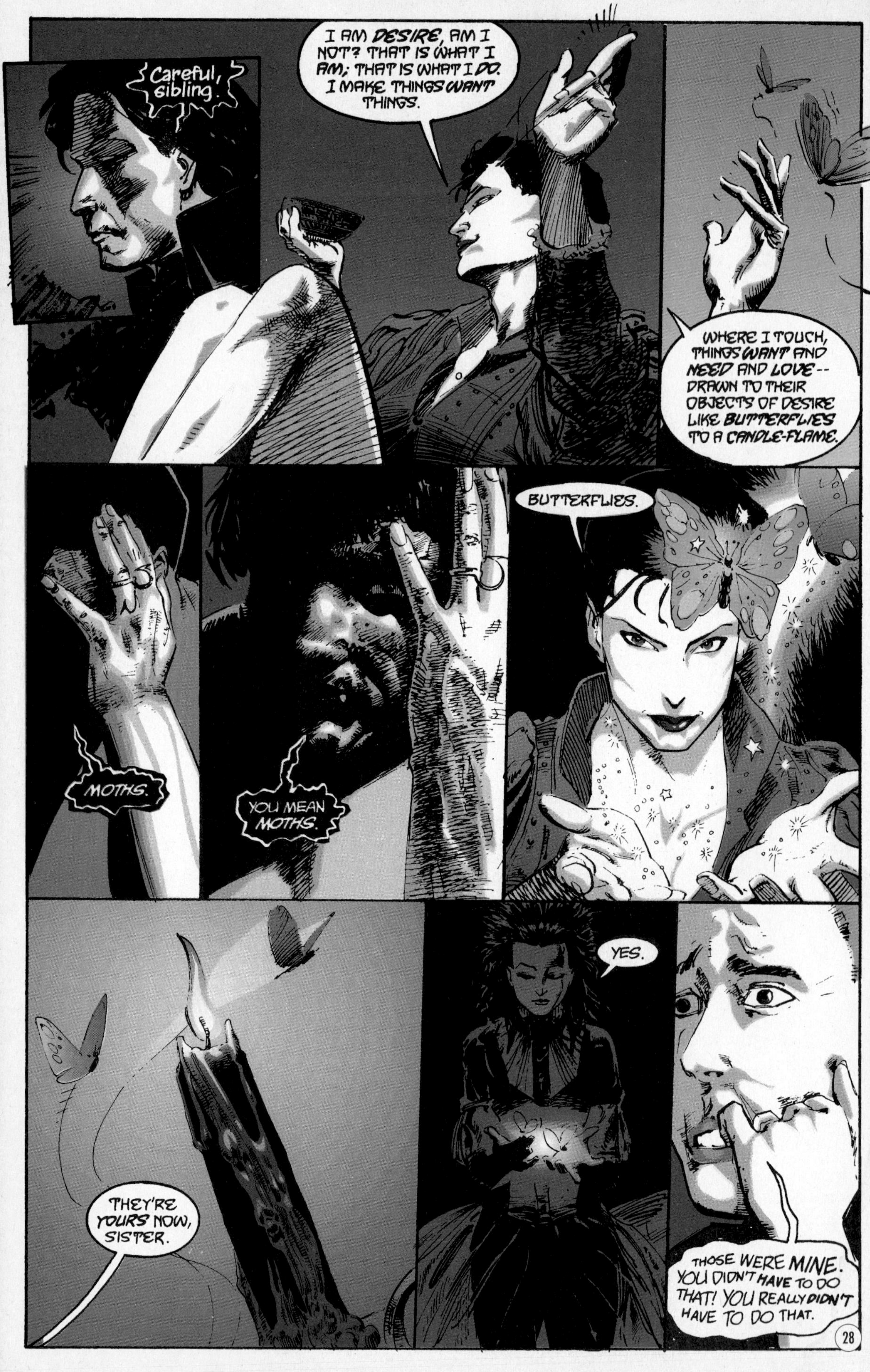
I AM DESIRE, AM I NOT? THAT IS WHAT I AM; THAT IS WHAT I DO. I MAKE THINGS WANT THINGS.
Careful, sibling.
WHERE I TOUCH, THINGS WANT AND NEED AND LOVE-- DRAWN TO THEIR OBJECTS OF DESIRE LIKE BUTTERFLIES TO A CANDLE-FLAME.
MOTHS.
YOU MEAN MOTHS.
BUTTERFLIES.
THEY'RE YOURS NOW, SISTER.
YES.
THOSE WERE MINE. YOU DIDN'T HAVE TO DO THAT! YOU REALLY DIDN'T HAVE TO DO THAT.

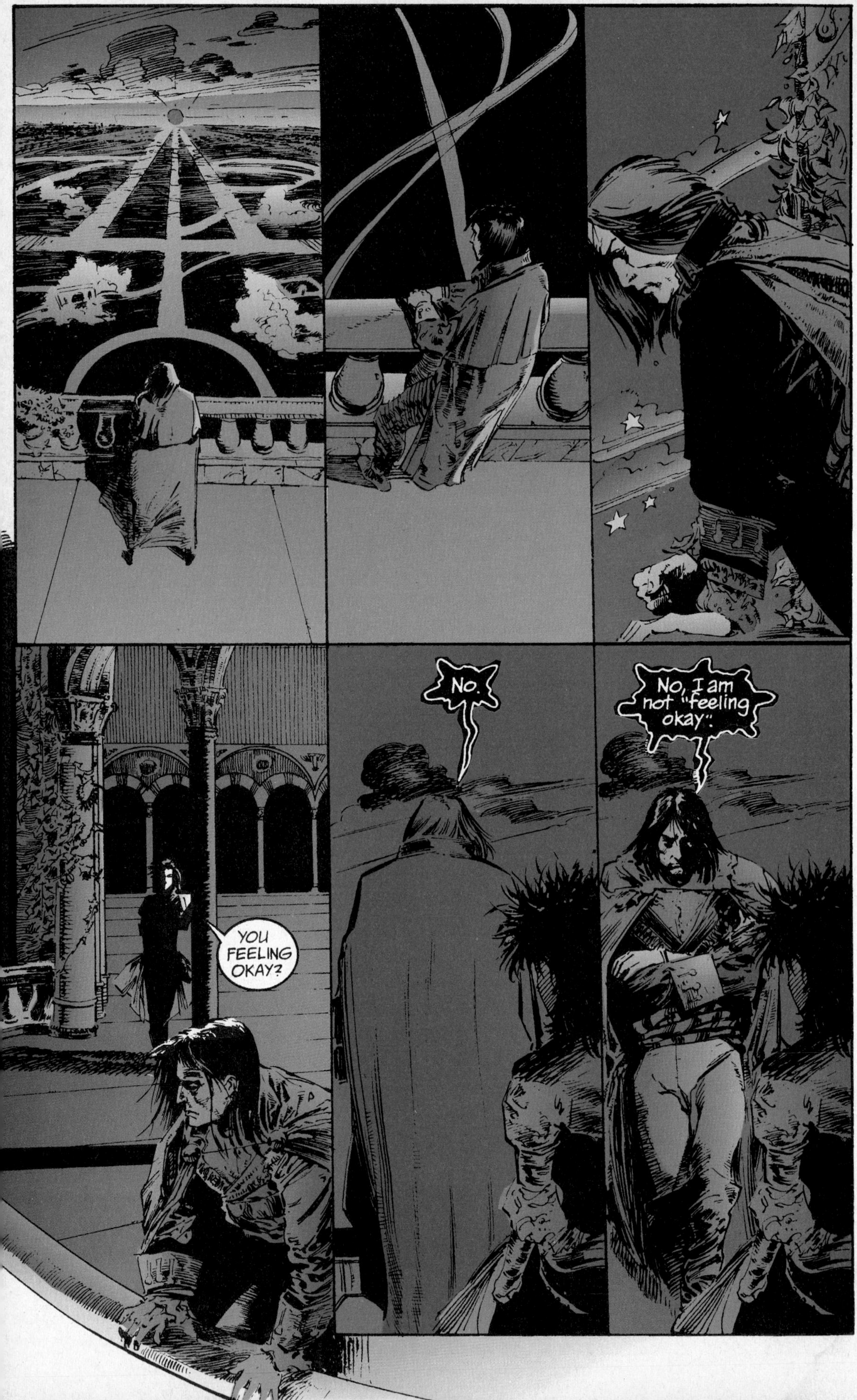
YOU FEELING OKAY?
No.
No, I am not "feeling okay".

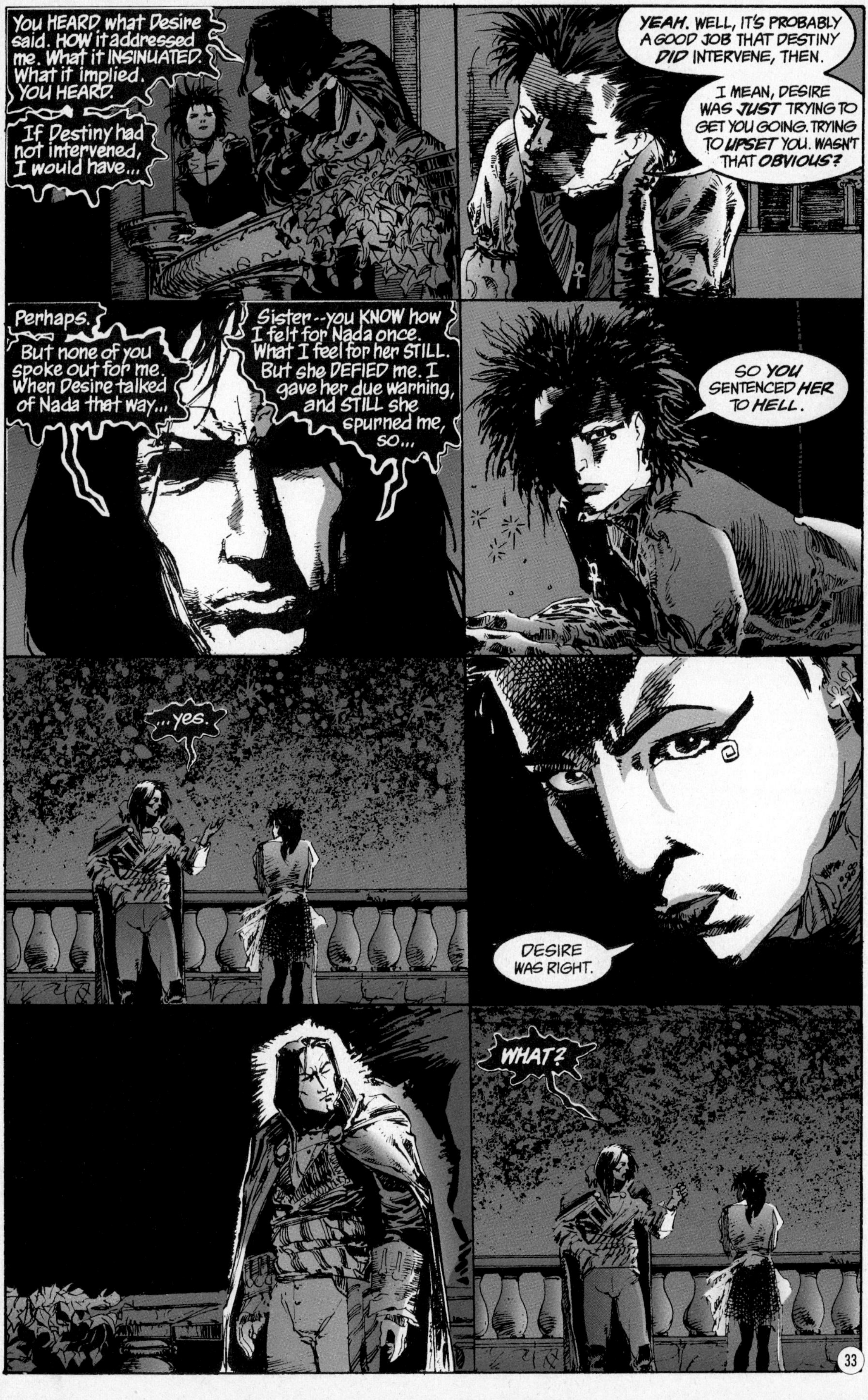
You HEARD what Desire said. HOW it addressed me. What it INSINUATED. What it implied. YOU HEARD.
If Destiny had not intervened, I would have...
YEAH. WELL, IT'S PROBABLY A GOOD JOB THAT DESTINY DID INTERVENE, THEN.
I MEAN, DESIRE WAS JUST TRYING TO GET YOU GOING. TRYING TO UPSET YOU. WASN'T THAT OBVIOUS?
Perhaps.
But none of you spoke out for me. When Desire talked of Nada that way...
Sister--you KNOW how I felt for Nada once. What I feel for her STILL. But she DEFIED me. I gave her due warning, and STILL she spurned me, so...
SO YOU SENTENCED HER TO HELL.
...yes.
DESIRE WAS RIGHT.
WHAT?

I had not wished to return to Hell. Not yet.

Lucifer Morningstar is not one to forgive a slight, nor to forget an injury.

But if I have committed a wrong, then I have but one course.

It must be made right.

I must go to my own realm, first, to prepare.

And then, though it might mean my doom, I must journey to Hell.

My sister, I pray you tell our siblings that I was needed elsewhere, and I could not stay.

Adieu.

YOU TOO.

HEY! DREAM?

My lady?

DON'T DO ANYTHING STUPID.

I am afraid it is too late for that admonition. But I shall do my best. I can do no more.

Either I shall bring Nada out of Hell...

...or I shall see you again soon, my sister.

See you for one final time.

35

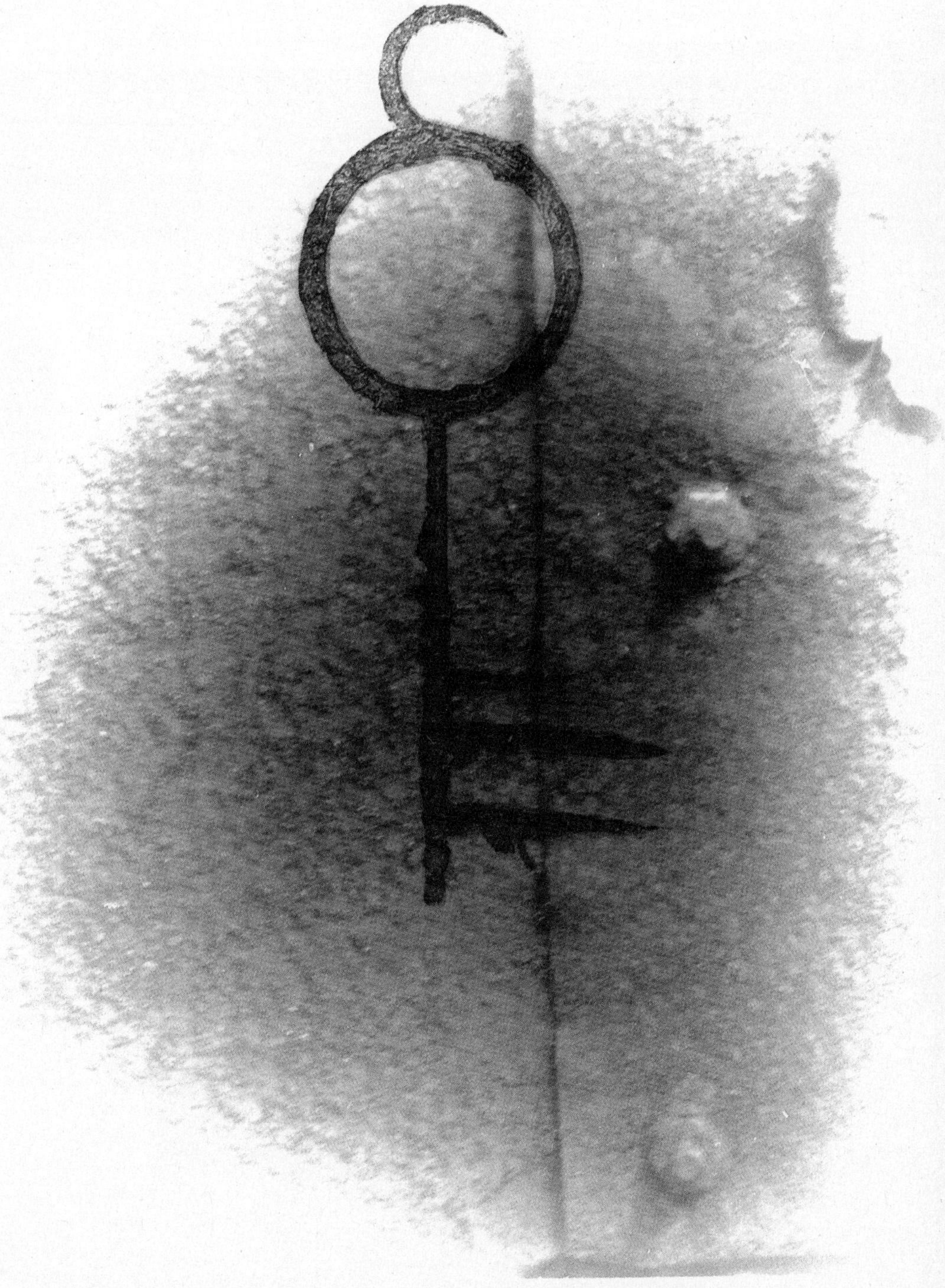

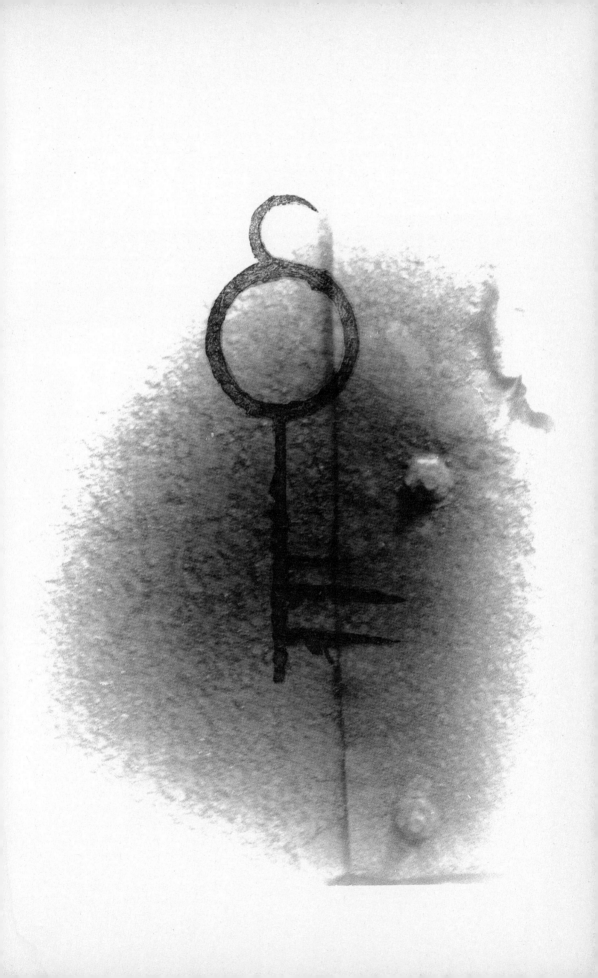

In which the Lord of Dreams makes preparations to visit the realms infernal; farewell's are said; a toast is drunk; and in Hell the Adversary makes certain preparations of his own.

EPISODE 1

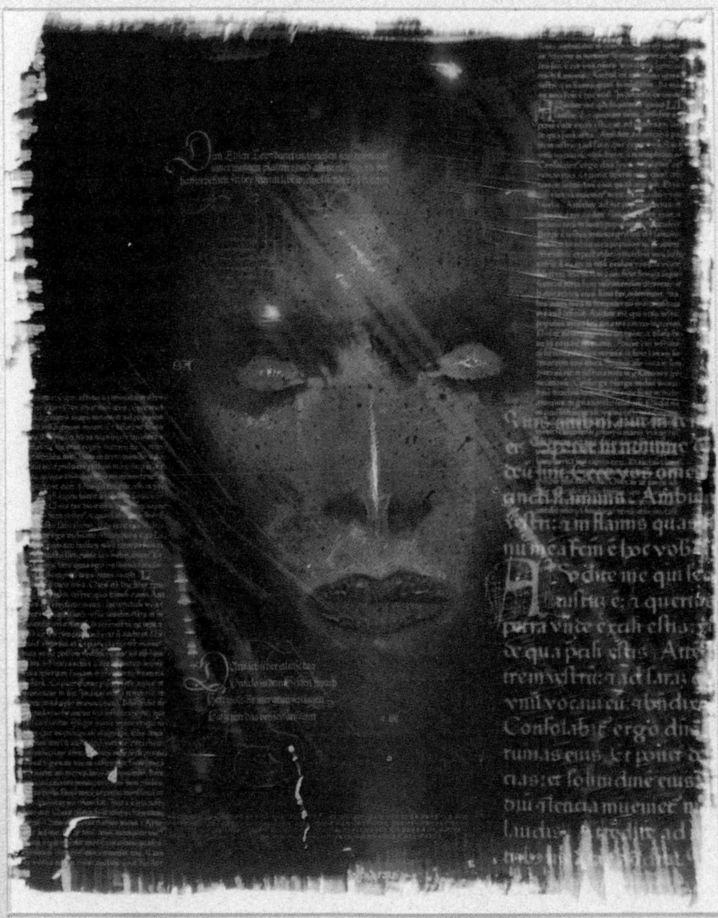

ONCE UPON A TIME, THERE WAS A PLACE THAT WASN'T A PLACE.

IT HAD MANY NAMES: AVERNUS, GEHENNA, TARTARUS, HADES, ABADDON, SHEOL...

IT WAS AN INFERNO OF PAIN AND FLAME AND ICE, WHERE EVERY NIGHTMARE HAD COME TRUE LONG SINCE.

WE'LL CALL IT HELL.

IT WAS NOT CONSIDERED A PLEASANT PLACE BY THE MAJORITY OF ITS INHABITANTS; HOWEVER, BEING DEAD, AND BEING THERE (AS THEY IMAGINED) AGAINST THEIR WILL, THEIR OPINIONS COUNTED FOR LITTLE.

THE OTHER INHABITANTS OF THIS PLACE WERE NOT DEAD; HOWEVER, NEITHER WERE THEY ALIVE, IN ANY BIOLOGICAL SENSE OF THE WORD.

HUMANITY CALLED THEM DEMONS WITHOUT UNDERSTANDING WHAT IT HAD NAMED.

AND INDEED, HAD HELL BEEN PLEASANT, THEY WOULD HAVE FELT CHEATED: THEY WERE THERE FOR PAIN, FOR SUFFERING, FOR TORMENT.

WHICH THEY RECEIVED IN ABUNDANCE.

THERE WAS LITTLE THAT DEMONKIND HAD IN COMMON WITH THE LEGIONS OF DAMNED SOULS WITH WHOM THEY SHARED THE INFERNAL MARCHES.

HOWEVER, THEY WERE ALL AGREED ON ONE THING.

THIS WAS AS BAD AS IT GOT.

IT *COULDN'T* GET ANY *WORSE*.

SO *THIS* IS YOUR LIBRARY, HUH, LUCIEN? IT'S A *BIG* PLACE.

WHAT'S SO *SPECIAL* ABOUT IT, THEN?

THEY'RE *JUST* BOOKS.

PSMITH AND JEEVES P.G. WODEHOUSE

LOVE CAN BE MURDER RAYMOND CHANDLER

THE DARK GOD'S DARLINGS LORD DUNSANY

THE HAND OF GLORY ERASMUS FRY

THE RETURN OF EDWIN DROOD CHARLES DICKENS

THE CONSCIENCE OF SHERLOCK HOLMES ARTHUR CONAN DOYLE

POICTESME BABYLON JAMES BRANCH CABELL

THE MAN WHO WAS OCTOBER G. K. CHESTERTON

THE LOST ROAD J.R.R. TOLKIEN

ALICE'S L...

...NEY BEHIND THE MO...

R... CARROLL

OH YES. BUT *UNUSUAL* BOOKS. YOU'LL FIND NONE OF THEM ON EARTH. IN *THIS* SECTION, FOR EXAMPLE, ARE NOVELS THEIR AUTHORS NEVER *WROTE*, OR NEVER *FINISHED*, EXCEPT IN DREAMS.

MM. I WAS NEVER A BIG READER, TO BE HONEST. I WAS MORE A MAN OF ACTION WHEN I WAS ALIVE.

ANYWAY, YOU *MUST* BE PLEASED TO HAVE THE LIBRARY BACK.

OH, IT'S A *VERY* UNUSUAL LIBRARY, MATTHEW. SOMEWHERE IN HERE IS *EVERY* STORY THAT HAS *EVER* BEEN DREAMED.

NEVERMORE!

GOOD, HUH?

HUH? LUCIEN, I WAS DOING *PETER LORRE* IN THAT *ROGER CORMAN* MOVIE...

I AM THE *KEEPER* OF THE *LIBRARY*, MATTHEW. WITHOUT IT I AM *NOTHING*.

WERE IT TO BE *DESTROYED* AGAIN, IT WOULD DESTROY *ME* AS WELL.

YEAH?-- SAY, WATCH THIS...

THE *COMPLETE POE* IS IN THE *SOUTHERN ANNEX*. ALL THE *BOOKS* AND TALES AND PLAYS AND *POEMS* HE NEVER WROTE, ALL HERE. WOULD YOU LIKE ME TO *READ* SOME TO YOU?

Lucien. Matthew. We must talk.

I will be in the Great Hall.

IMMEDIATELY, LORD.

I DIDN'T KNOW HE COULD DO THAT.

MATTHEW-- OUR LORD IS DREAM...

THIS IS HIS CASTLE, HIS SEAT OF POWER, AT THE *HEART* OF THE DREAMING.

IN THIS PLACE, HE CAN DO *WHATEVER* HE WISHES.

ONE MOMENT. I MUST LOCK THE DOOR--CAN'T HAVE ANY BOOKS GETTING OUT...

I WONDER *WHY* HE WANTS TO TALK TO US.

I, UH, DON'T THINK HE JUST WANTS TO TALK TO US, LUCIEN...

GANGWAY, AMIGOS!

I THINK HE WANTS TO TALK TO EVERYBODY.

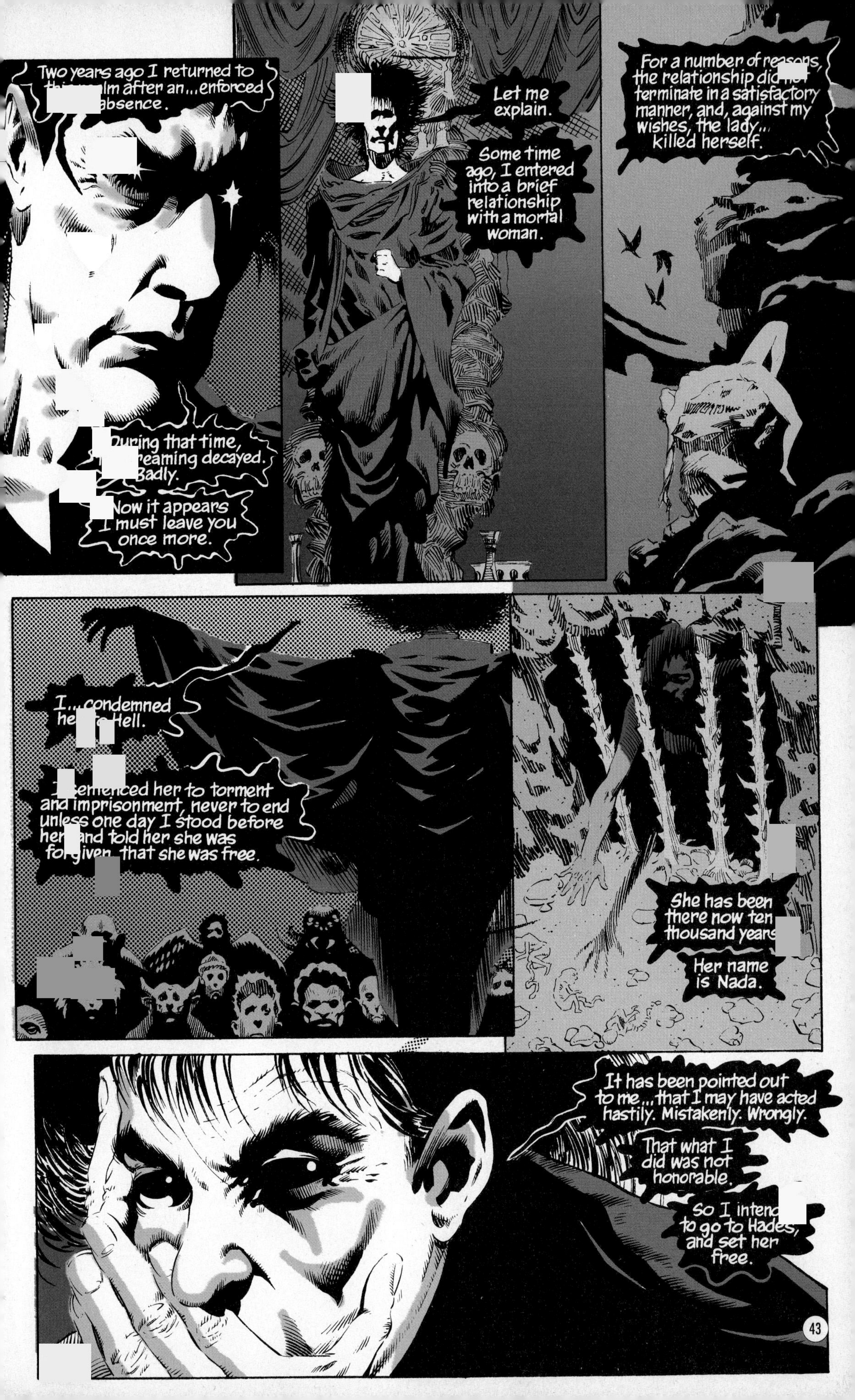

Two years ago I returned to this realm after an...enforced absence.
Let me explain.
Some time ago, I entered into a brief relationship with a mortal woman.
For a number of reasons, the relationship did not terminate in a satisfactory manner, and, against my wishes, the lady... killed herself.
During that time, Dreaming decayed. Badly.
Now it appears I must leave you once more.
I...condemned her to Hell.
I sentenced her to torment and imprisonment, never to end unless one day I stood before her and told her she was forgiven, that she was free.
She has been there now ten thousand years.
Her name is Nada.
It has been pointed out to me...that I may have acted hastily. Mistakenly. Wrongly.
That what I did was not honorable.
So I intend to go to Hades, and set her free.

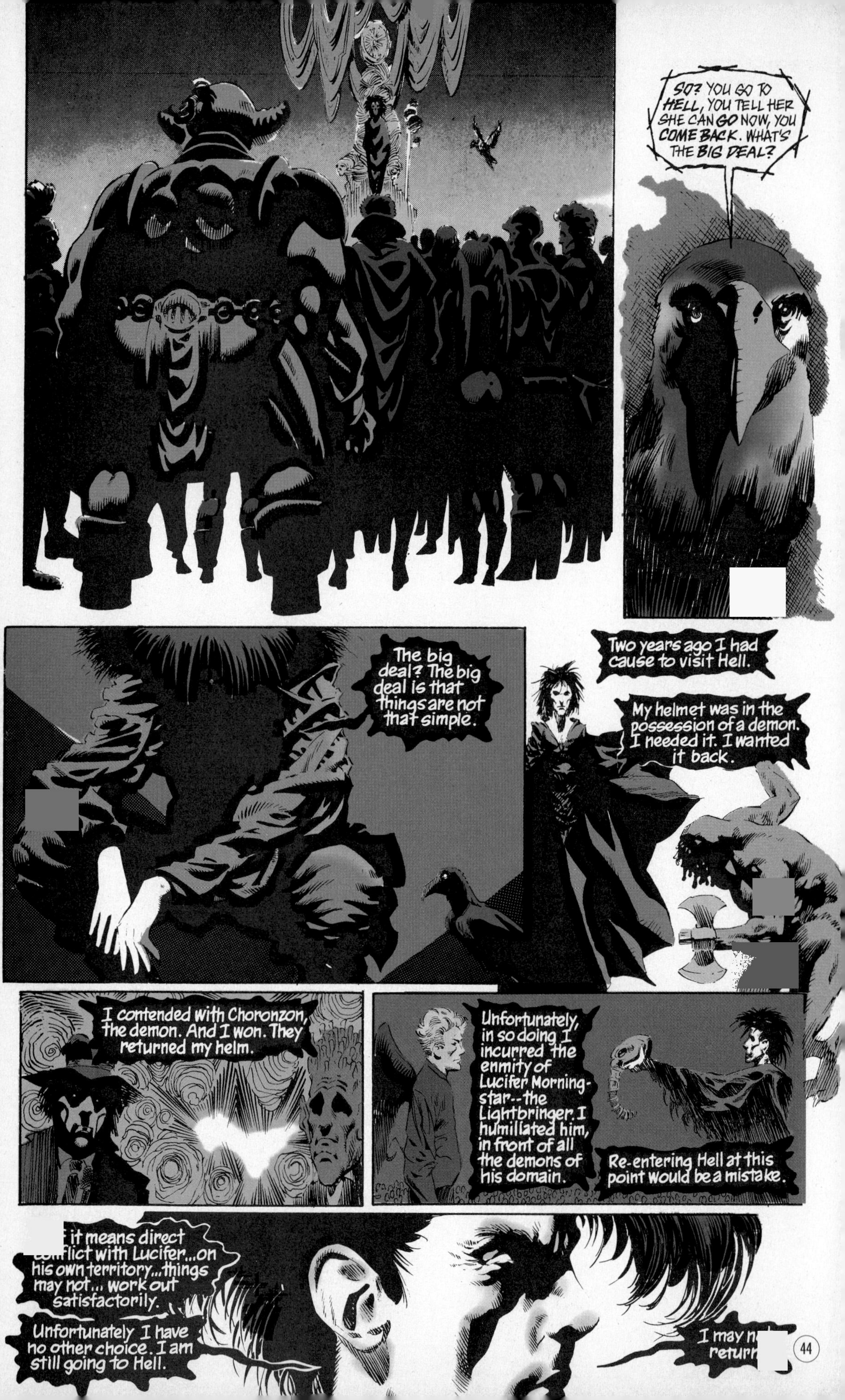
SO? YOU GO TO HELL, YOU TELL HER SHE CAN GO NOW, YOU COME BACK. WHAT'S THE BIG DEAL?
The big deal? The big deal is that things are not that simple.
Two years ago I had cause to visit Hell.
My helmet was in the possession of a demon. I needed it. I wanted it back.
I contended with Choronzon, the demon. And I won. They returned my helm.
Unfortunately, in so doing I incurred the enmity of Lucifer Morningstar--the Lightbringer. I humiliated him, in front of all the demons of his domain.
Re-entering Hell at this point would be a mistake.
it means direct onflict with Lucifer...on his own territory...things may not... work out satisfactorily.
Unfortunately I have no other choice. I am still going to Hell.
I may n
return

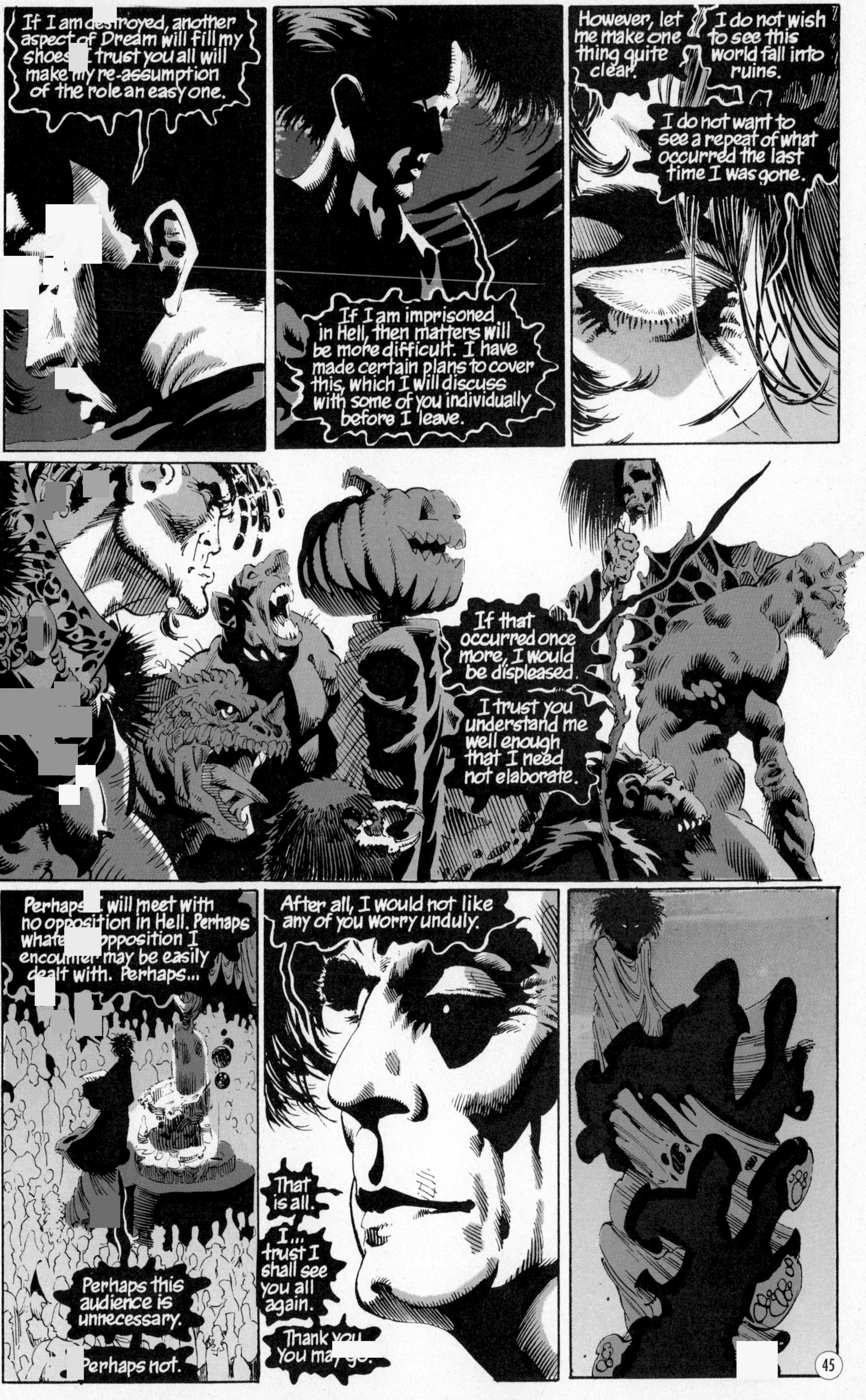
If I am destroyed, another aspect of Dream will fill my shoes. I trust you all will make my re-assumption of the role an easy one.
If I am imprisoned in Hell, then matters will be more difficult. I have made certain plans to cover this, which I will discuss with some of you individually before I leave.
However, let me make one thing quite clear.
I do not wish to see this world fall into ruins.
I do not want to see a repeat of what occurred the last time I was gone.
If that occurred once more, I would be displeased.
I trust you understand me well enough that I need not elaborate.
Perhaps I will meet with no opposition in Hell. Perhaps whatever opposition I encounter may be easily dealt with. Perhaps...
Perhaps this audience is unnecessary.
Perhaps not.
After all, I would not like any of you worry unduly.
That is all.
I... trust I shall see you all again.
Thank you. You may go.

GREAT PRINCE?

mm?

WE HAVE A PRISONER, SIRE.

SO?

HE CLAIMS TO BE A HERALD. AN ENVOY FROM THE REALM OF THE DREAM KING.

ah?

THEN BRING HIM TO US, ALICHINO.

THE PRISONER, SIRE.

AH. PRINCE LUCIFER--

SCHUCK UCK, SGUN. SHVEEG VHEN ZHU AH SCHVOGEN TZU. GHETCH DOWNG ONG HYOUH KNEES.

WE...KNOW YOU.

YES, WE KNOW YOU OF OLD. THE FIRST MAN BORN OF WOMAN. WHAT IS YOUR NAME?

CAIN. LORD.

AH, YES. DELIVER YOUR MESSAGE, CAIN.

47

MESSAGE. YES. RIGHT. UM.

AHEM: "FROM THE LORD OF THE DREAMWORLD, PRINCE OF STORIES, MONARCH OF THE SLEEPING MARCHES, HIS DARKNESS DREAM OF THE ENDLESS, TO HIS INFERNAL MAJESTY, LUCIFER, CALLED MORNINGSTAR: GREETINGS.

"OUR RIGHT TRUSTY AND WELL-BELOVED COUSIN--"

NO. NOT THE MESSAGE. JUST THE CONTENT.

HE IS COMING HERE. HE HOPES YOU WILL ALLOW HIM ACCESS TO YOUR REALM, BUT WHETHER YOU WILL OR NO, HE IS COMING.

THERE.

AH.

SHALL WE TAKE HIM OUT AND DESTROY HIM NOW, SIRE?

EAZCH HIZH FAZSHE...

"AND THE LORD SAID UNTO HIM, THEREFORE WHOSOEVER SLAYETH CAIN, VENGEANCE SHALL BE TAKEN ON HIM SEVENFOLD. AND THE LORD SET A MARK UPON CAIN, LEST ANY FINDING HIM SHOULD KILL HIM."

YOU CANNOT HURT HIM. WE MAY NOT GIVE YOU OUR PERMISSION.

CAIN IS UNDER THE PROTECTION OF ONE FAR GREATER THAN THE LORD OF DREAMS.

"AND CAIN WENT OUT FROM THE PRESENCE OF THE LORD, AND DWELT IN THE LAND OF NOD, ON THE EAST OF EDEN."

WHERE YOU STILL LIVE, EH?

YOU'RE UNDER HIS PROTECTION. DREAM WAS SENSIBLE TO SEND YOU AS HIS MESSENGER--ANY OTHER ENVOY WOULD HAVE BEEN RETURNED WITH HIS LIVER IN HIS MOUTH. BUT HE KNEW THAT.

LOOSE HIS BONDS AND LEAVE US.

VHUT NGY ROAHD RUSZCIVAH...

DO YOU WISH TO MAKE US REPEAT OURSELF?

NO, SIRE! YOUR PARDON, SIRE!

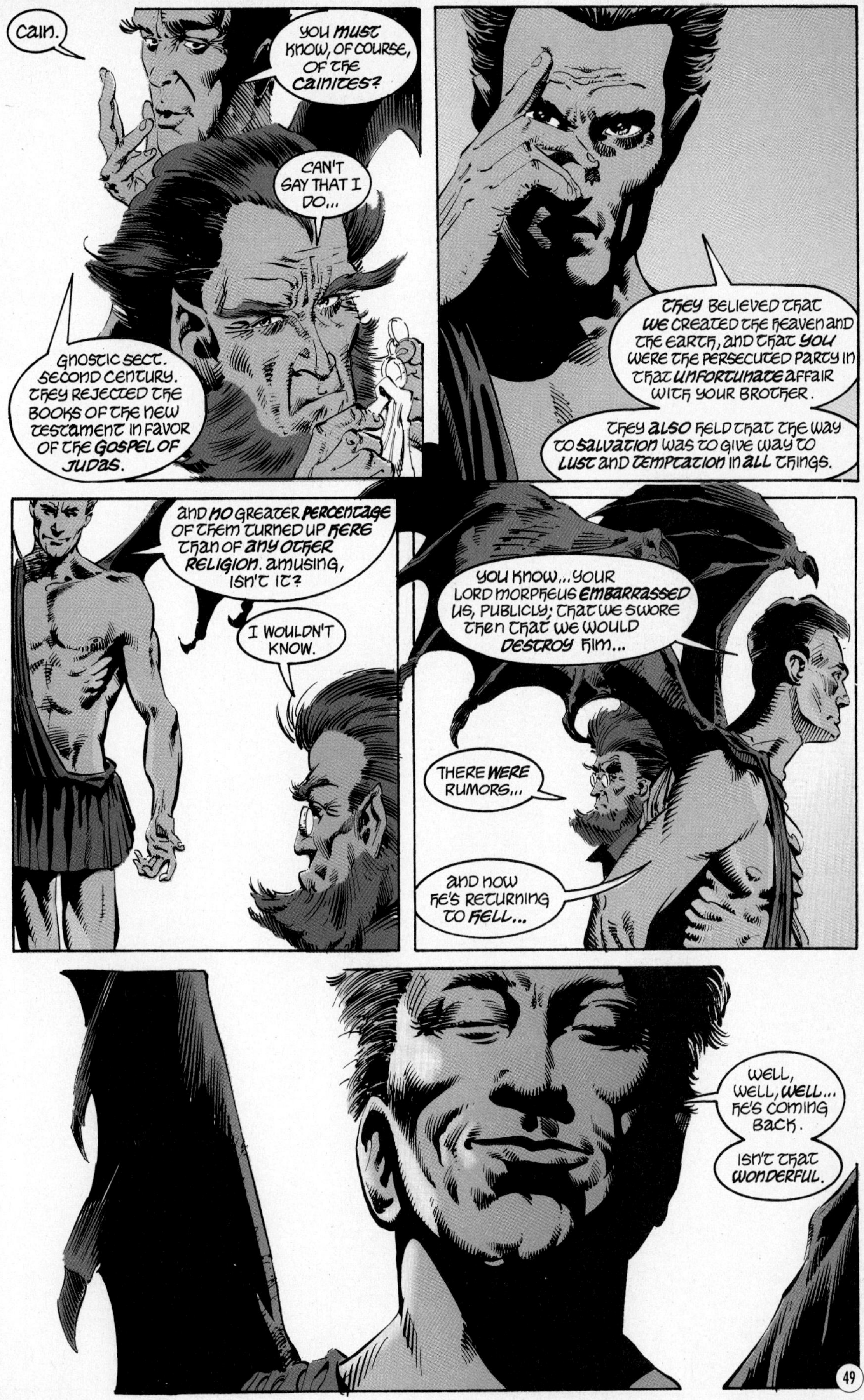
Cain.
YOU MUST KNOW, OF COURSE, OF THE CAINITES?
CAN'T SAY THAT I DO...
GNOSTIC SECT. SECOND CENTURY. THEY REJECTED THE BOOKS OF THE NEW TESTAMENT IN FAVOR OF THE GOSPEL OF JUDAS.
THEY BELIEVED THAT WE CREATED THE HEAVEN AND THE EARTH, AND THAT YOU WERE THE PERSECUTED PARTY IN THAT UNFORTUNATE AFFAIR WITH YOUR BROTHER.
THEY ALSO HELD THAT THE WAY TO SALVATION WAS TO GIVE WAY TO LUST AND TEMPTATION IN ALL THINGS.
AND NO GREATER PERCENTAGE OF THEM TURNED UP HERE THAN OF ANY OTHER RELIGION. AMUSING, ISN'T IT?
I WOULDN'T KNOW.
YOU KNOW... YOUR LORD MORPHEUS EMBARRASSED US, PUBLICLY; THAT WE SWORE THEN THAT WE WOULD DESTROY HIM...
THERE WERE RUMORS...
AND NOW HE'S RETURNING TO HELL...
WELL, WELL, WELL... HE'S COMING BACK.
ISN'T THAT WONDERFUL.

YOU?

YOU-- YOU GET *AWAY* FROM *MY CHILD*-- YOU-- DON'T YOU *TOUCH* HIM-- I'M *WARNING* YOU--

Calm yourself, Hippolyta. You have nothing to fear from me, today.

I have come to see your son. That is all.

YOU *KILLED HIS FATHER.* IF YOU *THINK* I'M GOING TO LET YOU *TOUCH* HIM ...

It is unusual for a child to gestate in dreams. It has not happened for so long...

A child formed in my realm...

Please. I have little enough time as it is. And your son is important.

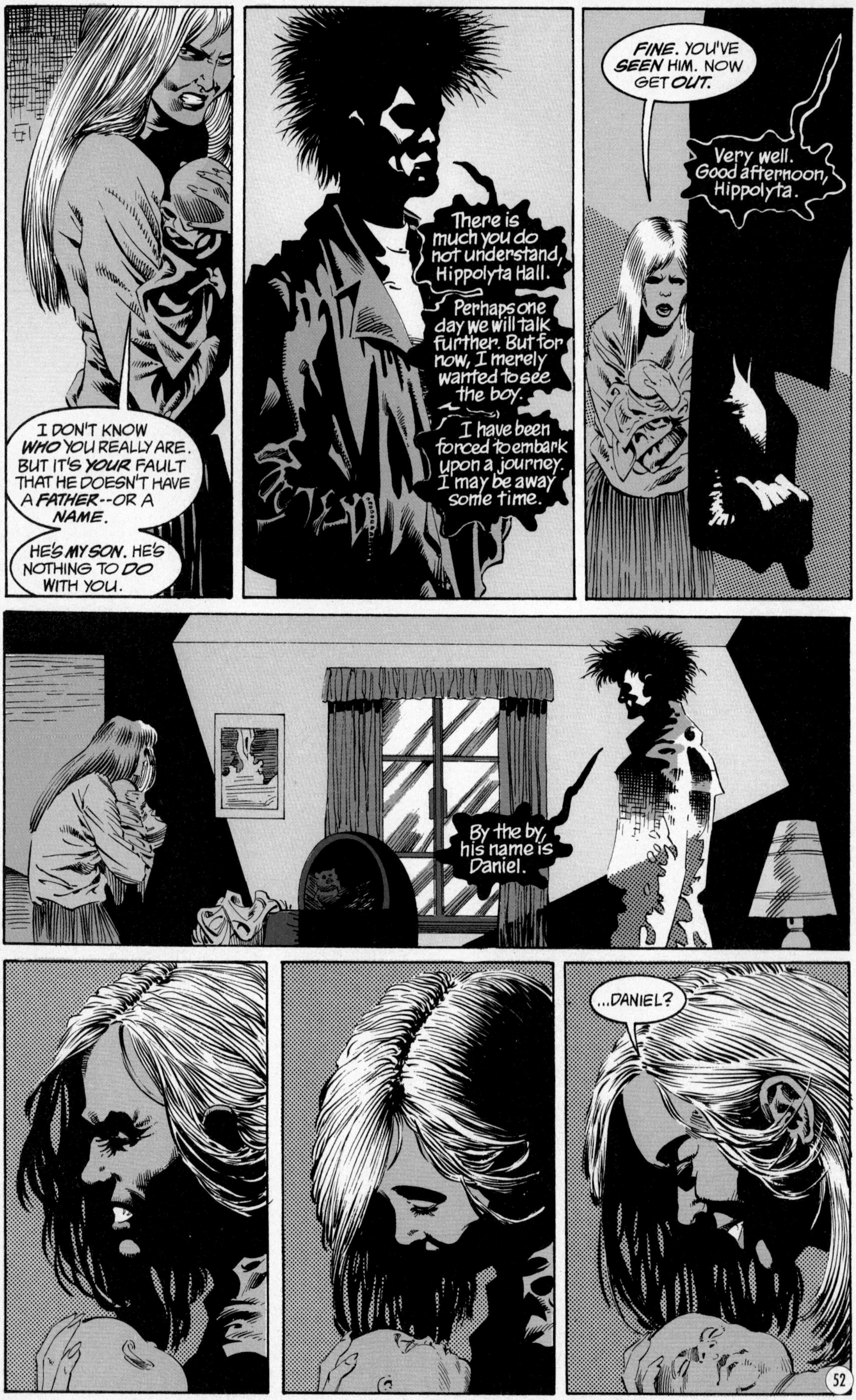
I DON'T KNOW WHO YOU REALLY ARE. BUT IT'S YOUR FAULT THAT HE DOESN'T HAVE A FATHER--OR A NAME.
HE'S MY SON. HE'S NOTHING TO DO WITH YOU.
There is much you do not understand, Hippolyta Hall.
Perhaps one day we will talk further. But for now, I merely wanted to see the boy.
I have been forced to embark upon a journey. I may be away some time.
FINE. YOU'VE SEEN HIM. NOW GET OUT.
Very well. Good afternoon, Hippolyta.
By the by, his name is Daniel.
...DANIEL?

I move from dreamer to dreamer, from dream to dream, hunting for what I need.

Slipping and sliding and flickering through dreams; and the dreamers will wake, and wonder why this dream seemed different, wonder how real their lives can truly be.

One more person to see, then. One final goodbye to be said, and then to Hell.

To Nada.

To Lucifer.

Here: in the dream of Cecilie Latour, as her father, now long dead, walks her through the family cellars.

PAY NO ATTENTION TO THAT MAN BEHIND THE CURTAIN, MA CHERIE.

There.

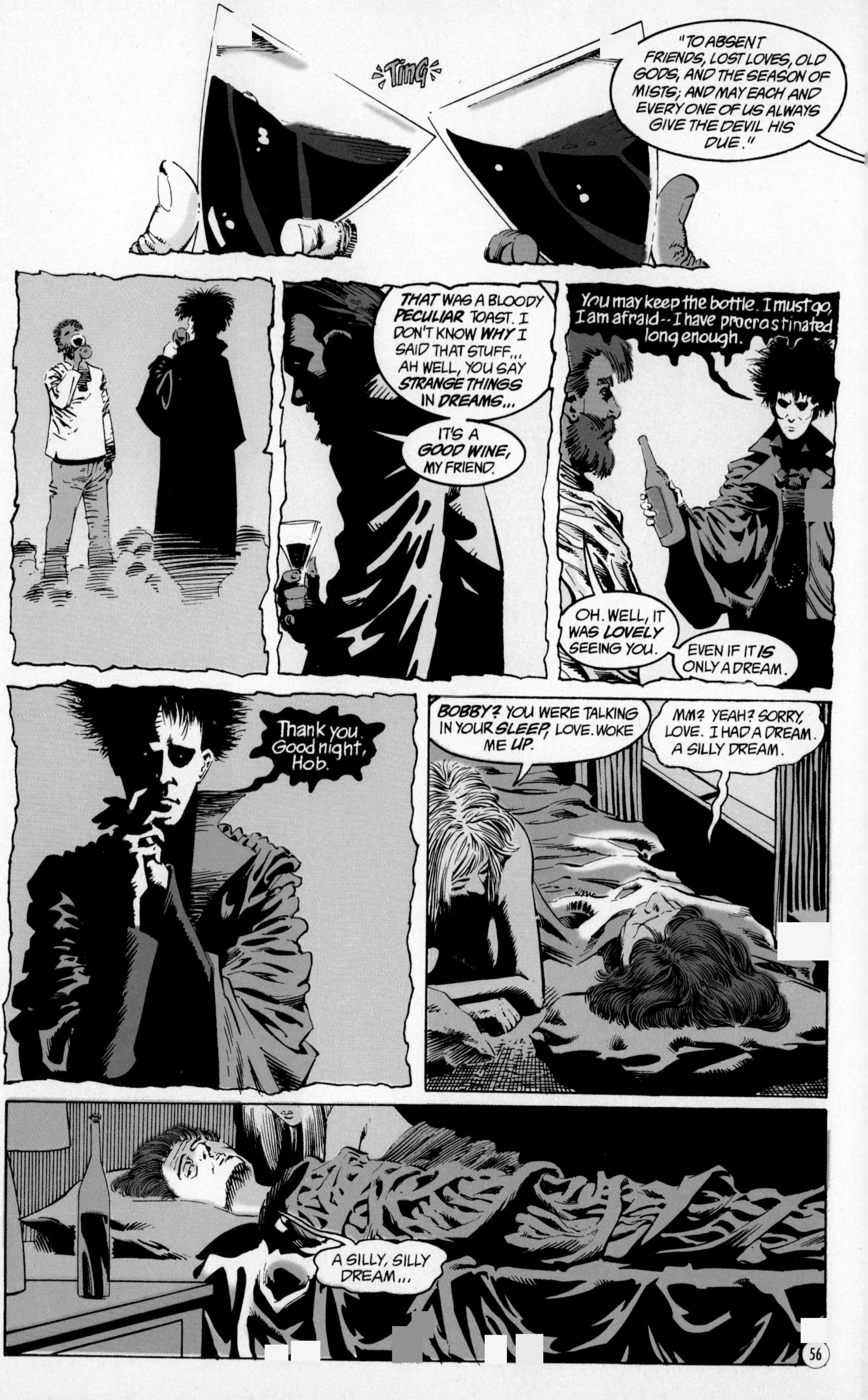
TING
"TO ABSENT FRIENDS, LOST LOVES, OLD GODS, AND THE SEASON OF MISTS; AND MAY EACH AND EVERY ONE OF US ALWAYS GIVE THE DEVIL HIS DUE."
THAT WAS A BLOODY PECULIAR TOAST. I DON'T KNOW WHY I SAID THAT STUFF... AH WELL, YOU SAY STRANGE THINGS IN DREAMS...
IT'S A GOOD WINE, MY FRIEND.
You may keep the bottle. I must go, I am afraid-- I have procrastinated long enough.
OH. WELL, IT WAS LOVELY SEEING YOU.
EVEN IF IT IS ONLY A DREAM.
Thank you. Good night, Hob.
BOBBY? YOU WERE TALKING IN YOUR SLEEP, LOVE. WOKE ME UP.
MM? YEAH? SORRY, LOVE. I HAD A DREAM. A SILLY DREAM.
A SILLY, SILLY DREAM...

BELOW YOU IS OUR DOMAIN, FIRST-BORN MAN. LOOK AT IT.

WHAT DO YOU THINK?

HOME TO MILLIONS OF DEMONS, TO AN UNCOUNTABLE NUMBER OF MORTAL SOULS. DO YOU THINK THEY ARE *HAPPY?*

AH. AH. AH.

WHY, JUST RECENTLY ONE OF THE *MINOR DEMONS* --SOME LITTLE YELLOW RHYMER-- THOUGHT TO DECLARE HIMSELF A *KING OF HELL,* TO USURP THE TRIUMVIRATE...

IT CAME TO NOTHING. THESE THINGS NEVER *DO.* BUT PERHAPS IT MADE HIM HAPPY. *BRIEFLY.*

AH. AH. OHNO. PLEASE. OHNO.

WHAT WE WONDER IS WHY THEY *BOTHER.* THESE LITTLE DEMONS...

THEY COME TO OUR PALACE AND SAY, "WE HAVE BATTLED: THERE WILL BE A COALITION." *WE* SAY, VERY WELL. AND THEY *OUST* EACH OTHER, AND *DESTROY* EACH OTHER, AND IT MATTERS *NOT.*

OR THEY SAY, "LUCIFER, YOU ARE DEPOSED, YOU ARE NO LONGER KING OF HELL-- AS IF MERELY *SAYING* SOMETHING WERE ENOUGH TO MAKE IT *TRUE.*

THEY BELIEVE THEMSELVES LUCIFER'S *EQUALS,* CAIN, ALL THESE PITIFUL LITTLE *GNATS.*

BUT THERE IS ONLY *ONE* THAT WE HAVE EVER OWNED TO BE OUR SUPERIOR. THERE IS BUT *ONE* GREATER THAN US. AND TO *HIM...*

TO HIM WE NO LONGER *SPEAK.*

OHTHANKYOULORD, THANKYOU THANKYOU THANK YOUTHANKYOU...

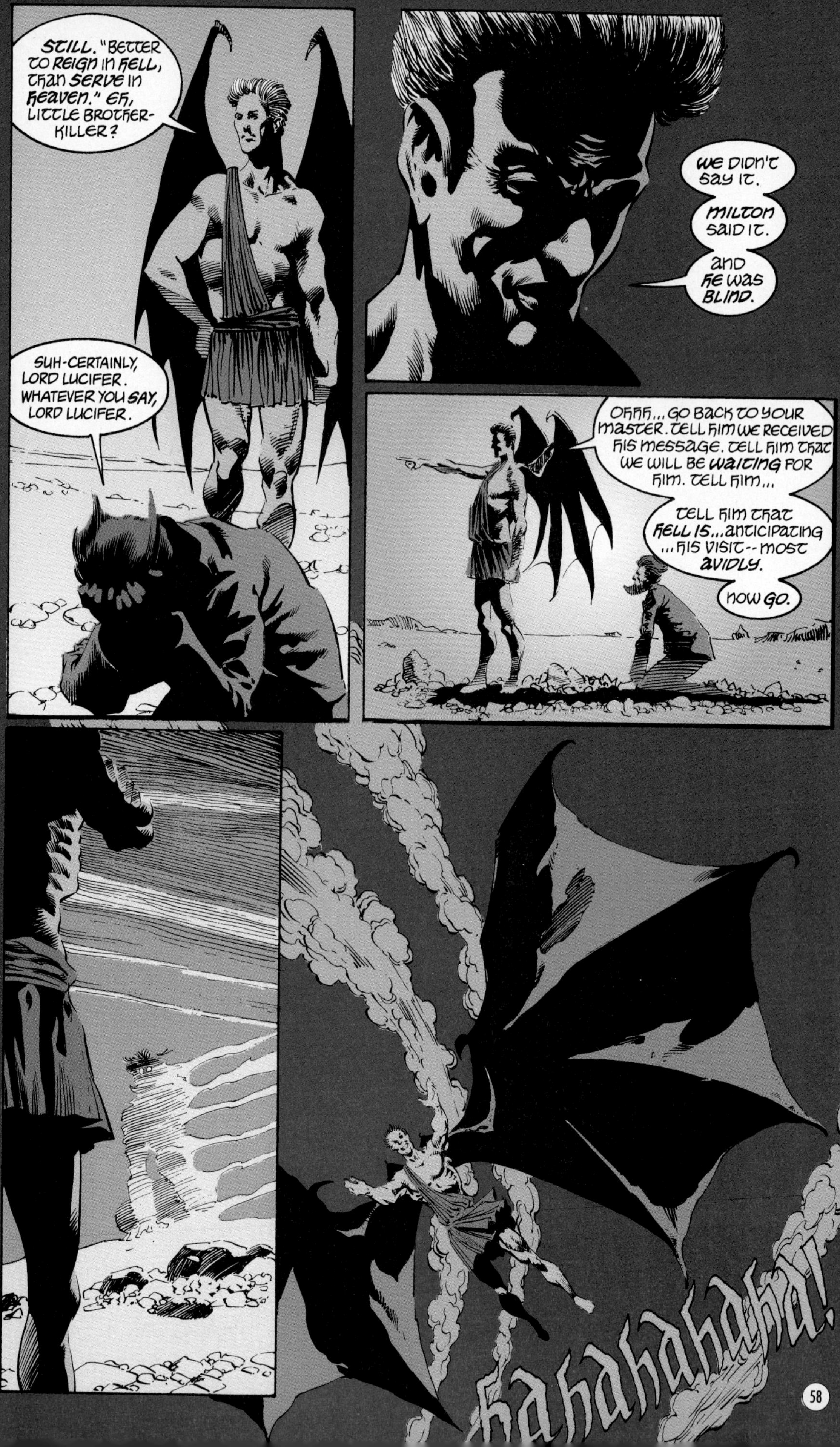
STILL. "BETTER TO REIGN IN HELL, THAN SERVE IN HEAVEN." EH, LITTLE BROTHER-KILLER?
WE DIDN'T SAY IT.
MILTON SAID IT.
AND HE WAS BLIND.
SUH-CERTAINLY, LORD LUCIFER. WHATEVER YOU SAY, LORD LUCIFER.
OHHH... GO BACK TO YOUR MASTER. TELL HIM WE RECEIVED HIS MESSAGE. TELL HIM THAT WE WILL BE WAITING FOR HIM. TELL HIM...
TELL HIM THAT HELL IS... ANTICIPATING ...HIS VISIT--MOST AVIDLY.
NOW GO.
HAHAHAHAHAHA!

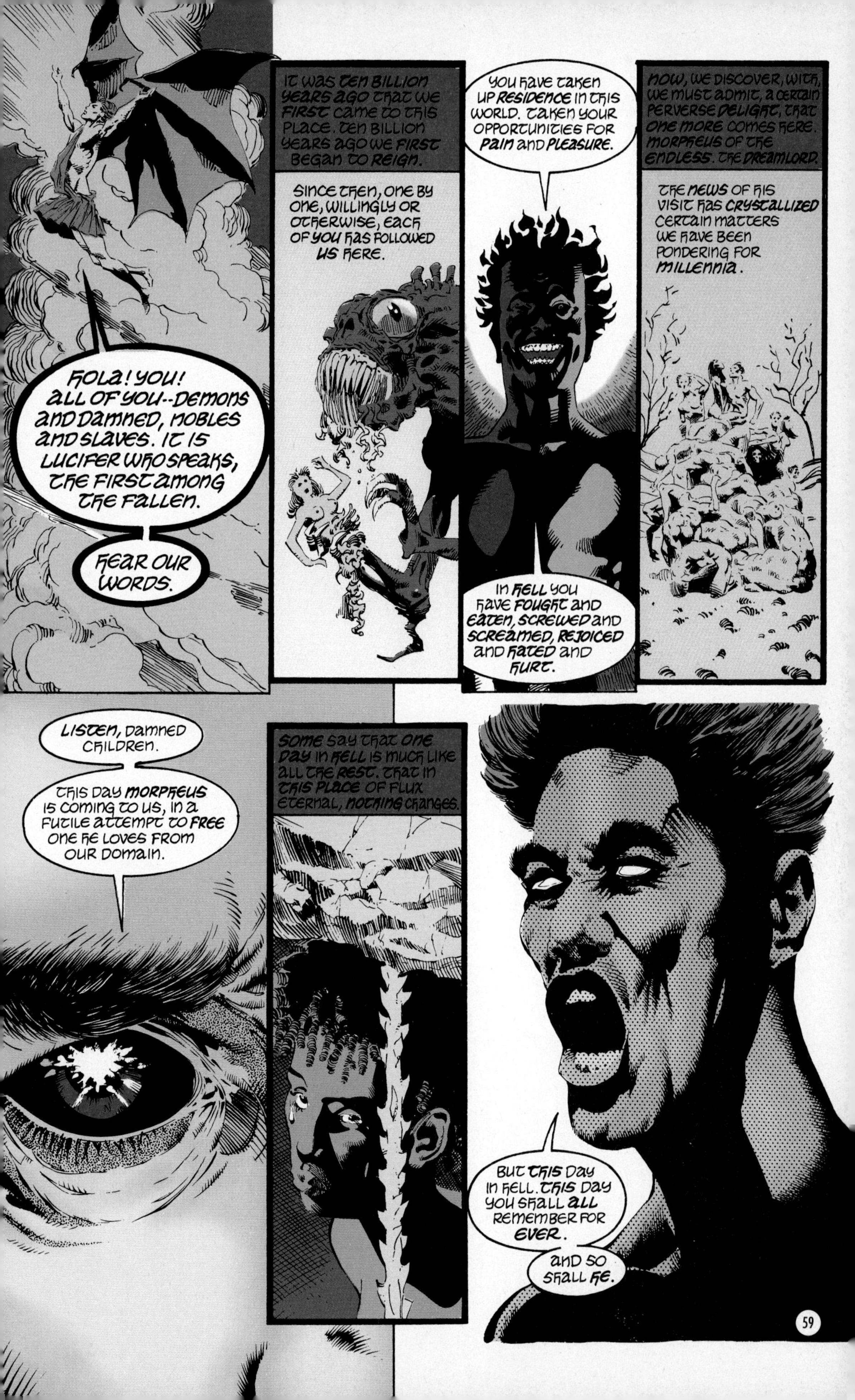
HOLA! YOU! ALL OF YOU--DEMONS AND DAMNED, NOBLES AND SLAVES. IT IS LUCIFER WHO SPEAKS, THE FIRST AMONG THE FALLEN.
HEAR OUR WORDS.
IT WAS TEN BILLION YEARS AGO THAT WE FIRST CAME TO THIS PLACE. TEN BILLION YEARS AGO WE FIRST BEGAN TO REIGN.
SINCE THEN, ONE BY ONE, WILLINGLY OR OTHERWISE, EACH OF YOU HAS FOLLOWED US HERE.
YOU HAVE TAKEN UP RESIDENCE IN THIS WORLD. TAKEN YOUR OPPORTUNITIES FOR PAIN AND PLEASURE.
IN HELL YOU HAVE FOUGHT AND EATEN, SCREWED AND SCREAMED, REJOICED AND HATED AND HURT.
NOW, WE DISCOVER, WITH, WE MUST ADMIT, A CERTAIN PERVERSE DELIGHT, THAT ONE MORE COMES HERE. MORPHEUS OF THE ENDLESS. THE DREAMLORD.
THE NEWS OF HIS VISIT HAS CRYSTALLIZED CERTAIN MATTERS WE HAVE BEEN PONDERING FOR MILLENNIA.
LISTEN, DAMNED CHILDREN.
THIS DAY MORPHEUS IS COMING TO US, IN A FUTILE ATTEMPT TO FREE ONE HE LOVES FROM OUR DOMAIN.
SOME SAY THAT ONE DAY IN HELL IS MUCH LIKE ALL THE REST. THAT IN THIS PLACE OF FLUX ETERNAL, NOTHING CHANGES.
BUT THIS DAY IN HELL. THIS DAY YOU SHALL ALL REMEMBER FOR EVER.
AND SO SHALL HE.

"SIRE -- CAIN HAS RETURNED. HE HAS *GIVEN* YOUR MESSAGE TO THE MORNINGSTAR."

"Ah. Where is he?"

...HIS *EYES*... MY LORD? I... I GAVE HIM YOUR MESSAGE. HE SAYS HE'LL BE WUH-WAITING FOR YOU... HE SAYS HE'S LOOKING *FORWARD* TO IT...

MY LORD -- HE IS MOST TERRIBLE. HE... HE DIDN'T CARE ABOUT MY MARK. HE JUST DIDN'T CARE. HE THOUGHT IT WAS *FUNNY*...

THERE, MY LORD.

Rest, my servant. You have done well.

MY LORD -- I *BEG* YOU TO RECONSIDER. PLEASE. ISN'T TOO LATE...

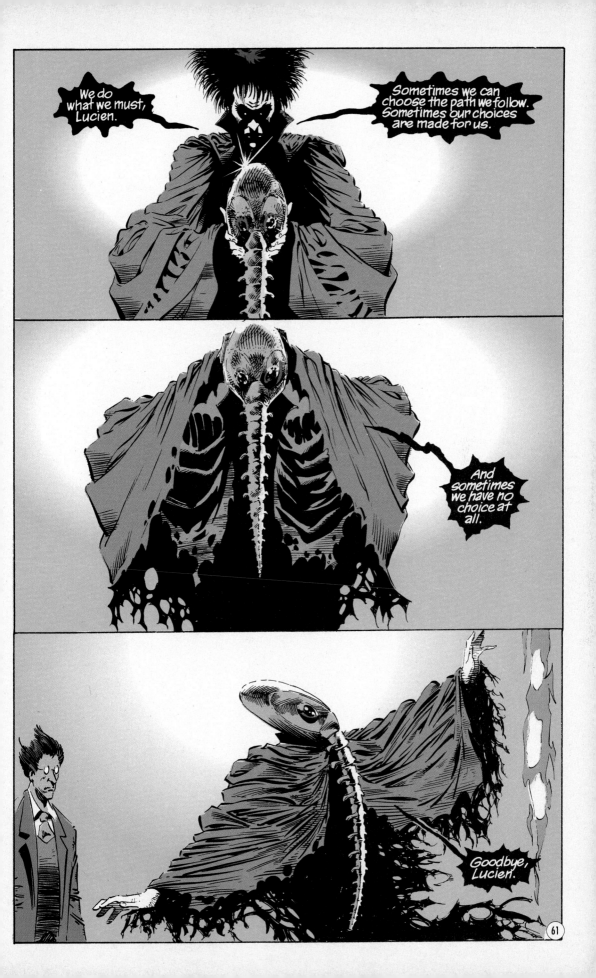

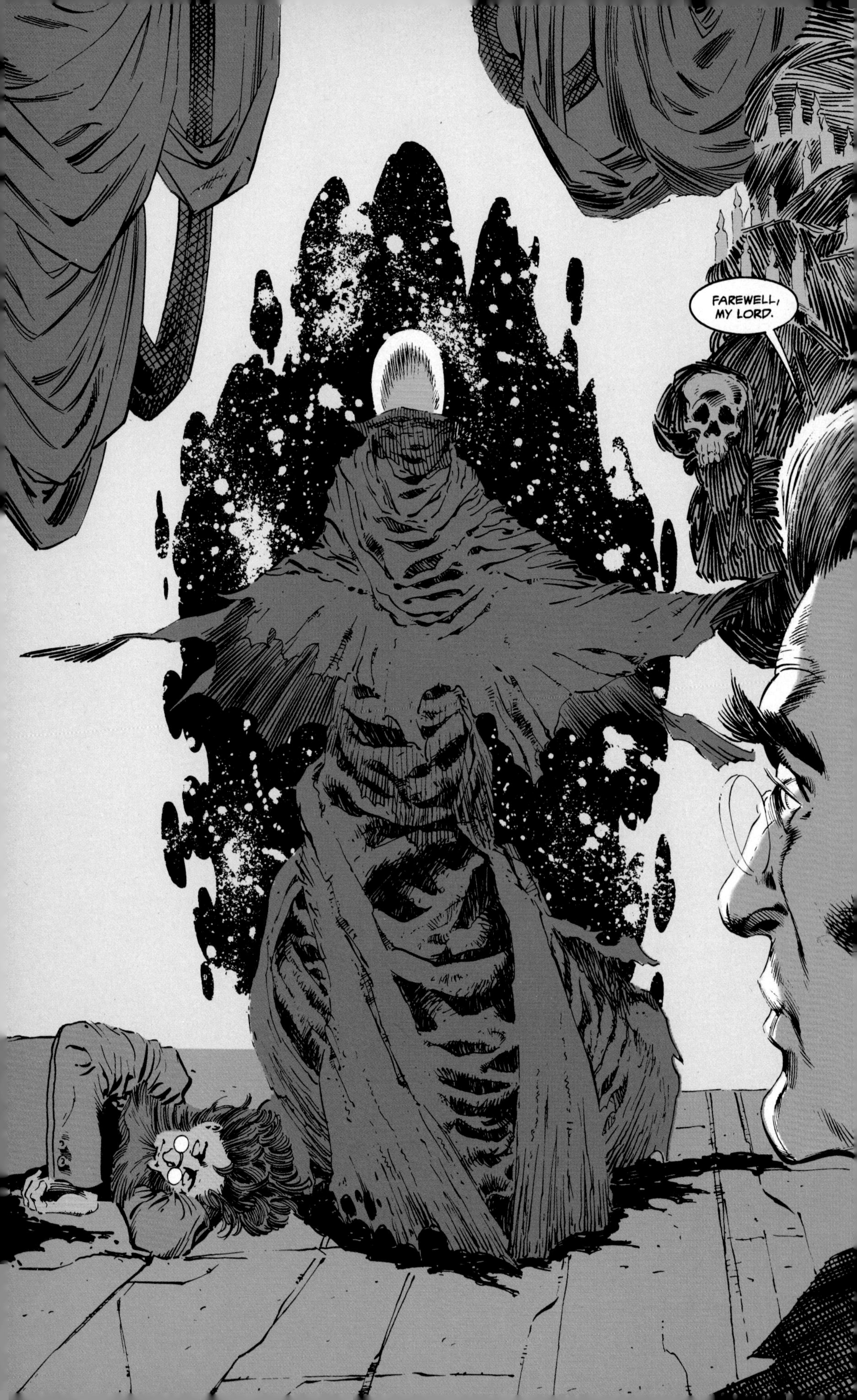
FAREWELL, MY LORD.

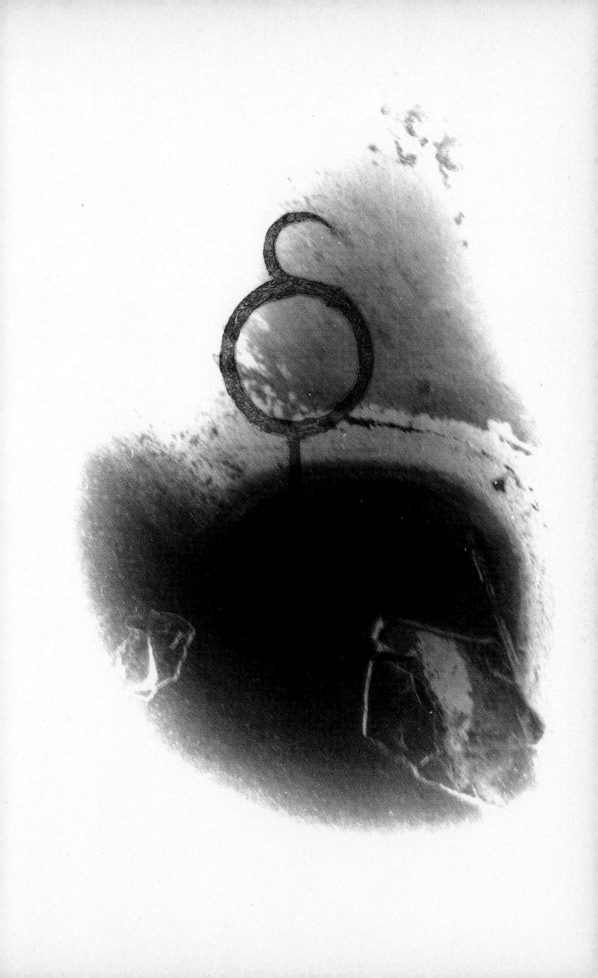

IN WHICH THE LORD OF DREAMS
RETURNS TO HELL, AND HIS
CONFRONTATION WITH THE LORD
OF THAT REALM; IN WHICH A
NUMBER OF DOORS ARE CLOSED FOR
THE LAST TIME; AND CONCERNING
THE STRANGE DISPOSITION OF
A KNIFE AND A KEY.

EPISODE 2

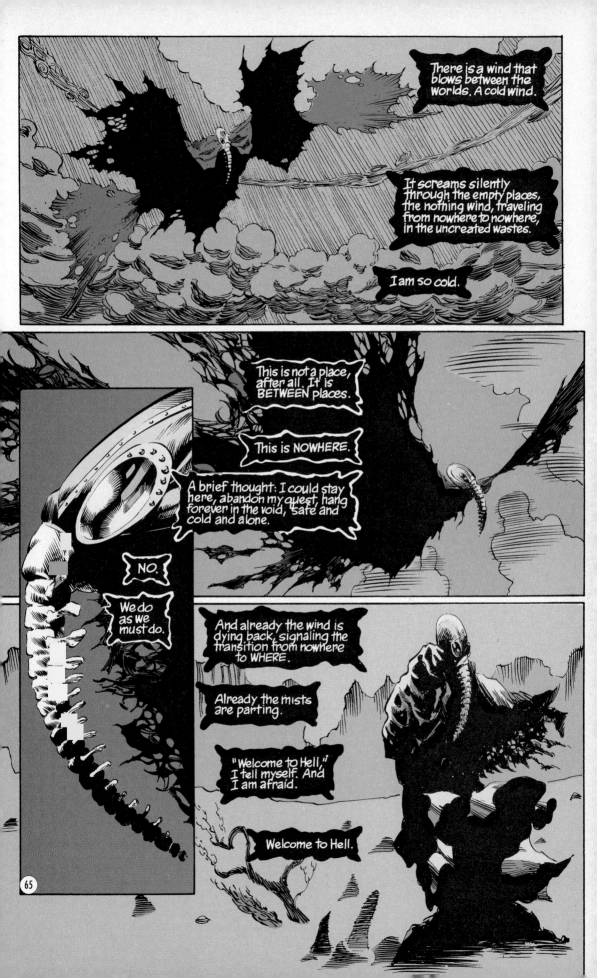

There is a wind that blows between the worlds. A cold wind.

It screams silently through the empty places, the nothing wind, traveling from nowhere to nowhere, in the uncreated wastes.

I am so cold.

This is not a place, after all. It is BETWEEN places.

This is NOWHERE.

A brief thought: I could stay here, abandon my quest, hang forever in the void, safe and cold and alone.

NO.

We do as we must do.

And already the wind is dying back, signaling the transition from nowhere to WHERE.

Already the mists are parting.

"Welcome to Hell," I tell myself. And I am afraid.

Welcome to Hell.

65

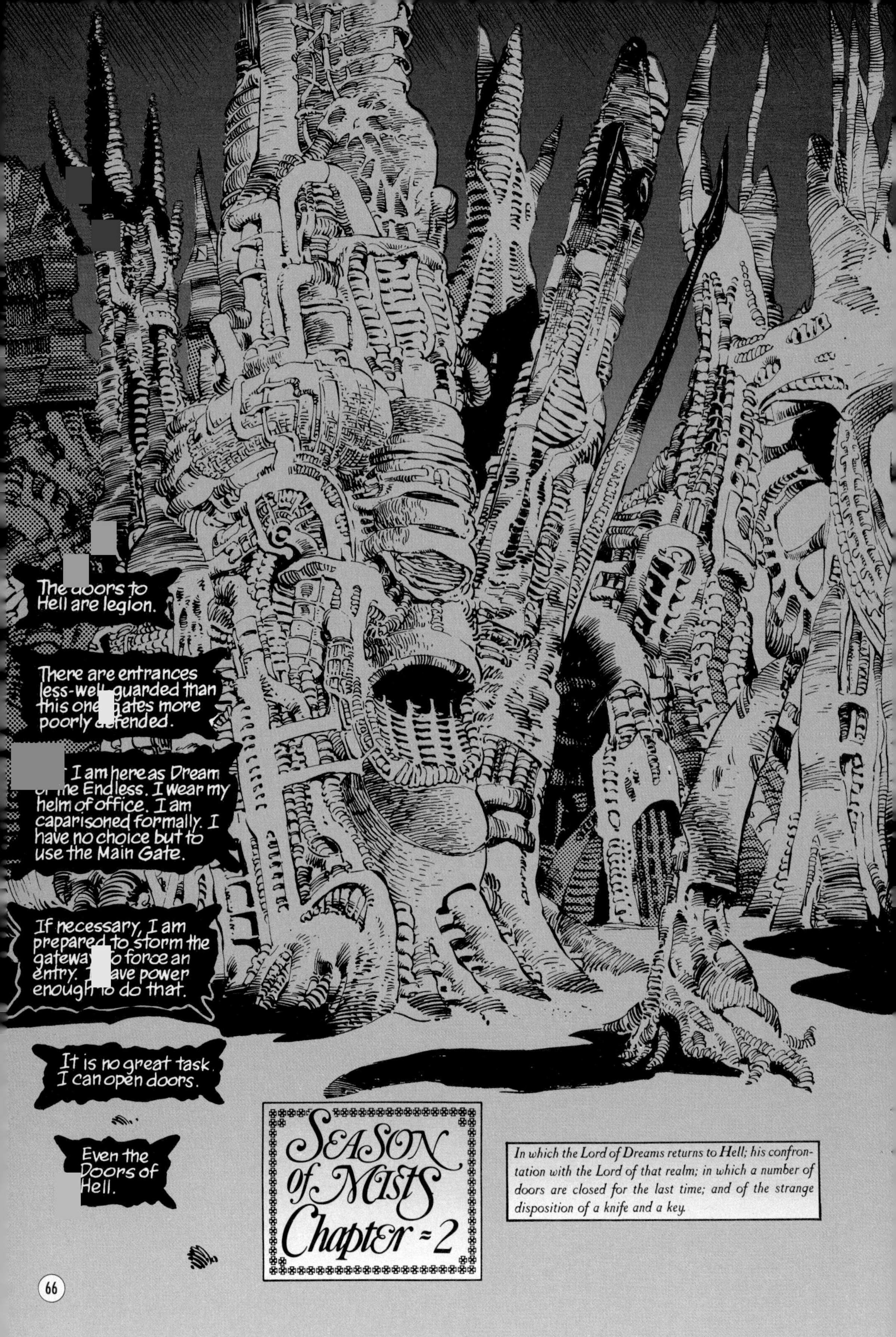
The doors to Hell are legion.
There are entrances less-well guarded than this one; gates more poorly defended.
For I am here as Dream of the Endless. I wear my helm of office. I am caparisoned formally. I have no choice but to use the Main Gate.
If necessary, I am prepared to storm the gateway, to force an entry. I have power enough to do that.
It is no great task. I can open doors.
Even the Doors of Hell.

Season of Mists Chapter 2

In which the Lord of Dreams returns to Hell; his confrontation with the Lord of that realm; in which a number of doors are closed for the last time; and of the strange disposition of a knife and a key.

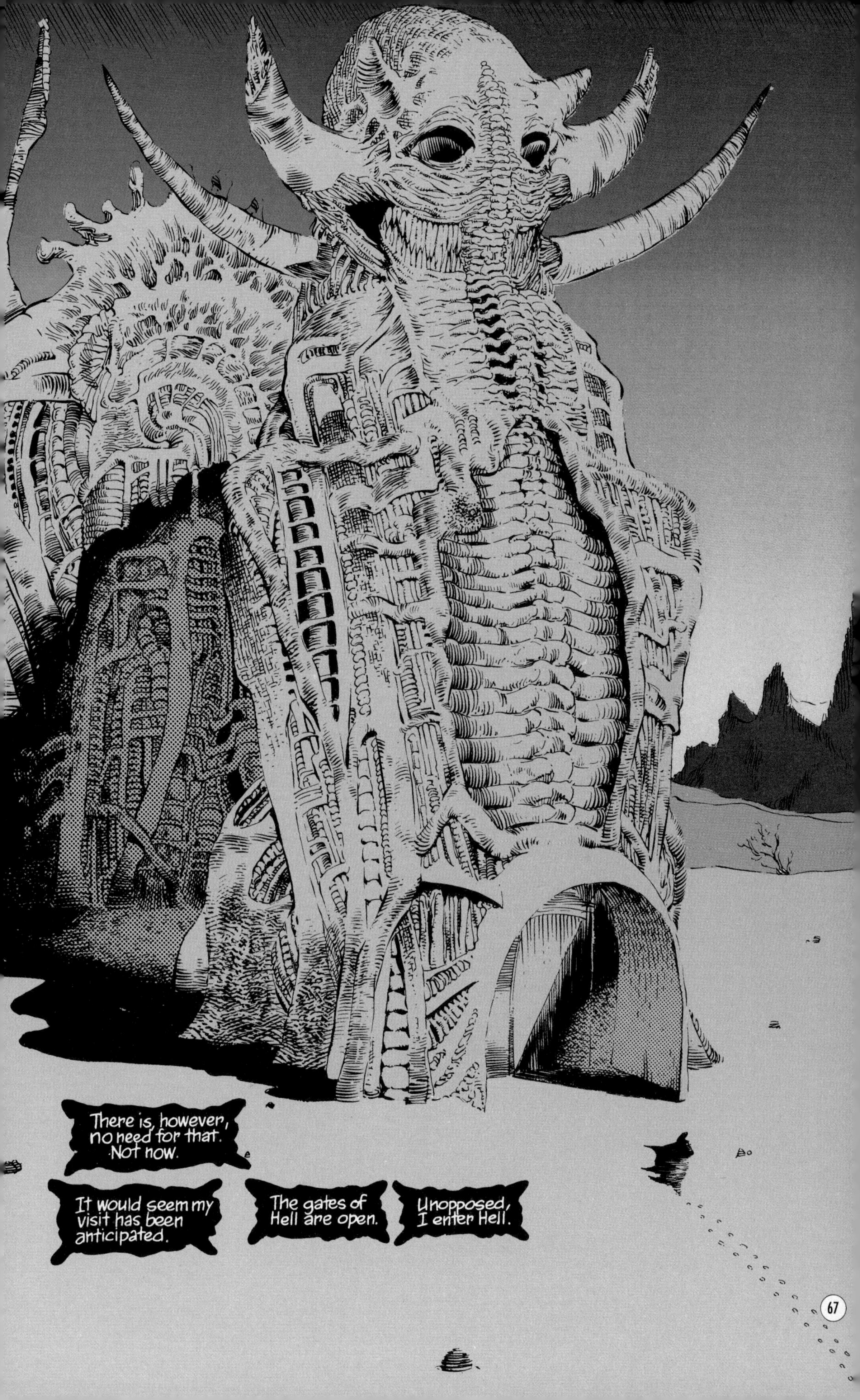
There is, however, no need for that. Not now.
It would seem my visit has been anticipated.
The gates of Hell are open.
Unopposed, I enter Hell.

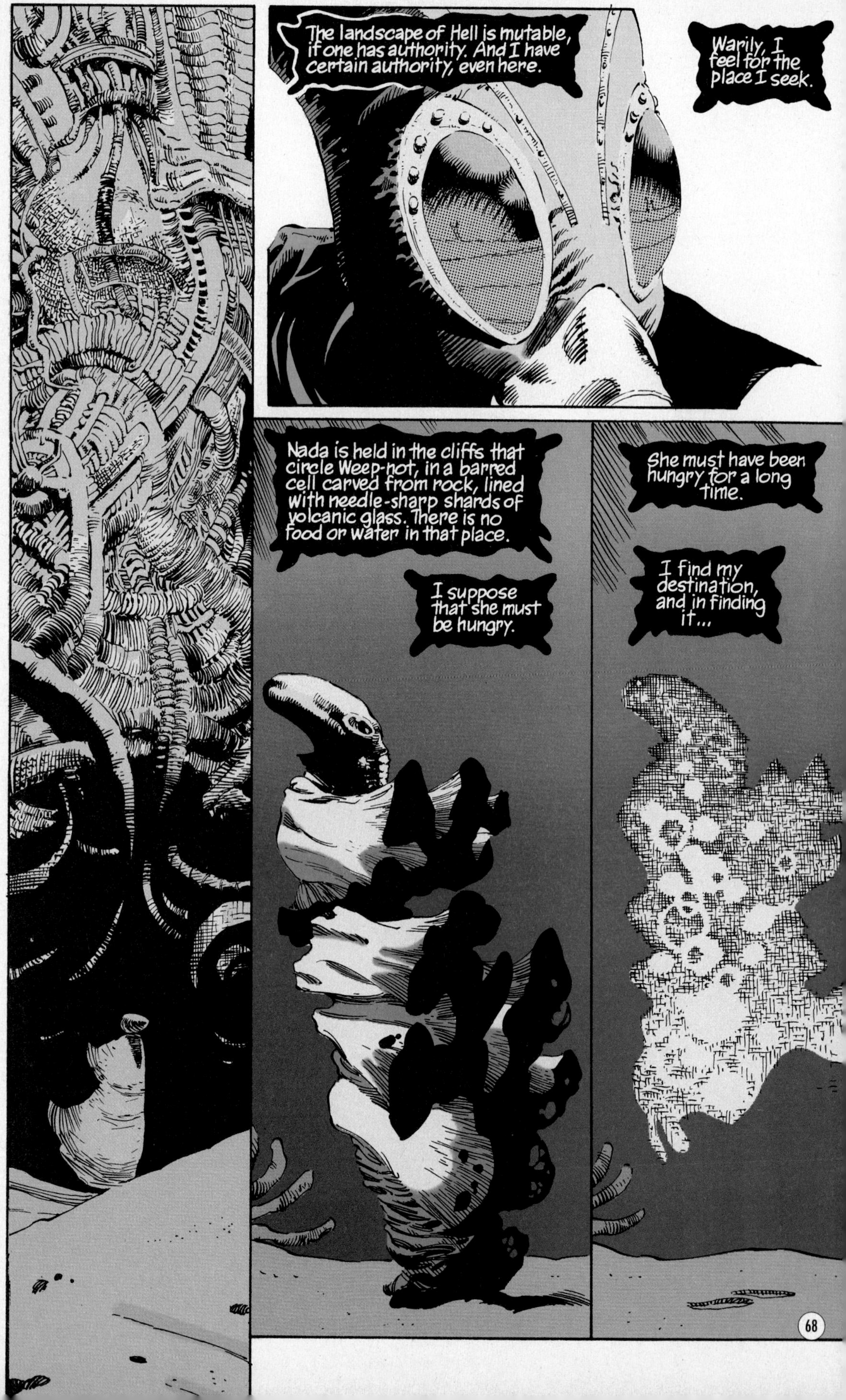
The landscape of Hell is mutable, if one has authority. And I have certain authority, even here.
Warily, I feel for the place I seek.
Nada is held in the cliffs that circle Weep-not, in a barred cell carved from rock, lined with needle-sharp shards of volcanic glass. There is no food or water in that place.
I suppose that she must be hungry.
She must have been hungry for a long time.
I find my destination, and in finding it...

And I think:

They have taken her.

They have hidden her from me.

And then I think:

There is something deeply wrong.

Even for Hell, there is something wrong...

I listen.

Silence, pure and dead.

I feel, with my mind.

Nothing.

It is not just Nada who has gone.

They have all gone. The dead, and the never-born. All of them.

Where are they?

Where is she?

What trickery is this?

70

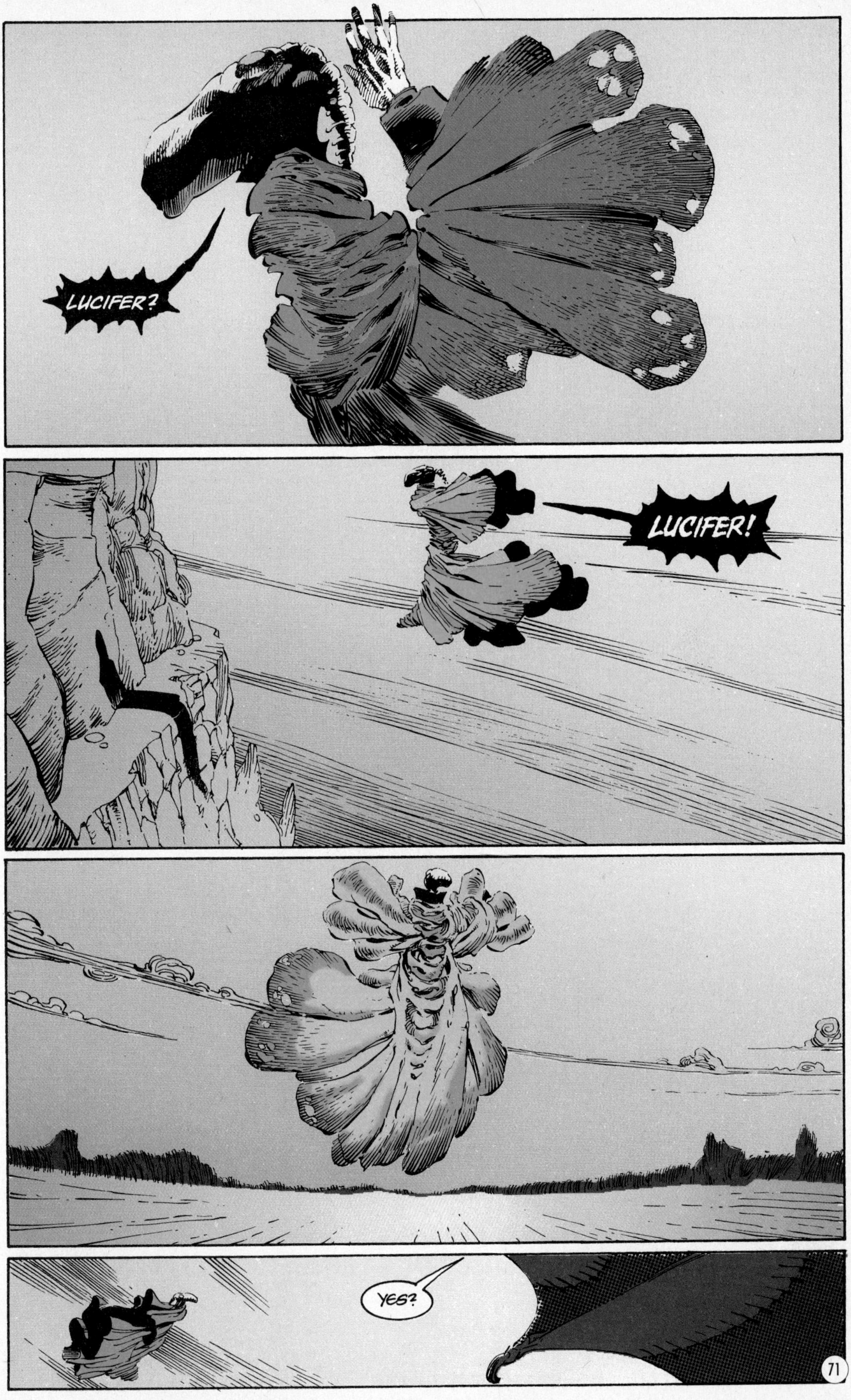
LUCIFER?
LUCIFER!
YES?

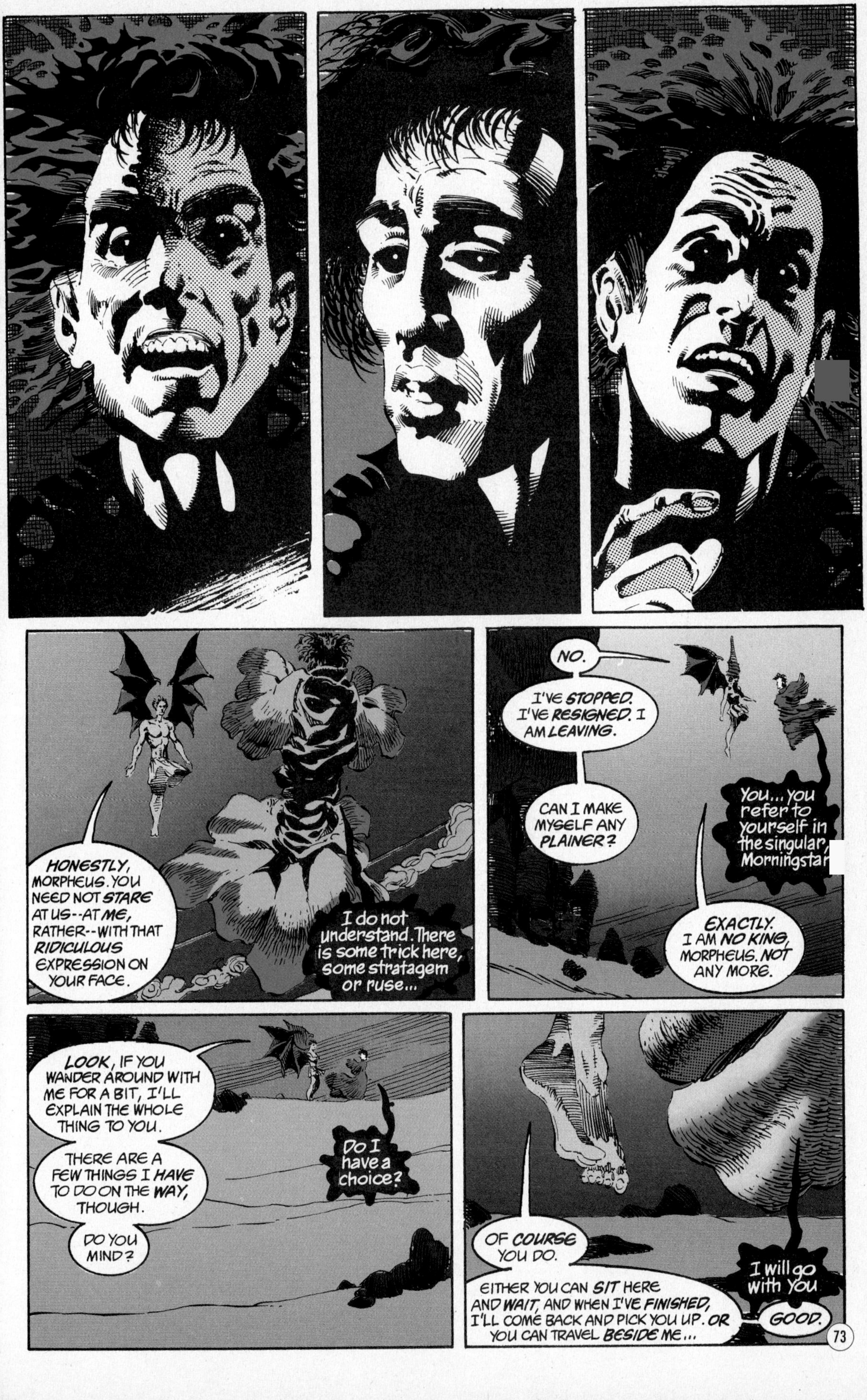

Lucifer.
Where is she? What have you done to her? Where have you hidden her?
HELLO, DREAM.
TAKE OFF THAT SILLY HELMET, AND WE'LL TALK.
I will not be tricked by you, Lucifer Morningstar.
WHY, SWEET MORPHEUS...
...ARE YOU SCARED OF ME?
Yes.
VERY WELL. THEN I GIVE YOU MY WORD THAT WHILE WE ARE WITHIN THE BOUNDS OF HELL, I WILL DO NOTHING TO HARM YOU.
THERE. NOW TAKE OFF YOUR HELMET, AND I'LL TELL YOU WHAT'S HAPPENED TO YOUR LADY-LOVE --AND THE REST OF THEM...
THERE. MUCH BETTER.
NOW, DO YOU STILL WANT TO KNOW WHAT'S GOING ON?
Yes.
ISN'T IT OBVIOUS, DREAM KING?
I'VE QUIT.

HONESTLY, MORPHEUS. YOU NEED NOT STARE AT US--AT ME, RATHER--WITH THAT RIDICULOUS EXPRESSION ON YOUR FACE.
I do not understand. There is some trick here, some stratagem or ruse...
NO.
I'VE STOPPED. I'VE RESIGNED. I AM LEAVING.
CAN I MAKE MYSELF ANY PLAINER?
You... you refer to yourself in the singular, Morningsta
EXACTLY. I AM NO KING, MORPHEUS. NOT ANY MORE.
LOOK, IF YOU WANDER AROUND WITH ME FOR A BIT, I'LL EXPLAIN THE WHOLE THING TO YOU.
THERE ARE A FEW THINGS I HAVE TO DO ON THE WAY, THOUGH.
DO YOU MIND?
Do I have a choice?
OF COURSE YOU DO.
EITHER YOU CAN SIT HERE AND WAIT, AND WHEN I'VE FINISHED, I'LL COME BACK AND PICK YOU UP. OR YOU CAN TRAVEL BESIDE ME...
I will go with You
GOOD.

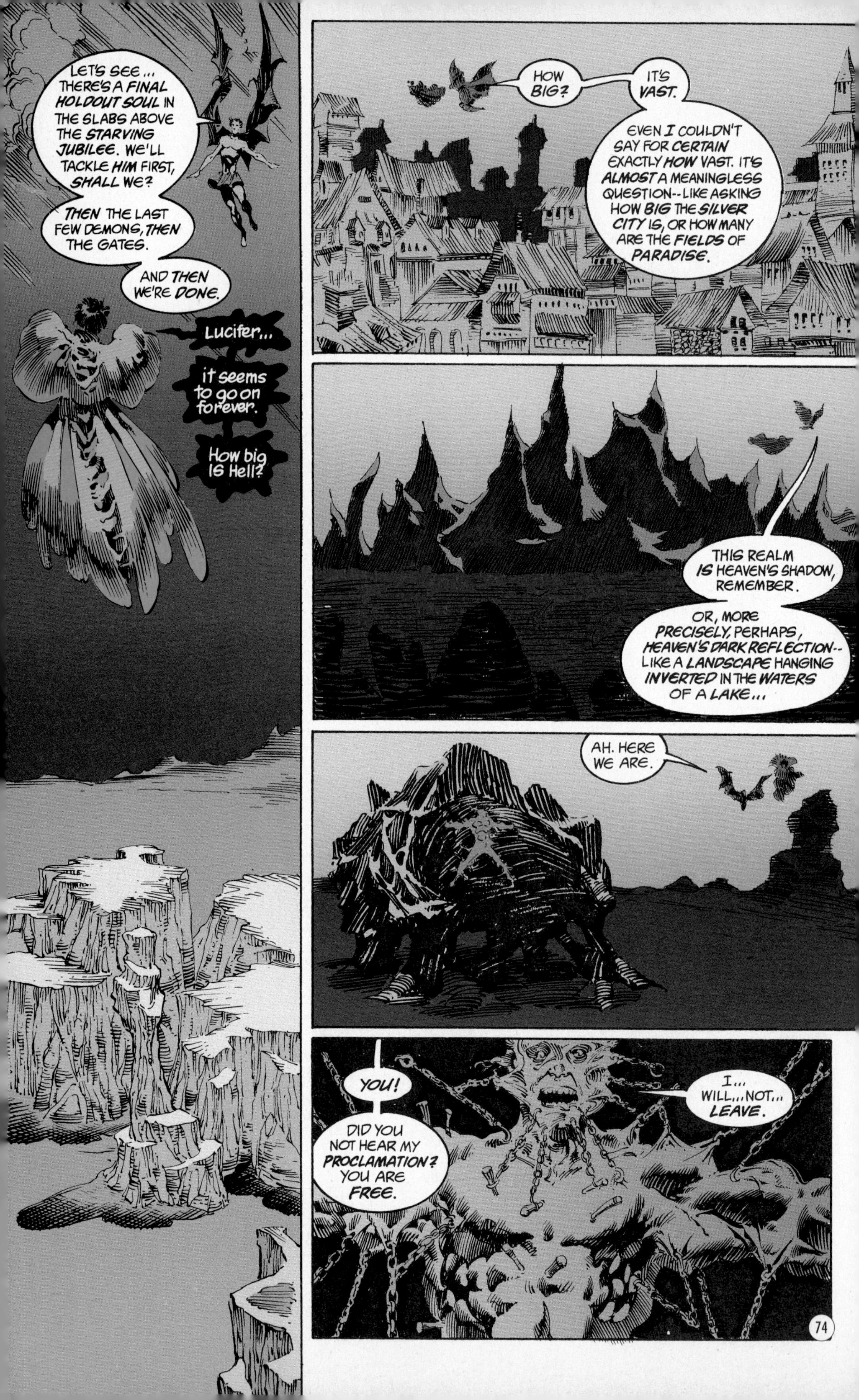

LET'S SEE... THERE'S A FINAL HOLDOUT SOUL IN THE SLABS ABOVE THE STARVING JUBILEE. WE'LL TACKLE HIM FIRST, SHALL WE?
THEN THE LAST FEW DEMONS, THEN THE GATES.
AND THEN WE'RE DONE.
Lucifer...
it seems to go on forever.
How big IS Hell?
HOW BIG?
IT'S VAST.
EVEN I COULDN'T SAY FOR CERTAIN EXACTLY HOW VAST. IT'S ALMOST A MEANINGLESS QUESTION--LIKE ASKING HOW BIG THE SILVER CITY IS, OR HOW MANY ARE THE FIELDS OF PARADISE.
THIS REALM IS HEAVEN'S SHADOW, REMEMBER.
OR, MORE PRECISELY, PERHAPS, HEAVEN'S DARK REFLECTION--LIKE A LANDSCAPE HANGING INVERTED IN THE WATERS OF A LAKE...
AH. HERE WE ARE.
YOU!
DID YOU NOT HEAR MY PROCLAMATION? YOU ARE FREE.
I... WILL... NOT... LEAVE.

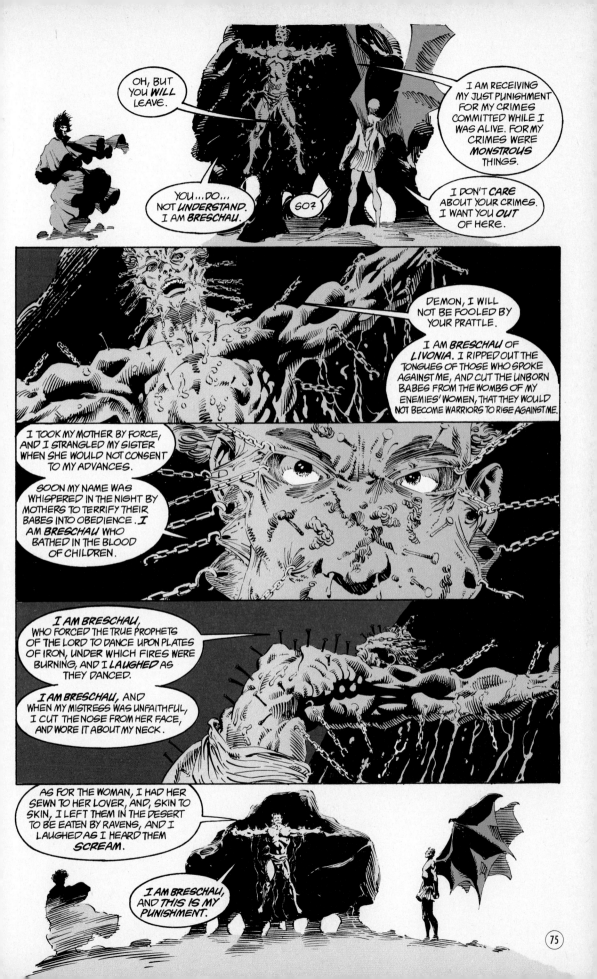

YOU MUST GO.

IT'S NOT ME THAT IS TORTURING ME. IT'S THE *VENGEANCE OF THE LORD* -- DID YOU NOT HEAR? I--

--AM BRESCHAU. YES, I KNOW.

DID YOU NOT *HEAR* ME, FIEND? I HAVE *KILLED*--

I HEARD. YOU KILLED A *NUMBER* OF PEOPLE WHO BY *NOW* WOULD BE *LONG-SINCE DEAD* ANYWAY. SO *WHAT?*

YOU'VE BEEN *CHAINED* TO THIS SLAB FOR ELEVEN HUNDRED YEARS. HAVEN'T YOU TORTURED YOURSELF ENOUGH?

BUT NO ONE TODAY REMEMBERS BRESCHAU.

NO ONE.

I DOUBT *ONE* LIVING MORTAL IN A *HUNDRED THOUSAND* COULD EVEN POINT TO WHERE LIVONIA *USED* TO BE, ON A *MAP.*

THE WORLD HAS *FORGOTTEN* YOU.

BUT... I... AM...

ENOUGH. GO.

Where has he gone?

AWAY.

HMM -- NOW, DOWN TO THE WANING STRAND FOR THE LAST FEW *STRAGGLERS.*

LUCIFER-- I do not understand--

BUT IT'S PERFECTLY *PLAIN,* MORPHEUS. IT'S OVER.

76

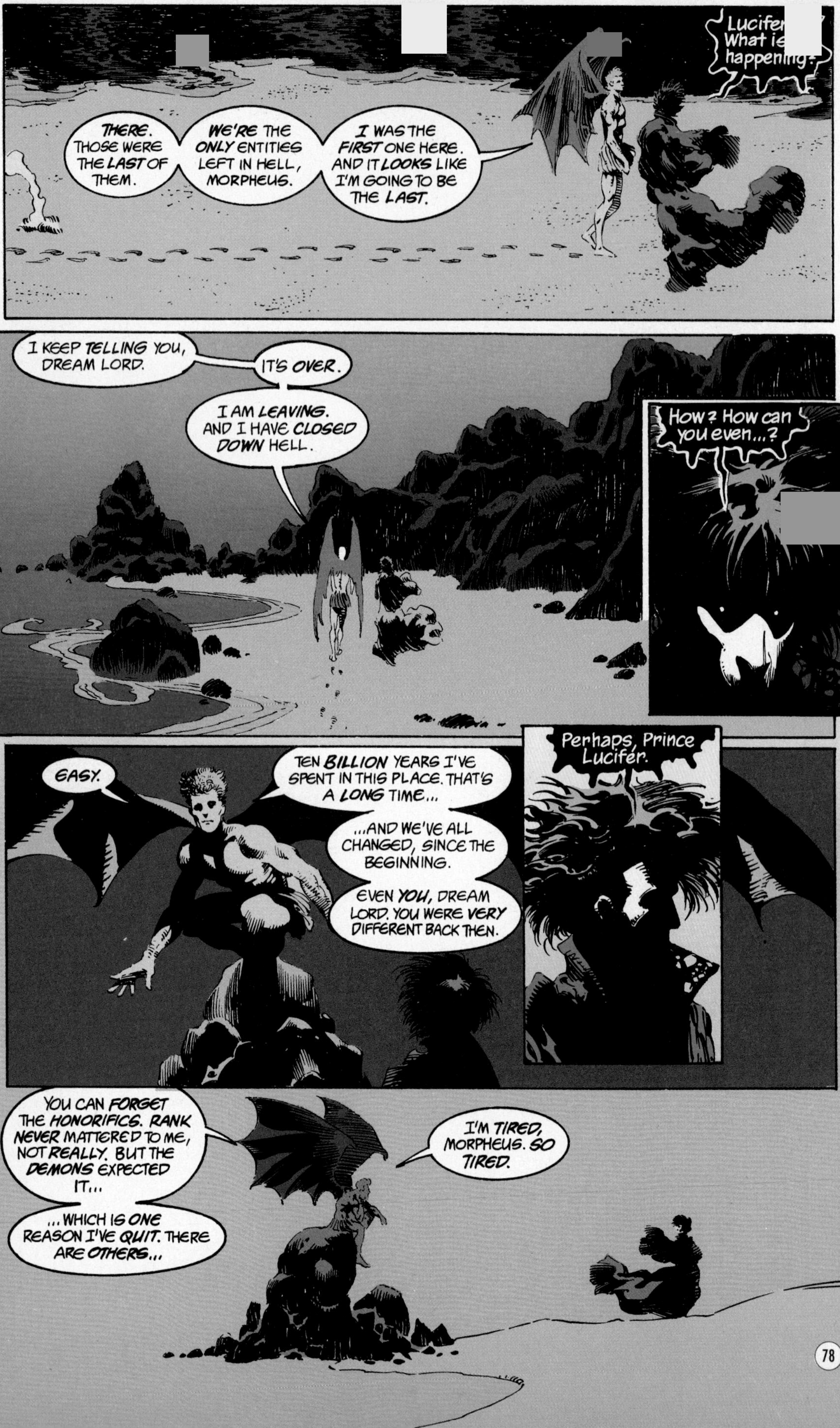

Lucifer What is happening?
THERE. THOSE WERE THE LAST OF THEM.
WE'RE THE ONLY ENTITIES LEFT IN HELL, MORPHEUS.
I WAS THE FIRST ONE HERE. AND IT LOOKS LIKE I'M GOING TO BE THE LAST.
I KEEP TELLING YOU, DREAM LORD.
IT'S OVER.
I AM LEAVING. AND I HAVE CLOSED DOWN HELL.
How? How can you even...?
EASY.
TEN BILLION YEARS I'VE SPENT IN THIS PLACE. THAT'S A LONG TIME...
...AND WE'VE ALL CHANGED, SINCE THE BEGINNING.
EVEN YOU, DREAM LORD. YOU WERE VERY DIFFERENT BACK THEN.
Perhaps, Prince Lucifer.
YOU CAN FORGET THE HONORIFICS. RANK NEVER MATTERED TO ME, NOT REALLY. BUT THE DEMONS EXPECTED IT...
...WHICH IS ONE REASON I'VE QUIT. THERE ARE OTHERS...
I'M TIRED, MORPHEUS. SO TIRED.

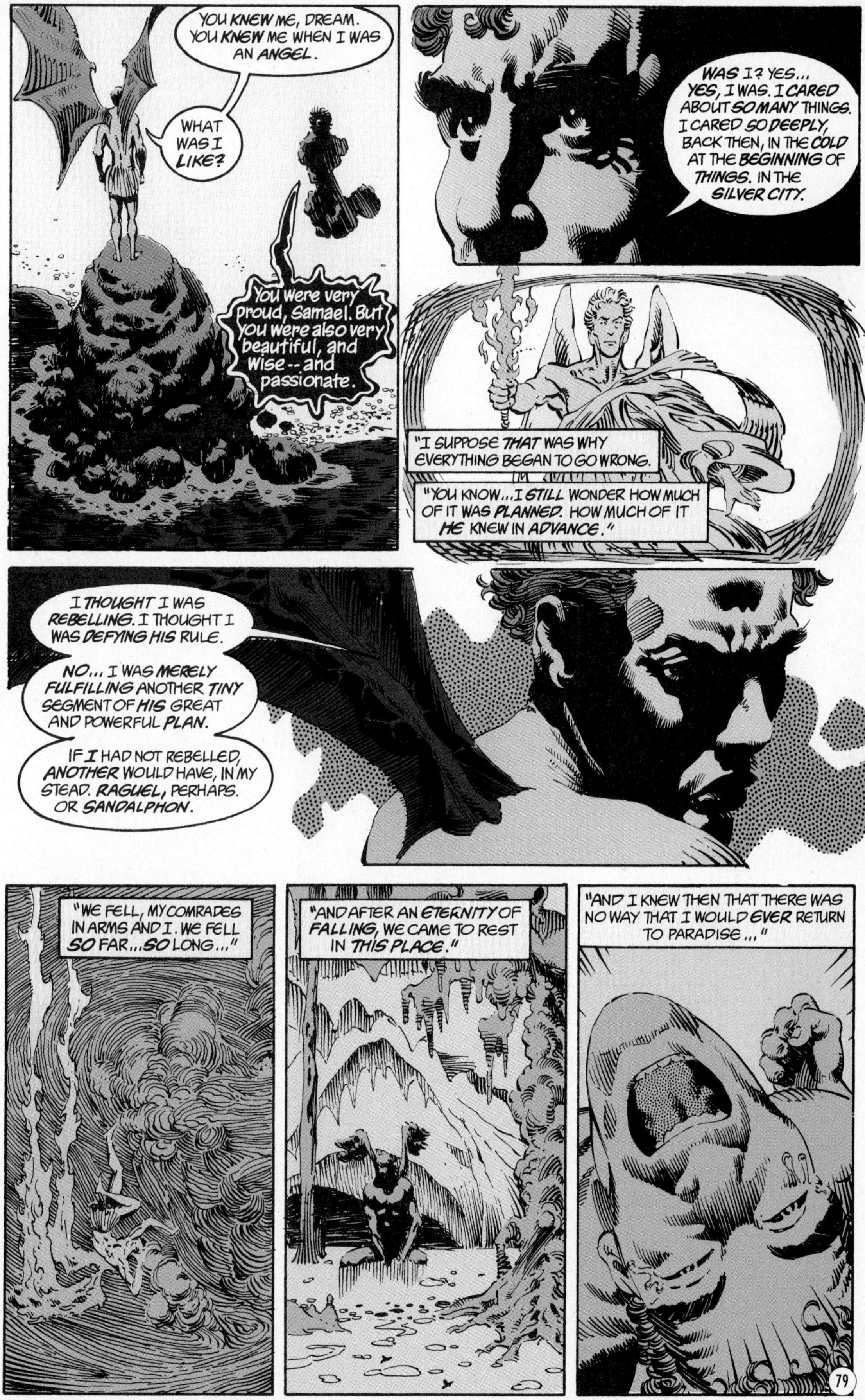

YOU KNEW ME, DREAM. YOU KNEW ME WHEN I WAS AN ANGEL.
WHAT WAS I LIKE?
You were very proud, Samael. But you were also very beautiful, and wise -- and passionate.
WAS I? YES... YES, I WAS. I CARED ABOUT SO MANY THINGS. I CARED SO DEEPLY, BACK THEN, IN THE COLD AT THE BEGINNING OF THINGS. IN THE SILVER CITY.
"I SUPPOSE THAT WAS WHY EVERYTHING BEGAN TO GO WRONG.
"YOU KNOW... I STILL WONDER HOW MUCH OF IT WAS PLANNED. HOW MUCH OF IT HE KNEW IN ADVANCE."
I THOUGHT I WAS REBELLING. I THOUGHT I WAS DEFYING HIS RULE.
NO... I WAS MERELY FULFILLING ANOTHER TINY SEGMENT OF HIS GREAT AND POWERFUL PLAN.
IF I HAD NOT REBELLED, ANOTHER WOULD HAVE, IN MY STEAD. RAGUEL, PERHAPS. OR SANDALPHON.
"WE FELL, MY COMRADES IN ARMS AND I. WE FELL SO FAR... SO LONG..."
"AND AFTER AN ETERNITY OF FALLING, WE CAME TO REST IN THIS PLACE."
"AND I KNEW THEN THAT THERE WAS NO WAY THAT I WOULD EVER RETURN TO PARADISE..."

BUT I'M **WOOLGATHERING.** I APOLOGIZE.

YOU DO NOT MIND IF I **WORK** AS WE TALK? THERE ARE **NO** MORE **ENTITIES** LEFT WITHIN THE BOUNDS INFERNAL. BUT I NEED TO **SECURE** THE LAST GATES.

No. I do not mind.

I HAVE **SEALED** OR **ERASED** MOST OF THE **GATEWAYS.** THERE ARE ONLY A **FEW** I NEED TO SECURE **PERSONALLY.**

YOU **ALSO** RULE A **WORLD,** MORPHEUS. A WORLD OF **SLEEPERS** AND **DREAMERS.** OF **STORIES.** A SIMPLE PLACE -- COMPARED TO **HELL.**

I **ENVY** YOU.

CAN YOU IMAGINE WHAT IT WAS **LIKE?**

TEN BILLION YEARS SPENT PROVIDING A PLACE FOR **DEAD MORTALS** TO **TORTURE** THEMSELVES.

AND LIKE **ALL** MASOCHISTS **THEY** CALLED THE SHOTS -- "BURN ME" "FREEZE ME" "EAT ME" "HURT ME"...

AND WE **DID.**

80

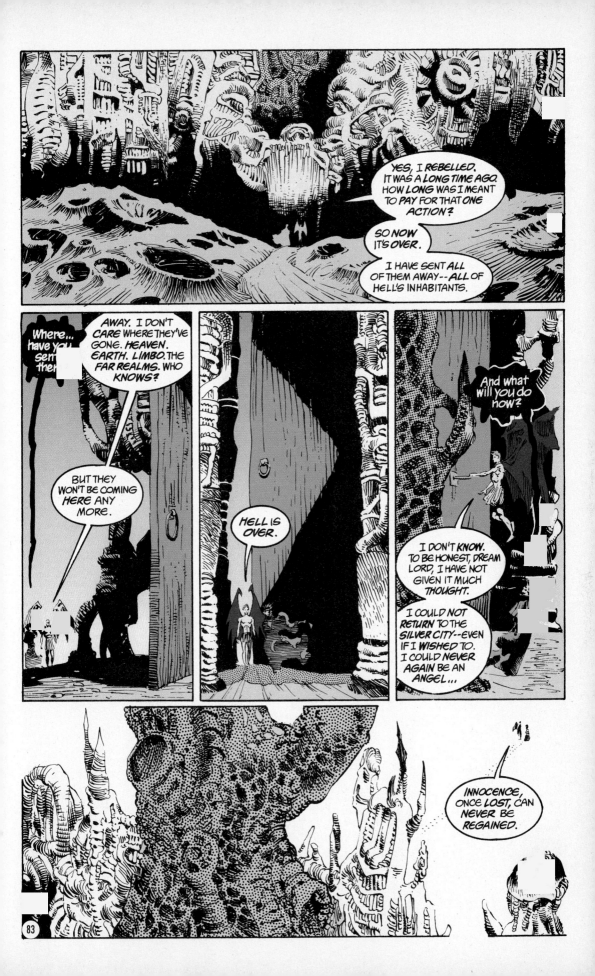

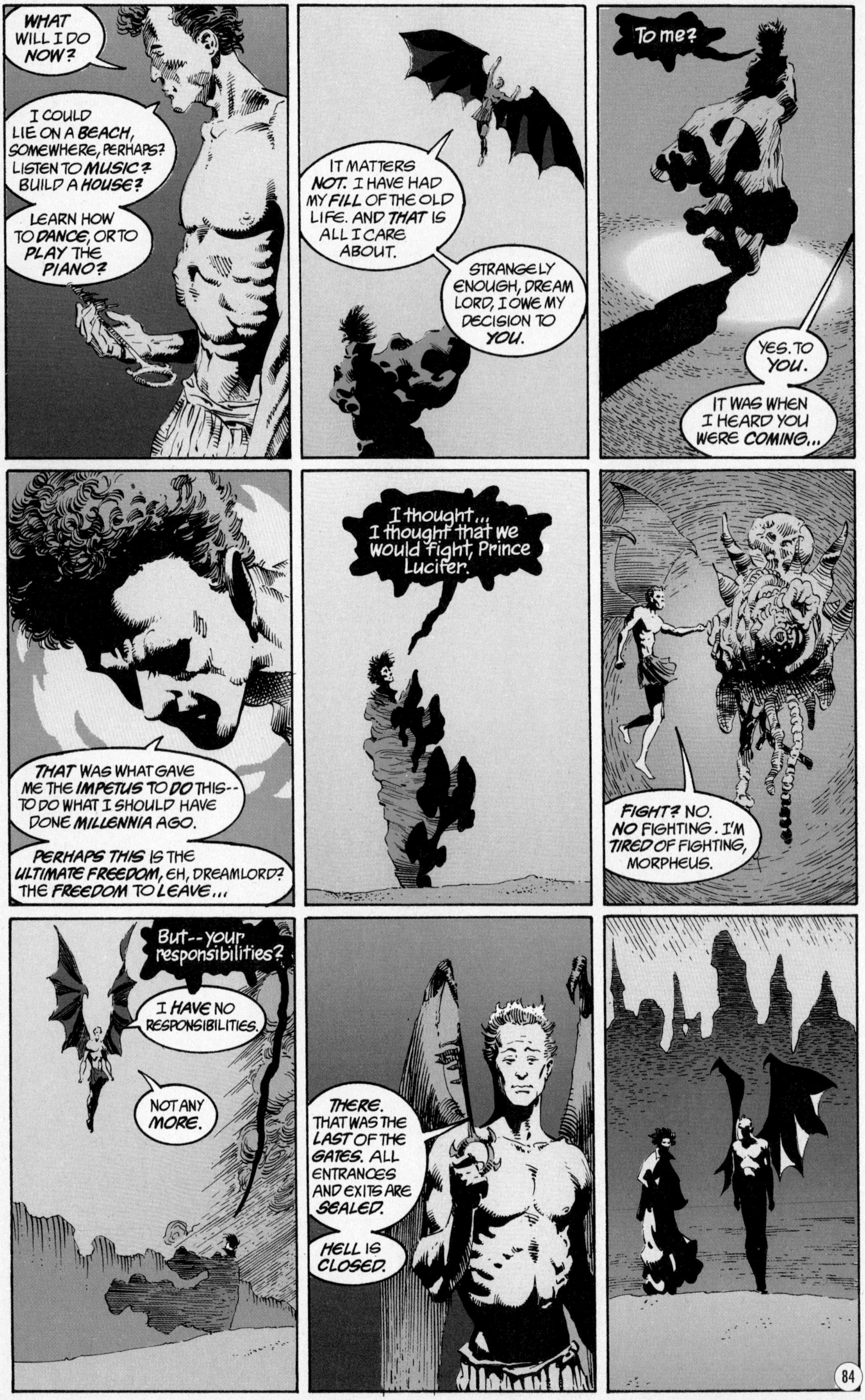
WHAT WILL I DO NOW?
I COULD LIE ON A BEACH, SOMEWHERE, PERHAPS? LISTEN TO MUSIC? BUILD A HOUSE?
LEARN HOW TO DANCE, OR TO PLAY THE PIANO?
IT MATTERS NOT. I HAVE HAD MY FILL OF THE OLD LIFE. AND THAT IS ALL I CARE ABOUT.
STRANGELY ENOUGH, DREAM LORD, I OWE MY DECISION TO YOU.
To me?
YES. TO YOU.
IT WAS WHEN I HEARD YOU WERE COMING...
THAT WAS WHAT GAVE ME THE IMPETUS TO DO THIS-- TO DO WHAT I SHOULD HAVE DONE MILLENNIA AGO.
PERHAPS THIS IS THE ULTIMATE FREEDOM, EH, DREAMLORD? THE FREEDOM TO LEAVE...
I thought... I thought that we would fight, Prince Lucifer.
FIGHT? NO. NO FIGHTING. I'M TIRED OF FIGHTING, MORPHEUS.
But--your responsibilities?
I HAVE NO RESPONSIBILITIES.
NOT ANY MORE.
THERE. THAT WAS THE LAST OF THE GATES. ALL ENTRANCES AND EXITS ARE SEALED.
HELL IS CLOSED.

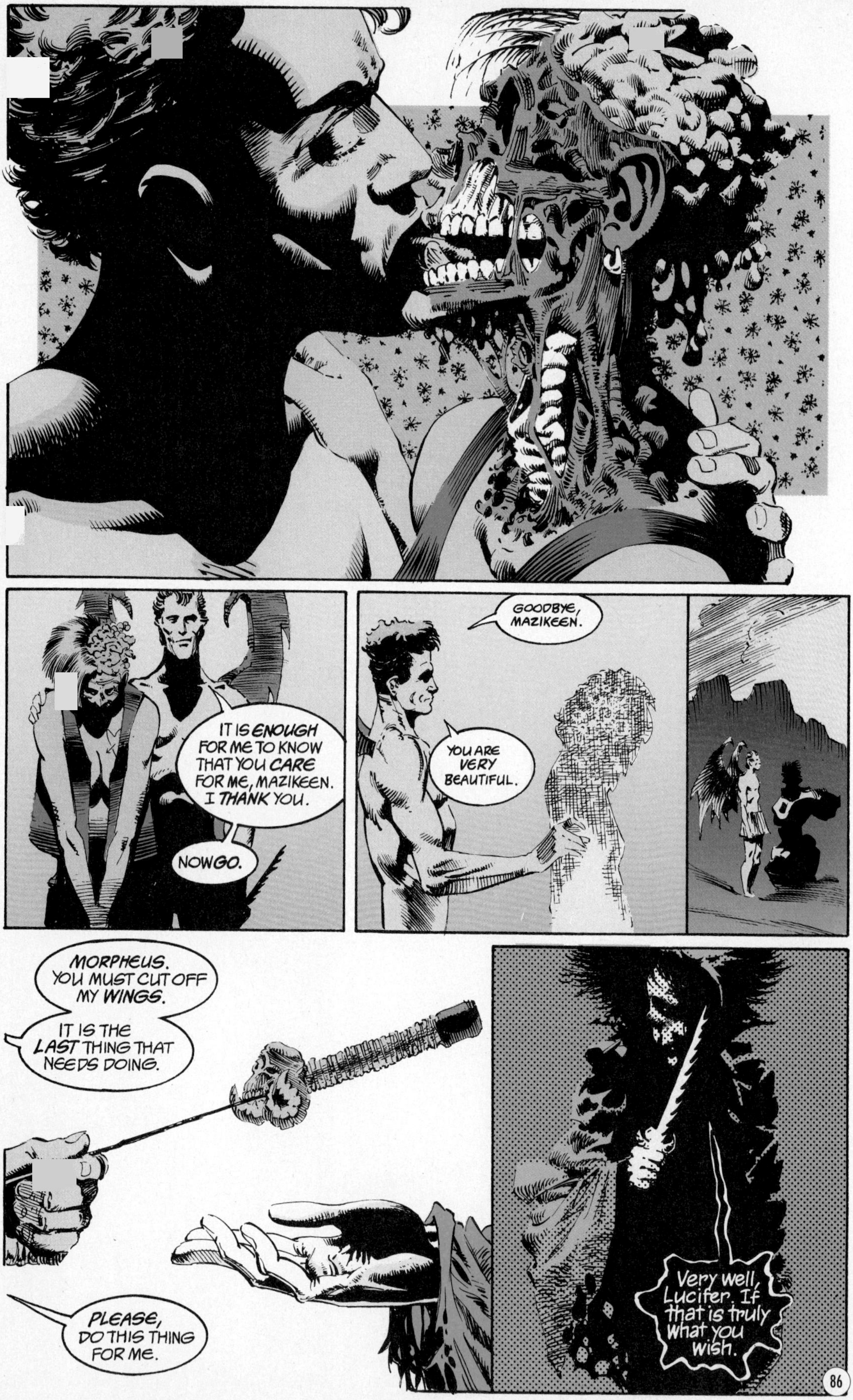
IT IS ENOUGH FOR ME TO KNOW THAT YOU CARE FOR ME, MAZIKEEN. I THANK YOU.
NOW GO.
GOODBYE, MAZIKEEN.
YOU ARE VERY BEAUTIFUL.
MORPHEUS. YOU MUST CUT OFF MY WINGS.
IT IS THE LAST THING THAT NEEDS DOING.
PLEASE, DO THIS THING FOR ME.
Very well, Lucifer. If that is truly what you wish.

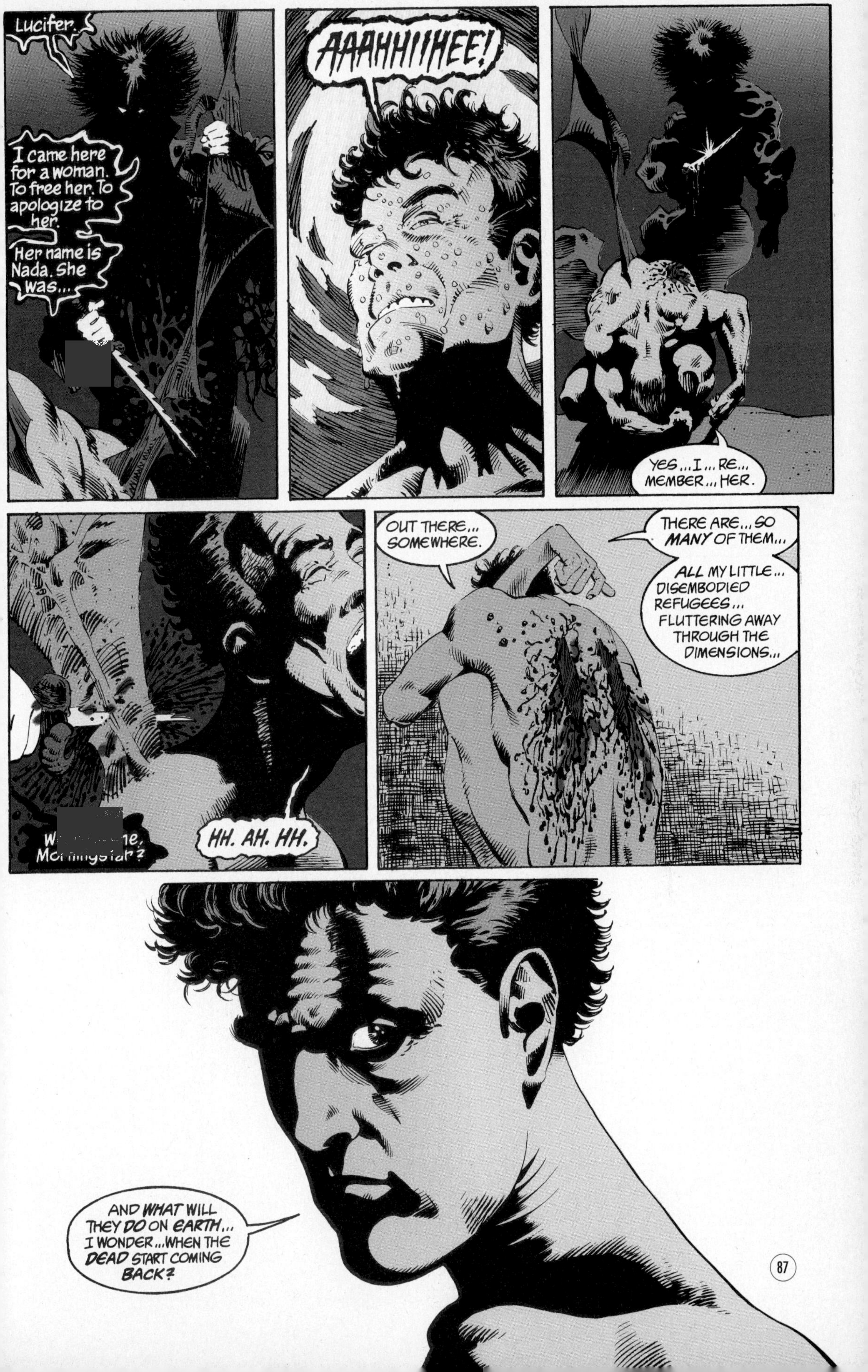
Lucifer.
I came here for a woman. To free her. To apologize to her.
Her name is Nada. She was...
AAAHHIIHEE!
YES... I... RE... MEMBER... HER.
W[redacted]me, Morningstar?
HH. AH. HH.
OUT THERE... SOMEWHERE.
THERE ARE... SO MANY OF THEM...
ALL MY LITTLE... DISEMBODIED REFUGEES... FLUTTERING AWAY THROUGH THE DIMENSIONS...
AND WHAT WILL THEY DO ON EARTH... I WONDER... WHEN THE DEAD START COMING BACK?

In which Lucifer's parting gift attracts unwanted attention; and the Dream Lord receives unwelcome visitors.

EPISODE 3

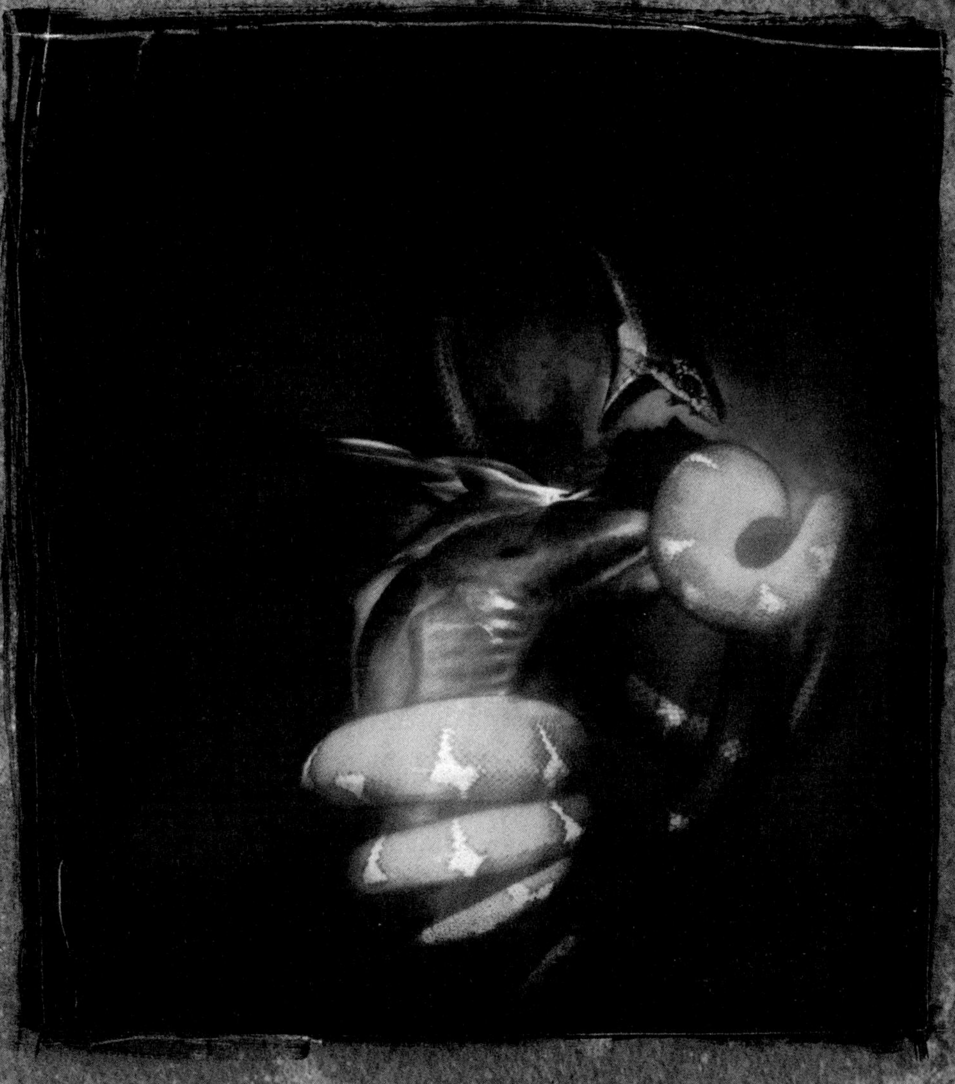

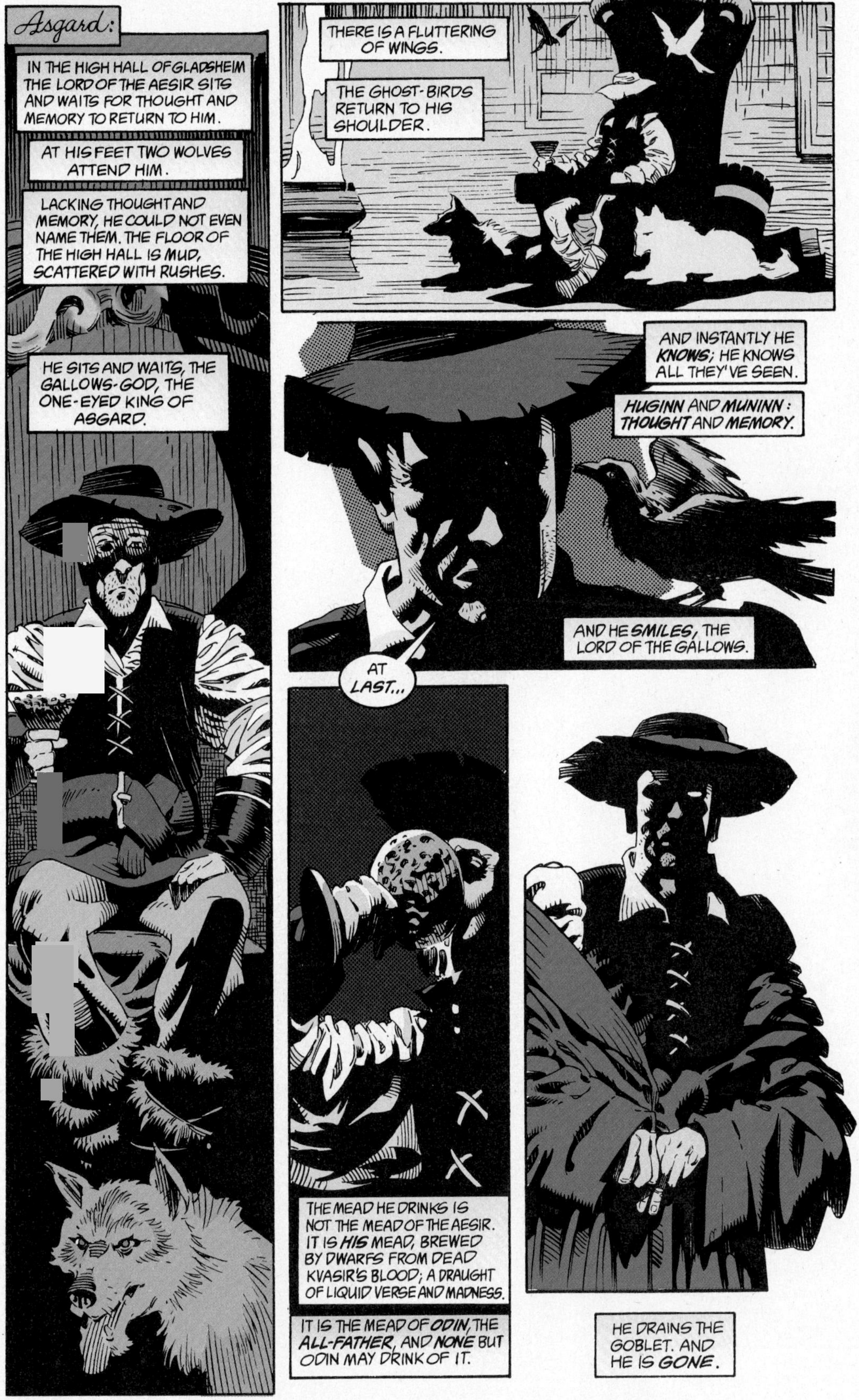
Asgard:
IN THE HIGH HALL OF GLADSHEIM THE LORD OF THE AESIR SITS AND WAITS FOR THOUGHT AND MEMORY TO RETURN TO HIM.
AT HIS FEET TWO WOLVES ATTEND HIM.
LACKING THOUGHT AND MEMORY, HE COULD NOT EVEN NAME THEM. THE FLOOR OF THE HIGH HALL IS MUD, SCATTERED WITH RUSHES.
HE SITS AND WAITS, THE GALLOWS-GOD, THE ONE-EYED KING OF ASGARD.
THERE IS A FLUTTERING OF WINGS.
THE GHOST-BIRDS RETURN TO HIS SHOULDER.
AND INSTANTLY HE *KNOWS*; HE KNOWS ALL THEY'VE SEEN.
HUGINN AND ***MUNINN***: ***THOUGHT*** AND ***MEMORY***.
AND HE ***SMILES***, THE LORD OF THE GALLOWS.
AT LAST...
THE MEAD HE DRINKS IS NOT THE MEAD OF THE AESIR. IT IS ***HIS*** MEAD, BREWED BY DWARFS FROM DEAD KVASIR'S BLOOD; A DRAUGHT OF LIQUID VERSE AND MADNESS.
IT IS THE MEAD OF ***ODIN***, THE ***ALL-FATHER***, AND ***NONE*** BUT ODIN MAY DRINK OF IT.
HE DRAINS THE GOBLET. AND HE IS ***GONE***.

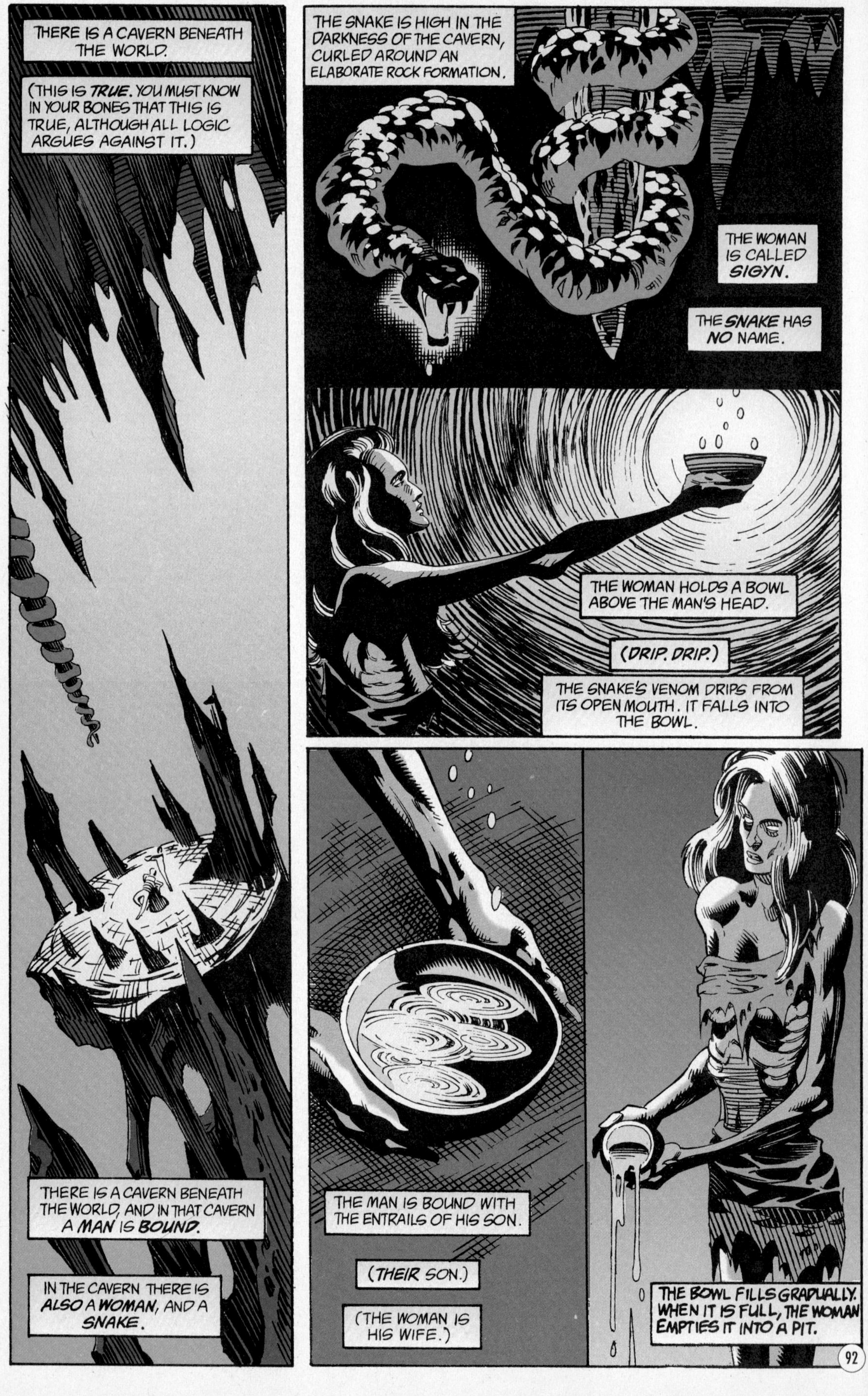
THERE IS A CAVERN BENEATH THE WORLD.
(THIS IS TRUE. YOU MUST KNOW IN YOUR BONES THAT THIS IS TRUE, ALTHOUGH ALL LOGIC ARGUES AGAINST IT.)
THERE IS A CAVERN BENEATH THE WORLD, AND IN THAT CAVERN A MAN IS BOUND.
IN THE CAVERN THERE IS ALSO A WOMAN, AND A SNAKE.
THE SNAKE IS HIGH IN THE DARKNESS OF THE CAVERN, CURLED AROUND AN ELABORATE ROCK FORMATION.
THE WOMAN IS CALLED SIGYN.
THE SNAKE HAS NO NAME.
THE WOMAN HOLDS A BOWL ABOVE THE MAN'S HEAD.
(DRIP. DRIP.)
THE SNAKE'S VENOM DRIPS FROM ITS OPEN MOUTH. IT FALLS INTO THE BOWL.
THE MAN IS BOUND WITH THE ENTRAILS OF HIS SON.
(THEIR SON.)
(THE WOMAN IS HIS WIFE.)
THE BOWL FILLS GRADUALLY. WHEN IT IS FULL, THE WOMAN EMPTIES IT INTO A PIT.

WHILE SHE IS GONE, THE SNAKE'S VENOM DRIPS ONTO THE MAN'S FACE.

WHEN HE WRITHES, THE *EARTH QUAKES.*

HE *TWISTS* AND *WRITHES* AS THE POISON EATS INTO HIS FLESH. HE *SCREAMS* AS IT ENTERS HIS *EYES.*

HE CURSES THE WOMAN, BUT STILL SHE STAYS WITH HIM.

THE *MAN.*
THE *WOMAN.*
THE *SNAKE.*
THE *BOWL.*

IT'S NOT NICE, OR PRETTY; BUT IT'S *TRUE.*

AND IT'S *NECESSARY.*

IT HAS BEEN GOING ON FOR A *VERY* LONG TIME

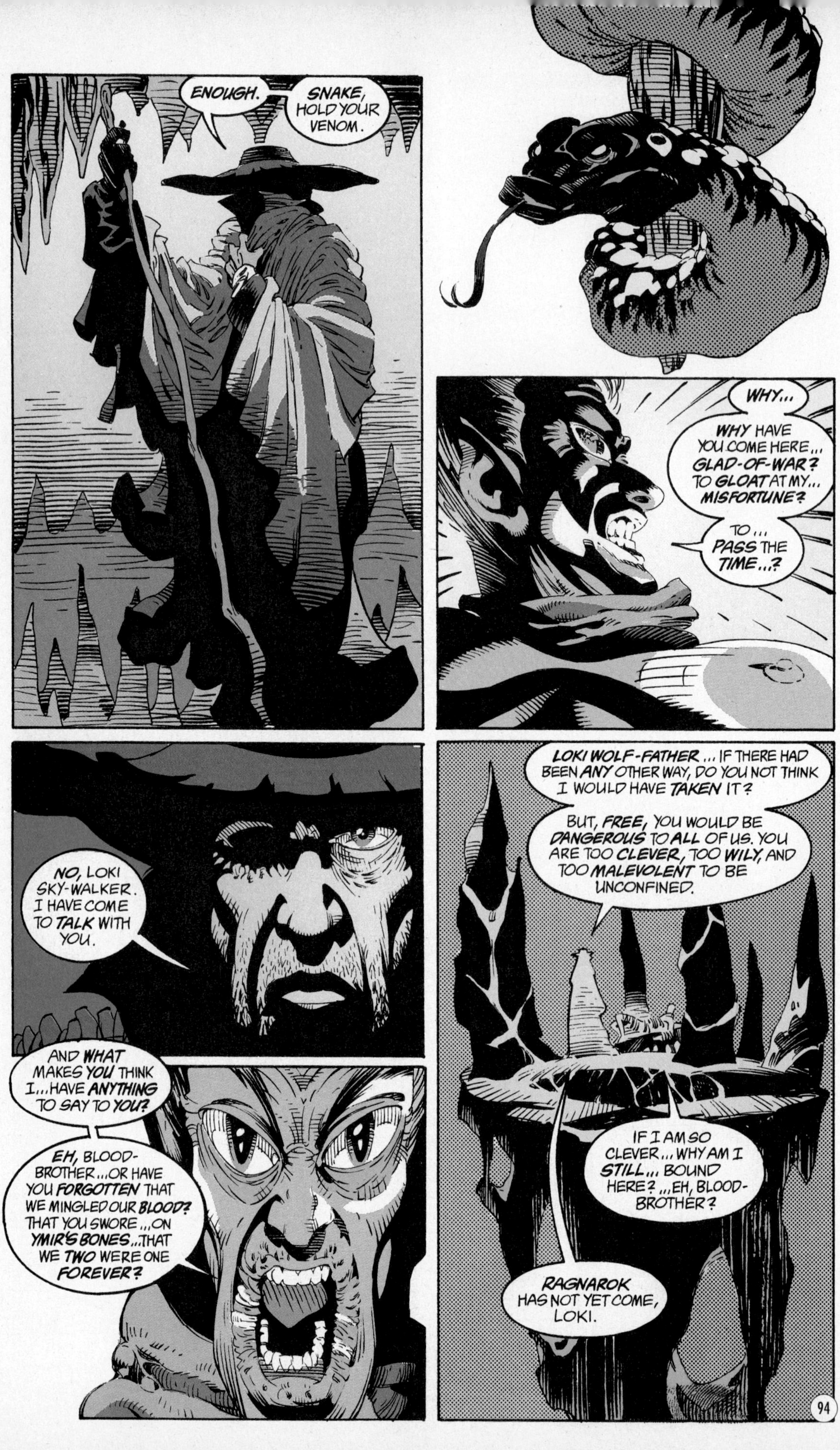
ENOUGH.
SNAKE, HOLD YOUR VENOM.
WHY...
WHY HAVE YOU COME HERE... GLAD-OF-WAR? TO GLOAT AT MY... MISFORTUNE?
TO... PASS THE TIME...?
NO, LOKI SKY-WALKER. I HAVE COME TO TALK WITH YOU.
AND WHAT MAKES YOU THINK I... HAVE ANYTHING TO SAY TO YOU?
EH, BLOOD-BROTHER... OR HAVE YOU FORGOTTEN THAT WE MINGLED OUR BLOOD? THAT YOU SWORE... ON YMIR'S BONES... THAT WE TWO WERE ONE FOREVER?
LOKI WOLF-FATHER... IF THERE HAD BEEN ANY OTHER WAY, DO YOU NOT THINK I WOULD HAVE TAKEN IT?
BUT, FREE, YOU WOULD BE DANGEROUS TO ALL OF US. YOU ARE TOO CLEVER, TOO WILY, AND TOO MALEVOLENT TO BE UNCONFINED.
IF I AM SO CLEVER... WHY AM I STILL... BOUND HERE? ...EH, BLOOD-BROTHER?
RAGNAROK HAS NOT YET COME, LOKI.

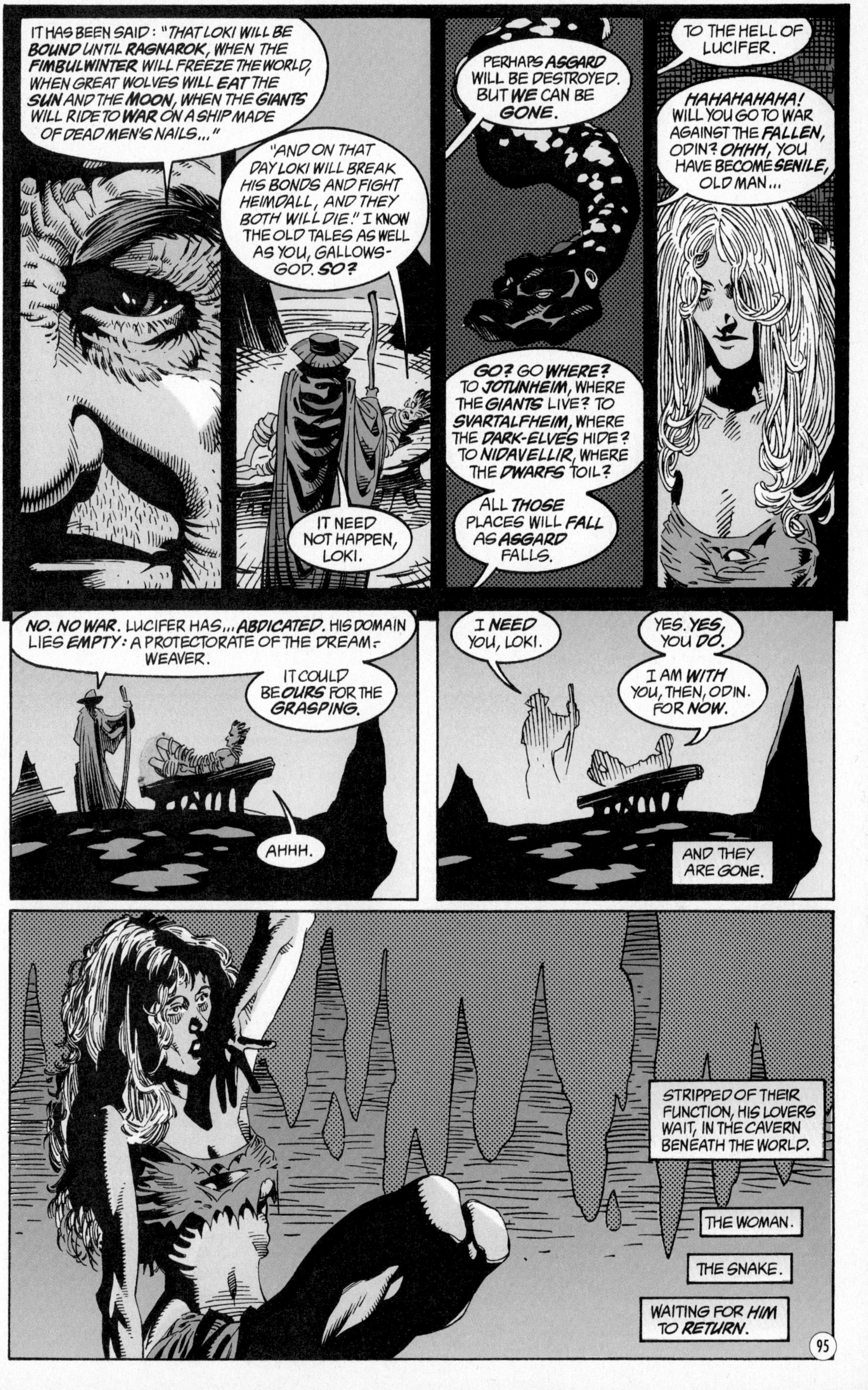
IT HAS BEEN SAID: "THAT LOKI WILL BE BOUND UNTIL RAGNAROK, WHEN THE FIMBULWINTER WILL FREEZE THE WORLD, WHEN GREAT WOLVES WILL EAT THE SUN AND THE MOON, WHEN THE GIANTS WILL RIDE TO WAR ON A SHIP MADE OF DEAD MEN'S NAILS..."
"AND ON THAT DAY LOKI WILL BREAK HIS BONDS AND FIGHT HEIMDALL, AND THEY BOTH WILL DIE." I KNOW THE OLD TALES AS WELL AS YOU, GALLOWS-GOD. SO?
IT NEED NOT HAPPEN, LOKI.
PERHAPS ASGARD WILL BE DESTROYED. BUT WE CAN BE GONE.
GO? GO WHERE? TO JOTUNHEIM, WHERE THE GIANTS LIVE? TO SVARTALFHEIM, WHERE THE DARK-ELVES HIDE? TO NIDAVELLIR, WHERE THE DWARFS TOIL?
ALL THOSE PLACES WILL FALL AS ASGARD FALLS.
TO THE HELL OF LUCIFER.
HAHAHAHAHA! WILL YOU GO TO WAR AGAINST THE FALLEN, ODIN? OHHH, YOU HAVE BECOME SENILE, OLD MAN...
NO. NO WAR. LUCIFER HAS... ABDICATED. HIS DOMAIN LIES EMPTY: A PROTECTORATE OF THE DREAM-WEAVER.
IT COULD BE OURS FOR THE GRASPING.
AHHH.
I NEED YOU, LOKI.
YES. YES, YOU DO.
I AM WITH YOU, THEN, ODIN. FOR NOW.
AND THEY ARE GONE.
STRIPPED OF THEIR FUNCTION, HIS LOVERS WAIT, IN THE CAVERN BENEATH THE WORLD.
THE WOMAN.
THE SNAKE.
WAITING FOR HIM TO RETURN.

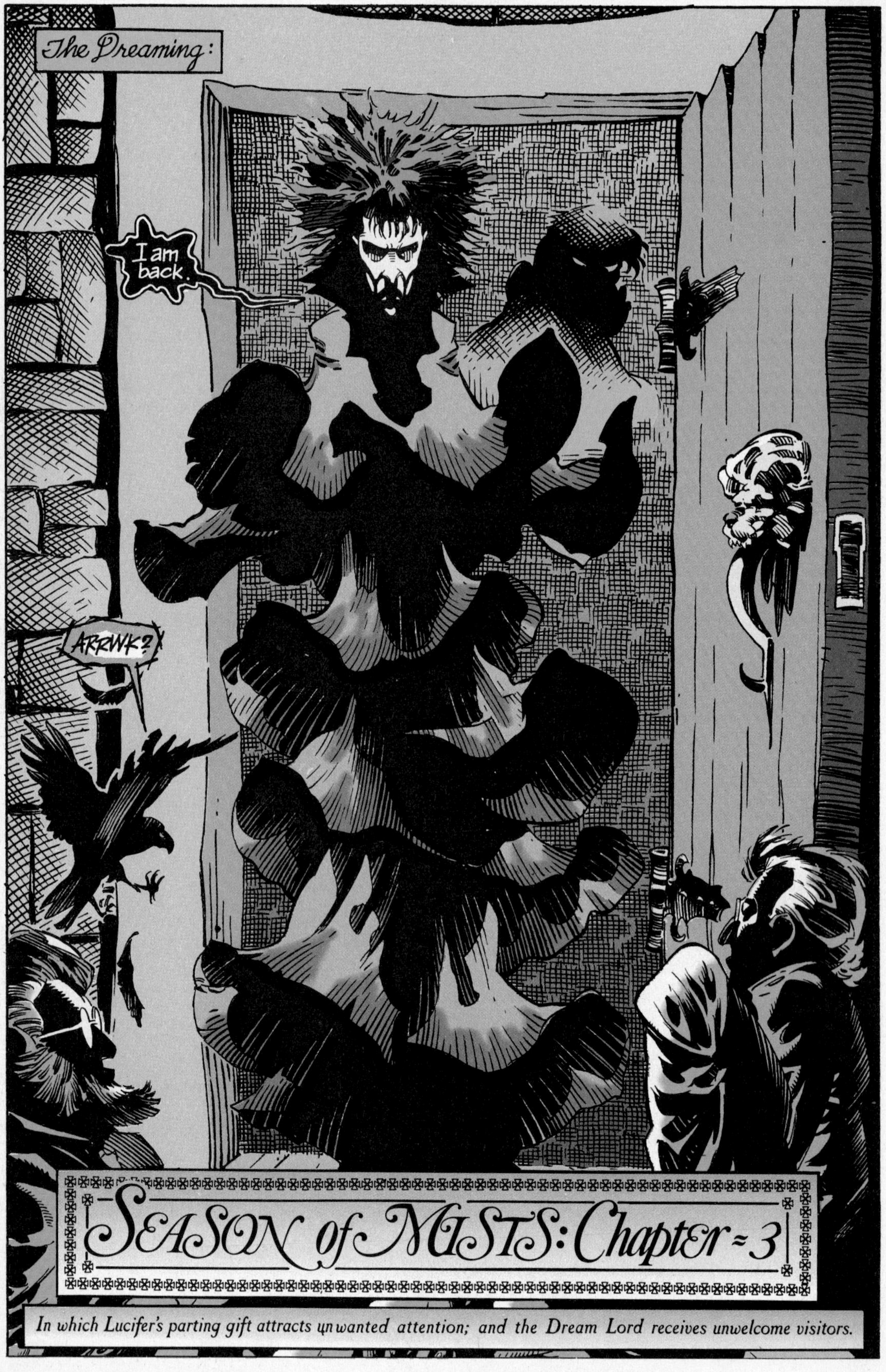
The Dreaming:
I am back.
ARRWK?
SEASON of MISTS: Chapter 3
In which Lucifer's parting gift attracts unwanted attention; and the Dream Lord receives unwelcome visitors.

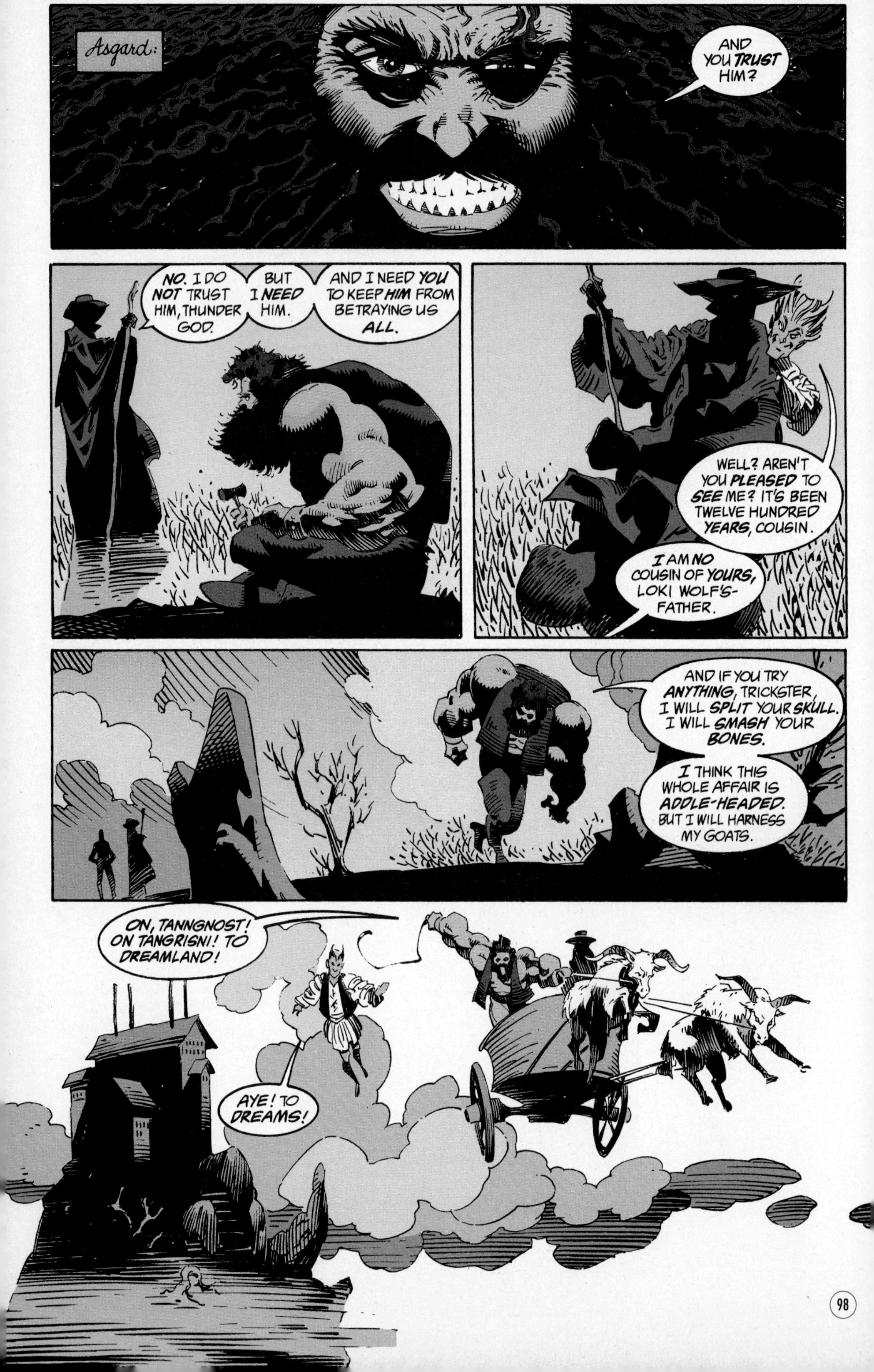
Asgard:
AND YOU TRUST HIM?
NO. I DO NOT TRUST HIM, THUNDER GOD.
BUT I NEED HIM.
AND I NEED YOU TO KEEP HIM FROM BETRAYING US ALL.
WELL? AREN'T YOU PLEASED TO SEE ME? IT'S BEEN TWELVE HUNDRED YEARS, COUSIN.
I AM NO COUSIN OF YOURS, LOKI WOLF'S-FATHER.
AND IF YOU TRY ANYTHING, TRICKSTER, I WILL SPLIT YOUR SKULL. I WILL SMASH YOUR BONES.
I THINK THIS WHOLE AFFAIR IS ADDLE-HEADED. BUT I WILL HARNESS MY GOATS.
ON, TANNGNOST! ON TANGRISNI! TO DREAMLAND!
AYE! TO DREAMS!

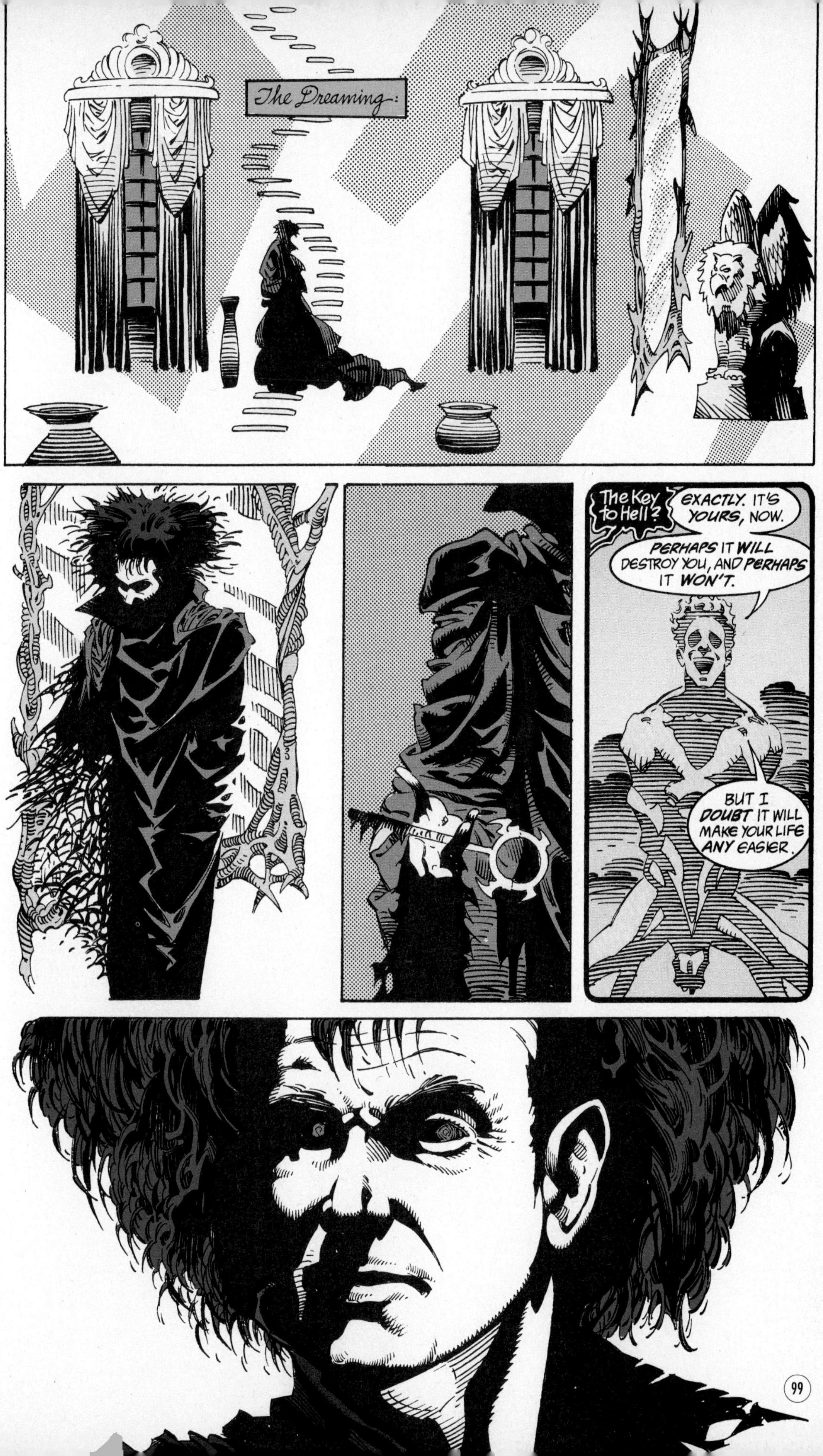
The Dreaming:
The Key to Hell?
EXACTLY. IT'S YOURS, NOW.
PERHAPS IT WILL DESTROY YOU, AND PERHAPS IT WON'T.
BUT I DOUBT IT WILL MAKE YOUR LIFE ANY EASIER.

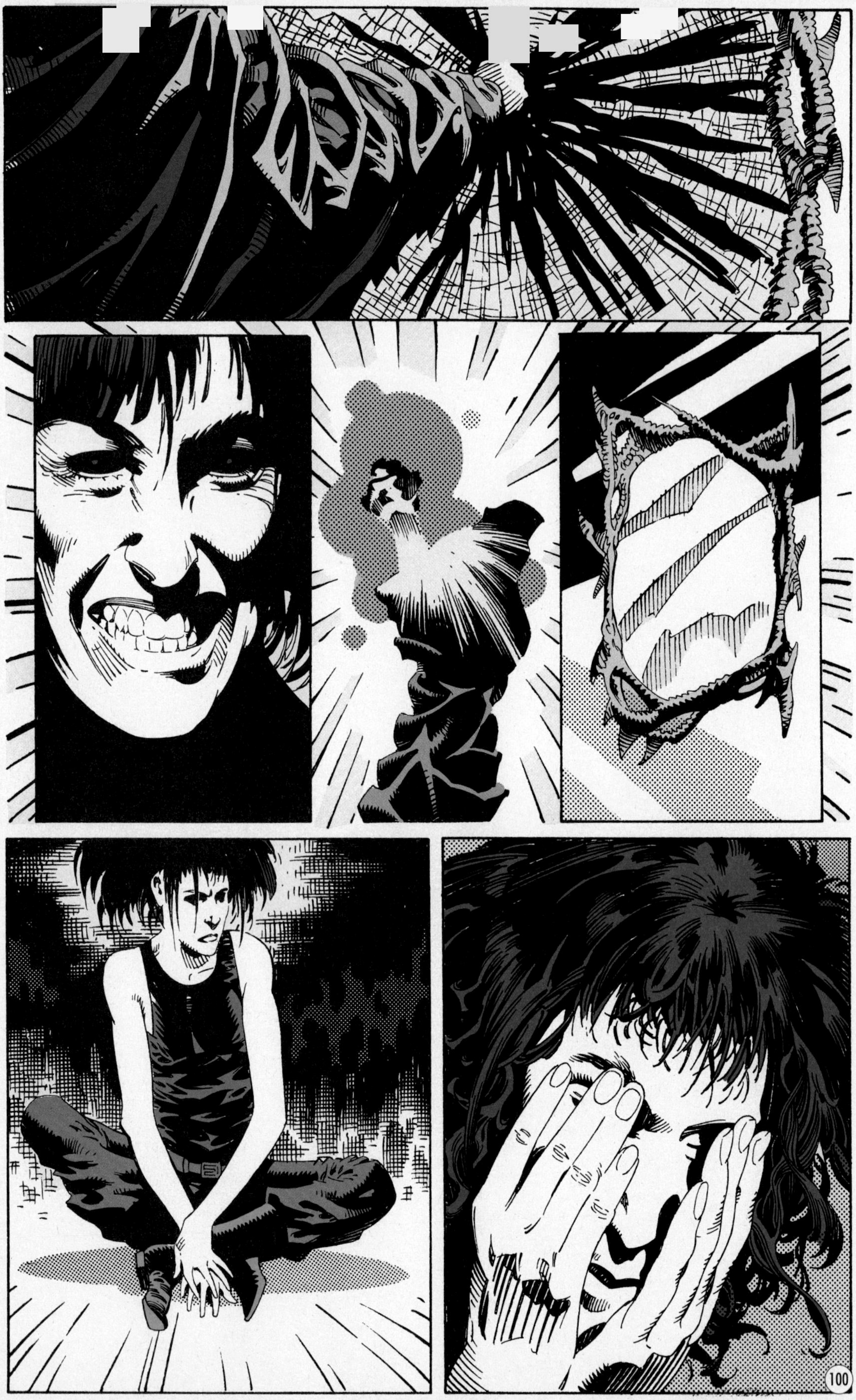

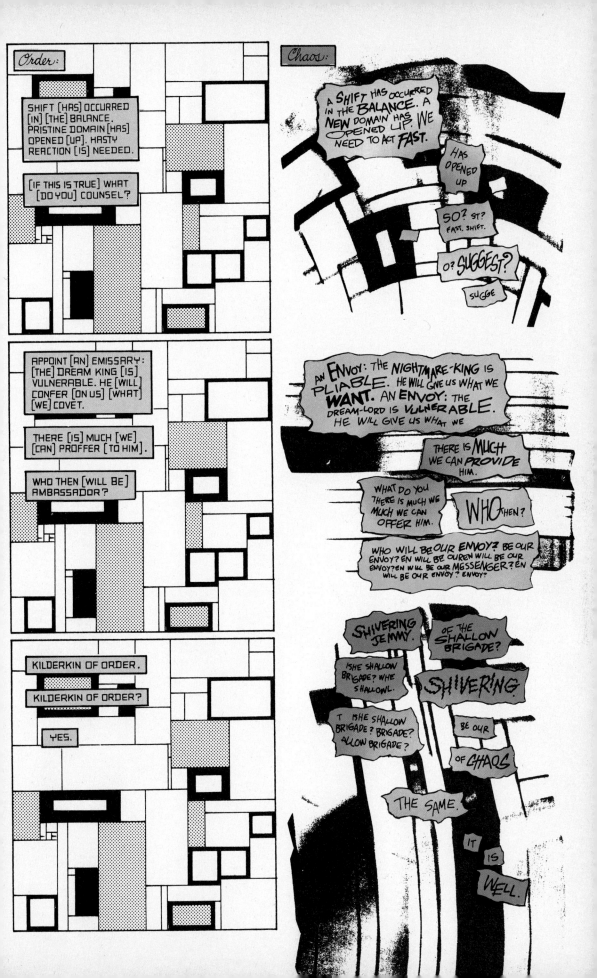

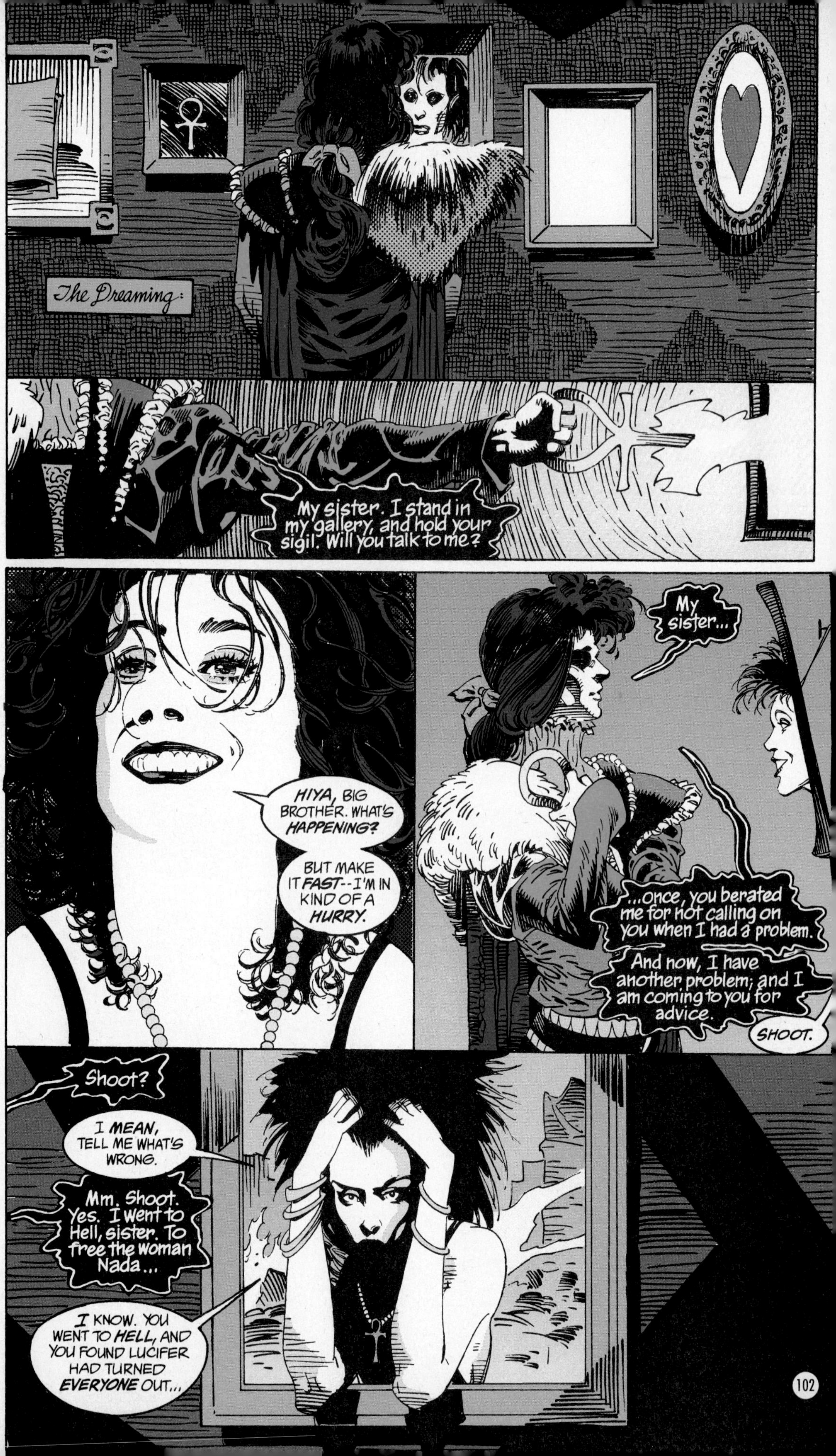
The Dreaming:
My sister. I stand in my gallery, and hold your sigil. Will you talk to me?
HIYA, BIG BROTHER. WHAT'S HAPPENING?
BUT MAKE IT FAST--I'M IN KIND OF A HURRY.
My sister...
...once, you berated me for not calling on you when I had a problem.
And now, I have another problem; and I am coming to you for advice.
SHOOT.
Shoot?
I MEAN, TELL ME WHAT'S WRONG.
Mm. Shoot. Yes. I went to Hell, sister. To free the woman Nada...
I KNOW. YOU WENT TO HELL, AND YOU FOUND LUCIFER HAD TURNED EVERYONE OUT...

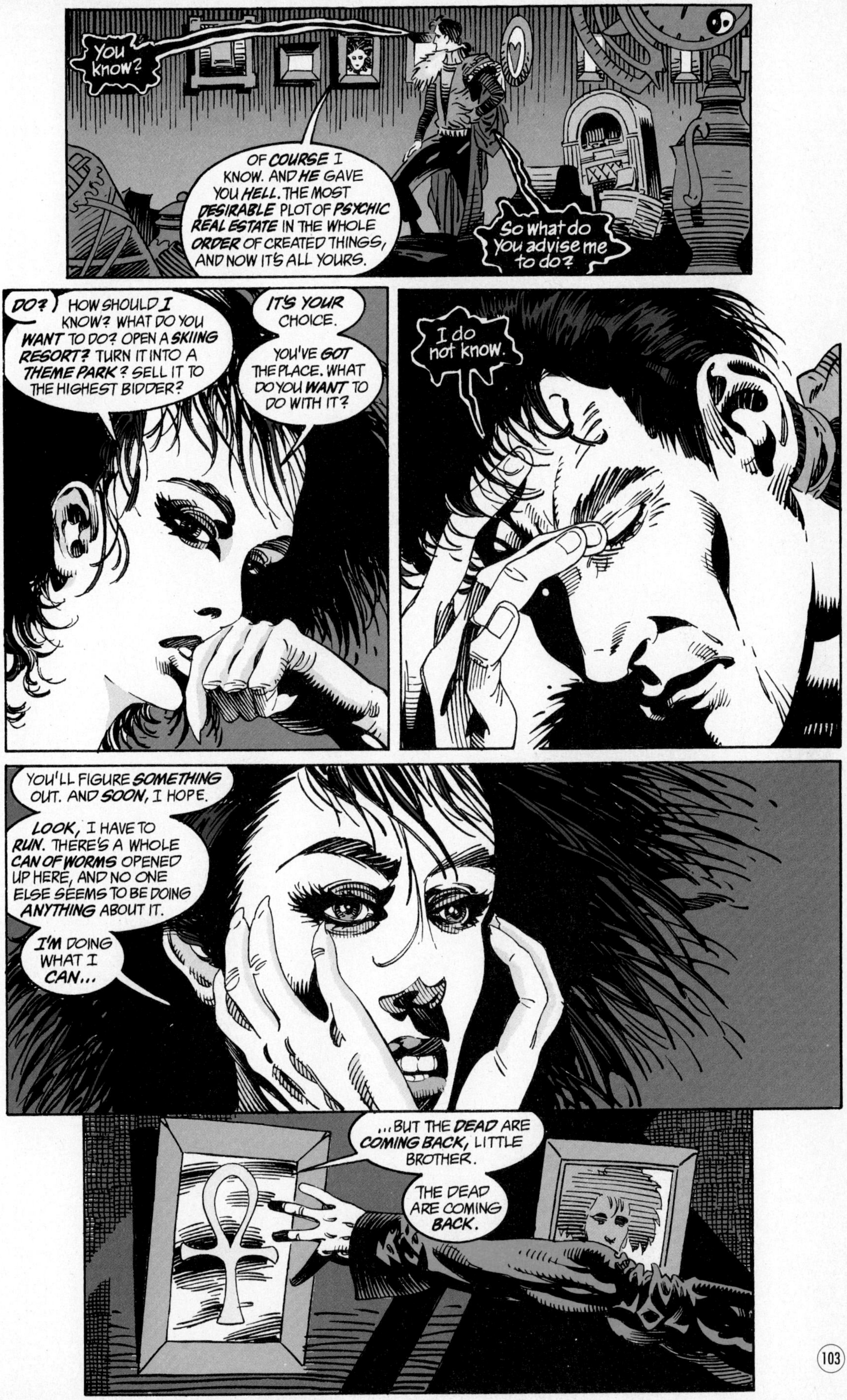
You know?
OF COURSE I KNOW. AND HE GAVE YOU HELL. THE MOST DESIRABLE PLOT OF PSYCHIC REAL ESTATE IN THE WHOLE ORDER OF CREATED THINGS, AND NOW IT'S ALL YOURS.
So what do you advise me to do?
DO? HOW SHOULD I KNOW? WHAT DO YOU WANT TO DO? OPEN A SKIING RESORT? TURN IT INTO A THEME PARK? SELL IT TO THE HIGHEST BIDDER?
IT'S YOUR CHOICE.
YOU'VE GOT THE PLACE. WHAT DO YOU WANT TO DO WITH IT?
I do not know.
YOU'LL FIGURE SOMETHING OUT. AND SOON, I HOPE.
LOOK, I HAVE TO RUN. THERE'S A WHOLE CAN OF WORMS OPENED UP HERE, AND NO ONE ELSE SEEMS TO BE DOING ANYTHING ABOUT IT.
I'M DOING WHAT I CAN...
...BUT THE DEAD ARE COMING BACK, LITTLE BROTHER.
THE DEAD ARE COMING BACK.

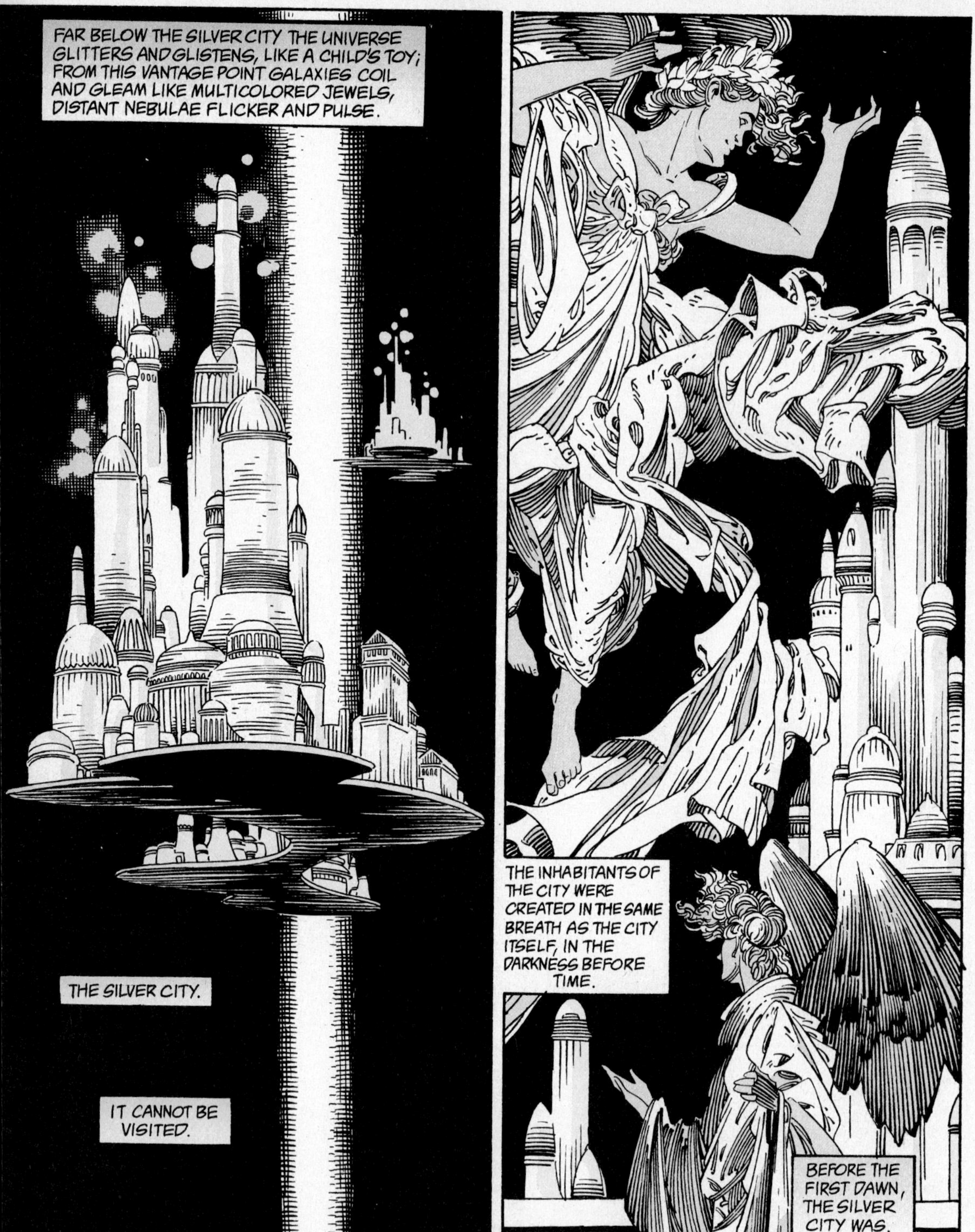
FAR BELOW THE SILVER CITY THE UNIVERSE GLITTERS AND GLISTENS, LIKE A CHILD'S TOY; FROM THIS VANTAGE POINT GALAXIES COIL AND GLEAM LIKE MULTICOLORED JEWELS, DISTANT NEBULAE FLICKER AND PULSE.
THE SILVER CITY.
IT CANNOT BE VISITED.
THE INHABITANTS OF THE CITY WERE CREATED IN THE SAME BREATH AS THE CITY ITSELF, IN THE DARKNESS BEFORE TIME.
BEFORE THE FIRST DAWN, THE SILVER CITY WAS.
IT IS NOT PARADISE.
IT IS NOT HEAVEN.
IT IS THE SILVER CITY, THAT IS NOT PART OF THE ORDER OF CREATED THINGS.

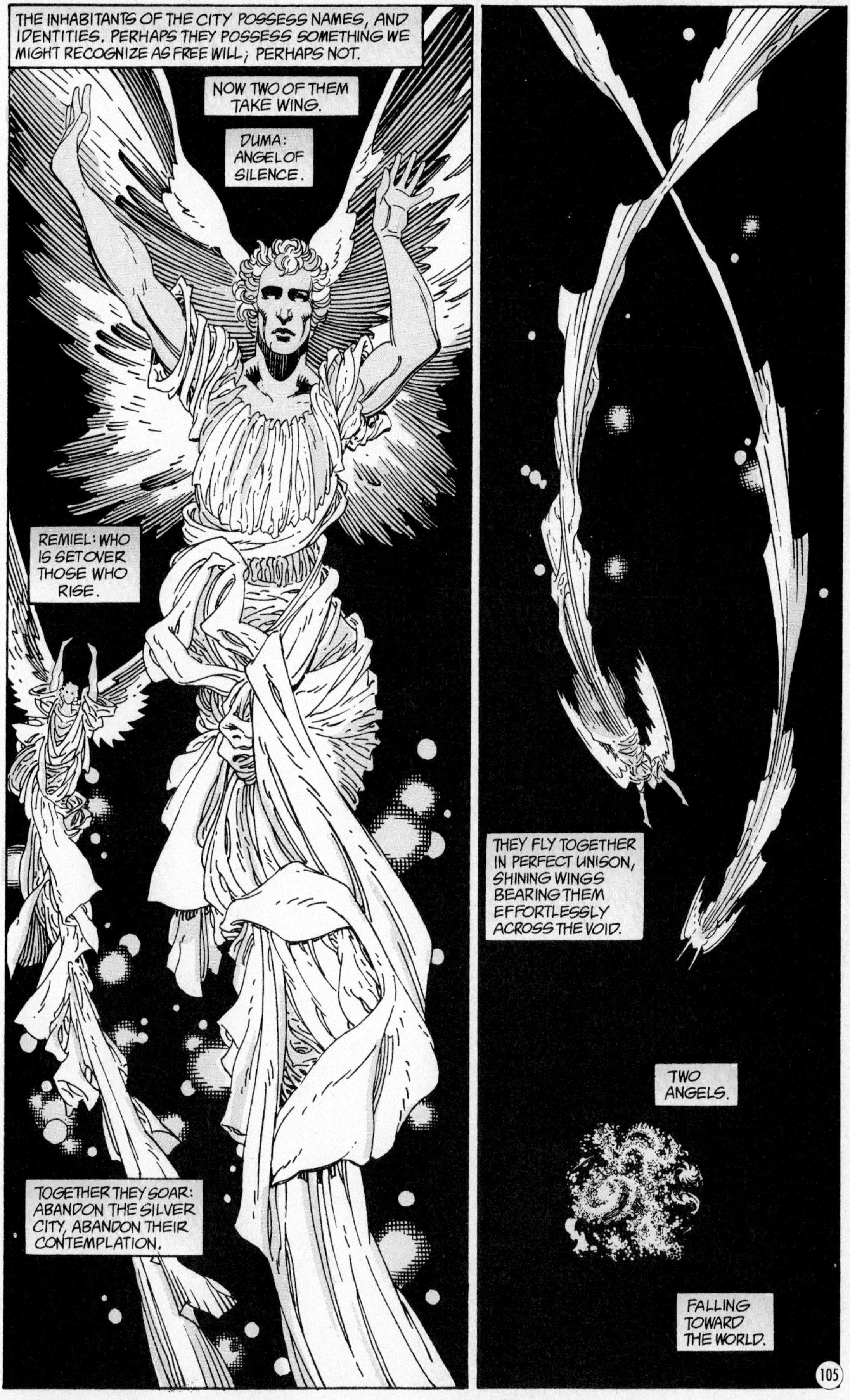
THE INHABITANTS OF THE CITY POSSESS NAMES, AND IDENTITIES. PERHAPS THEY POSSESS SOMETHING WE MIGHT RECOGNIZE AS FREE WILL; PERHAPS NOT.
NOW TWO OF THEM TAKE WING.
DUMA: ANGEL OF SILENCE.
REMIEL: WHO IS SET OVER THOSE WHO RISE.
TOGETHER THEY SOAR: ABANDON THE SILVER CITY, ABANDON THEIR CONTEMPLATION.
THEY FLY TOGETHER IN PERFECT UNISON, SHINING WINGS BEARING THEM EFFORTLESSLY ACROSS THE VOID.
TWO ANGELS.
FALLING TOWARD THE WORLD.

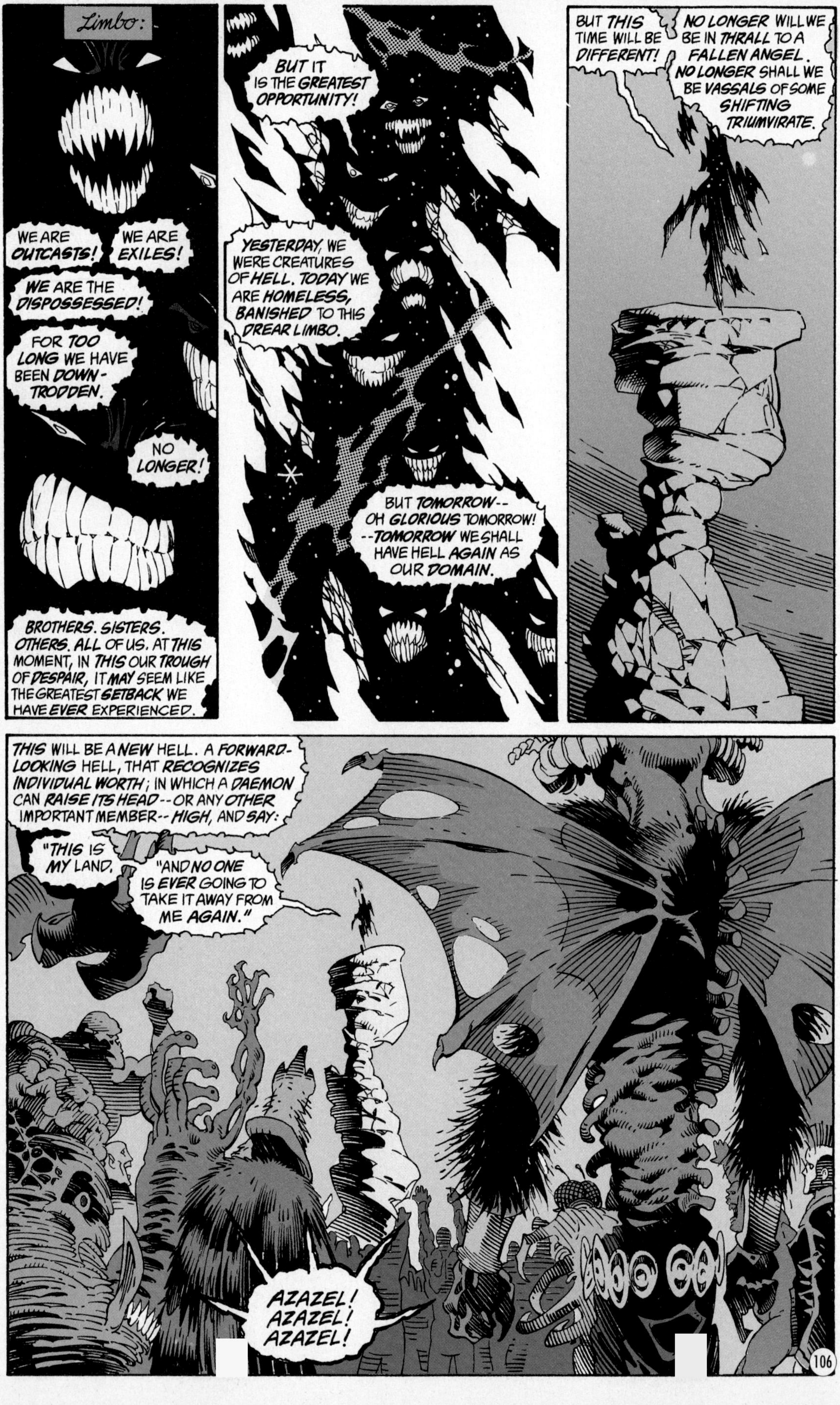
Limbo:
WE ARE OUTCASTS!
WE ARE EXILES!
WE ARE THE DISPOSSESSED!
FOR TOO LONG WE HAVE BEEN DOWN-TRODDEN.
NO LONGER!
BROTHERS. SISTERS. OTHERS. ALL OF US. AT THIS MOMENT, IN THIS OUR TROUGH OF DESPAIR, IT MAY SEEM LIKE THE GREATEST SETBACK WE HAVE EVER EXPERIENCED.
BUT IT IS THE GREATEST OPPORTUNITY!
YESTERDAY, WE WERE CREATURES OF HELL. TODAY WE ARE HOMELESS, BANISHED TO THIS DREAR LIMBO.
BUT TOMORROW-- OH GLORIOUS TOMORROW! --TOMORROW WE SHALL HAVE HELL AGAIN AS OUR DOMAIN.
BUT THIS TIME WILL BE DIFFERENT!
NO LONGER WILL WE BE IN THRALL TO A FALLEN ANGEL. NO LONGER SHALL WE BE VASSALS OF SOME SHIFTING TRIUMVIRATE.
THIS WILL BE A NEW HELL. A FORWARD-LOOKING HELL, THAT RECOGNIZES INDIVIDUAL WORTH; IN WHICH A DAEMON CAN RAISE ITS HEAD--OR ANY OTHER IMPORTANT MEMBER--HIGH, AND SAY:
"THIS IS MY LAND.
"AND NO ONE IS EVER GOING TO TAKE IT AWAY FROM ME AGAIN."
AZAZEL! AZAZEL! AZAZEL!

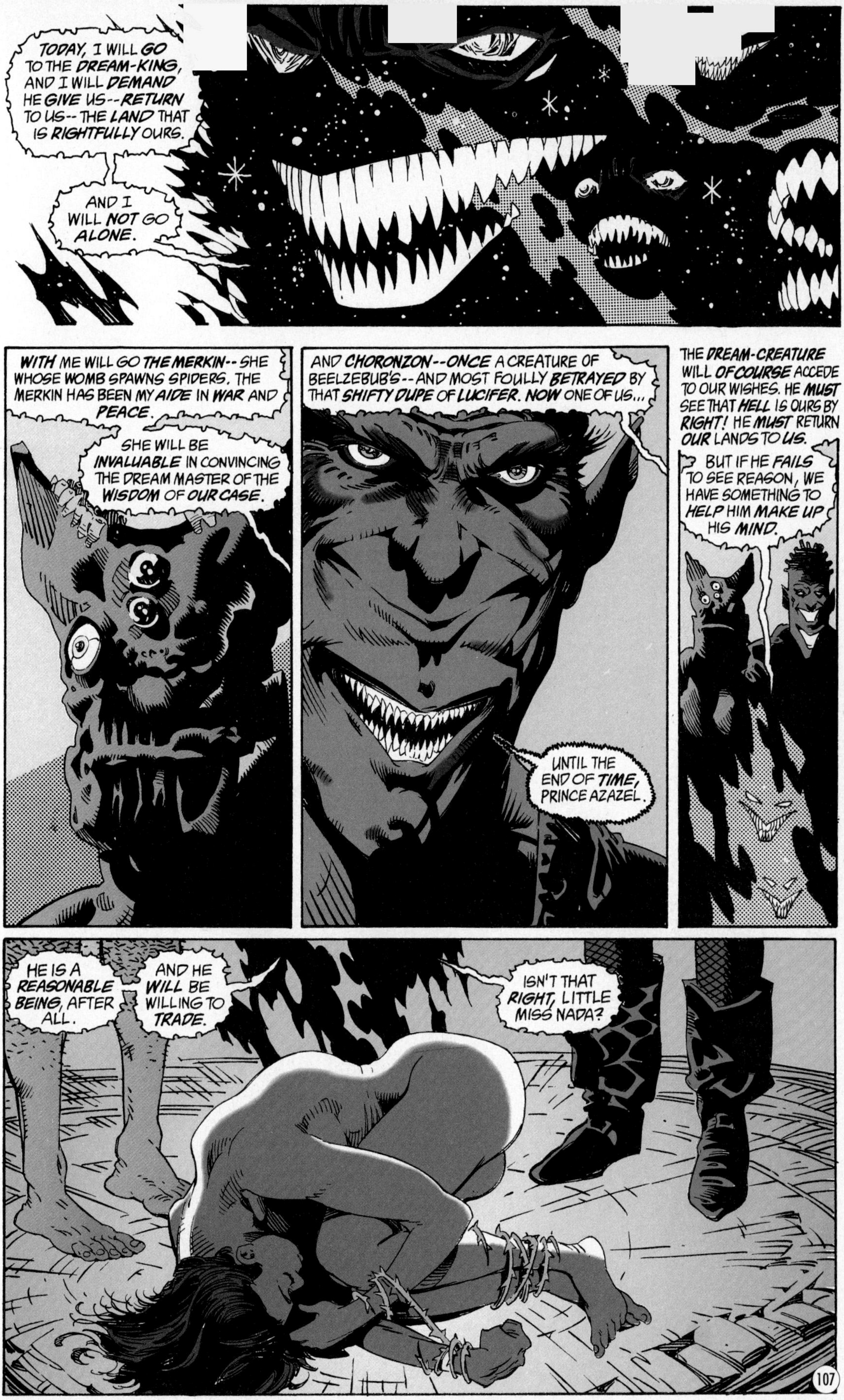
TODAY, I WILL GO TO THE DREAM-KING, AND I WILL DEMAND HE GIVE US--RETURN TO US--THE LAND THAT IS RIGHTFULLY OURS.
AND I WILL NOT GO ALONE.
WITH ME WILL GO THE MERKIN--SHE WHOSE WOMB SPAWNS SPIDERS. THE MERKIN HAS BEEN MY AIDE IN WAR AND PEACE.
SHE WILL BE INVALUABLE IN CONVINCING THE DREAM MASTER OF THE WISDOM OF OUR CASE.
AND CHORONZON--ONCE A CREATURE OF BEELZEBUB'S--AND MOST FOULLY BETRAYED BY THAT SHIFTY DUPE OF LUCIFER. NOW ONE OF US...
UNTIL THE END OF TIME, PRINCE AZAZEL.
THE DREAM-CREATURE WILL OF COURSE ACCEDE TO OUR WISHES. HE MUST SEE THAT HELL IS OURS BY RIGHT! HE MUST RETURN OUR LANDS TO US.
BUT IF HE FAILS TO SEE REASON, WE HAVE SOMETHING TO HELP HIM MAKE UP HIS MIND.
HE IS A REASONABLE BEING, AFTER ALL.
AND HE WILL BE WILLING TO TRADE.
ISN'T THAT RIGHT, LITTLE MISS NADA?

The Dreaming.

KAAARK!

EVE? YOU THERE?

MATTHEW. WELCOME BACK. WHAT NEWS?

OF THE *BOSS*? NOTHING REALLY. HE'S *STILL* HIDING OUT IN HIS *SUITE* IN THE *CASTLE*.

HE WON'T *TALK* TO *ANYONE*. NOT EVEN *ME*.

HMPH. HE'S LIKE A LITTLE *CHILD*.

OH--AND HE'S *MOVED* THE *CASTLE* TO THE TOP OF A MOUNTAIN.

HE'S EXPECTING UNWELCOME *VISITORS*, THEN. HE *ONLY* DOES *THAT* WHEN HE'S FEELING *ANTI-SOCIAL*.

I'M *SURE* THIS WILL SORT ITSELF OUT. THESE THINGS USUALLY *DO*.

I *HOPE* SO. I'VE NEVER SEEN HIM *THIS* OUT OF IT BEFORE.

NO. BUT YOU HAVE NOT BEEN WITH US *LONG*, LITTLE RAVEN. HE GETS *BLACKMOODS* ON HIM SOMETIMES.

WORSE THAN THIS ONE SOUNDS. *MUCH* WORSE.

IS THERE ANYTHING *WE* CAN DO?

OF *COURSE*, MY DARLING.

WE CAN *WAIT*.

BUT THEY ARE *ENVOYS,* MY LORD. I RECOGNIZE A *FEW* OF THEM. SOME HAVE BEEN HERE *BEFORE* -- AS *HONORED* GUESTS.

SOME OF THEM ARE *GODS.* ALL OF THEM ARE *PUISSANT.*

Enough.

WE *GATEKEEPERS* CANNOT KEEP THEM *ALL* OUT, SHOULD THEY *TAKE* IT TO *FORCE* THEIR WAY *IN.*

NOT UNLESS YOU LEND US *POWER,* LORD.

NOT UNLESS YOU LEND US *STRENGTH...*

WHAT SHALL WE *DO,* LORD?

Let them in.

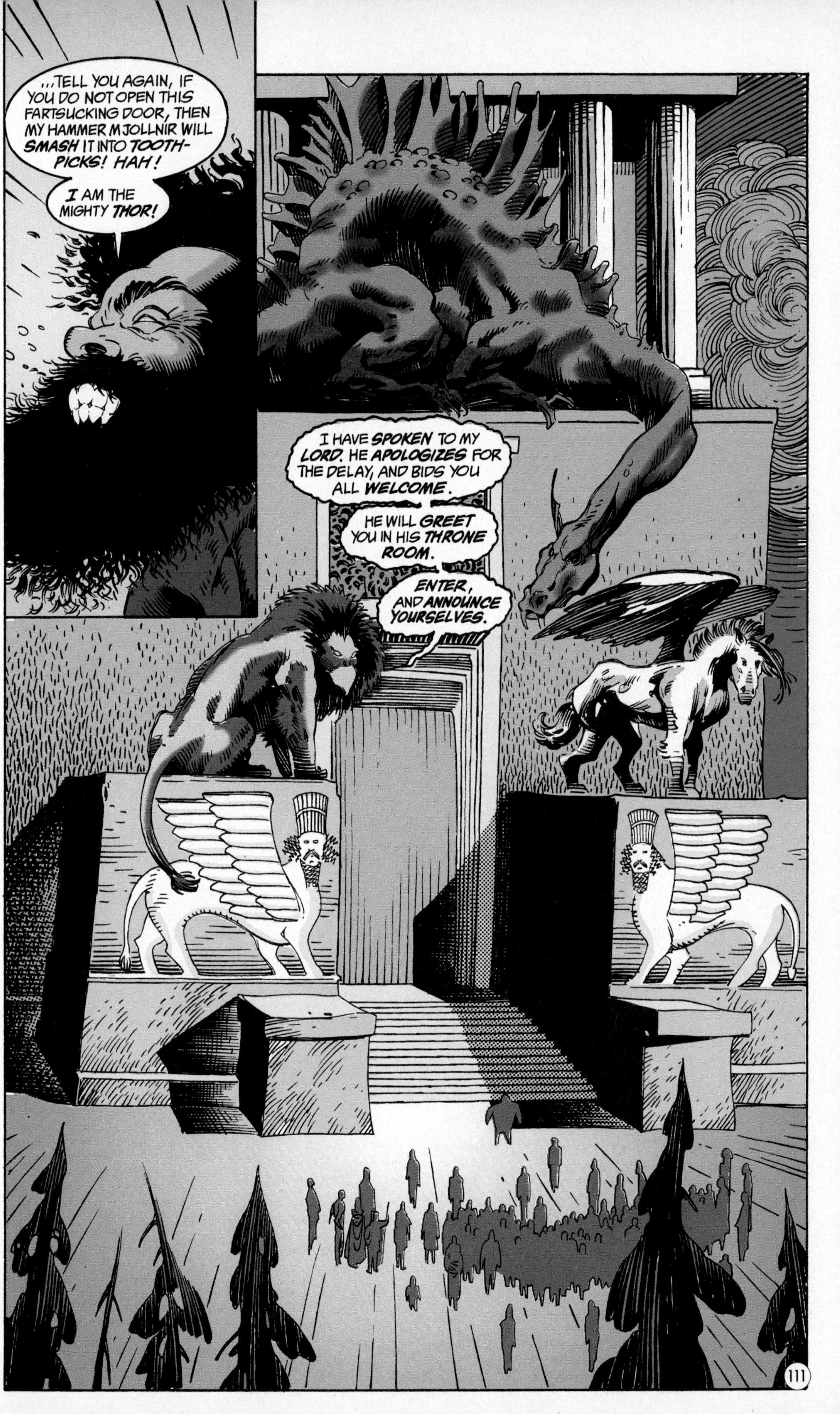
...TELL YOU AGAIN, IF YOU DO NOT OPEN THIS FARTSUCKING DOOR, THEN MY HAMMER MJOLLNIR WILL SMASH IT INTO TOOTH-PICKS! HAH!
I AM THE MIGHTY THOR!
I HAVE SPOKEN TO MY LORD. HE APOLOGIZES FOR THE DELAY, AND BIDS YOU ALL WELCOME.
HE WILL GREET YOU IN HIS THRONE ROOM.
ENTER, AND ANNOUNCE YOURSELVES.

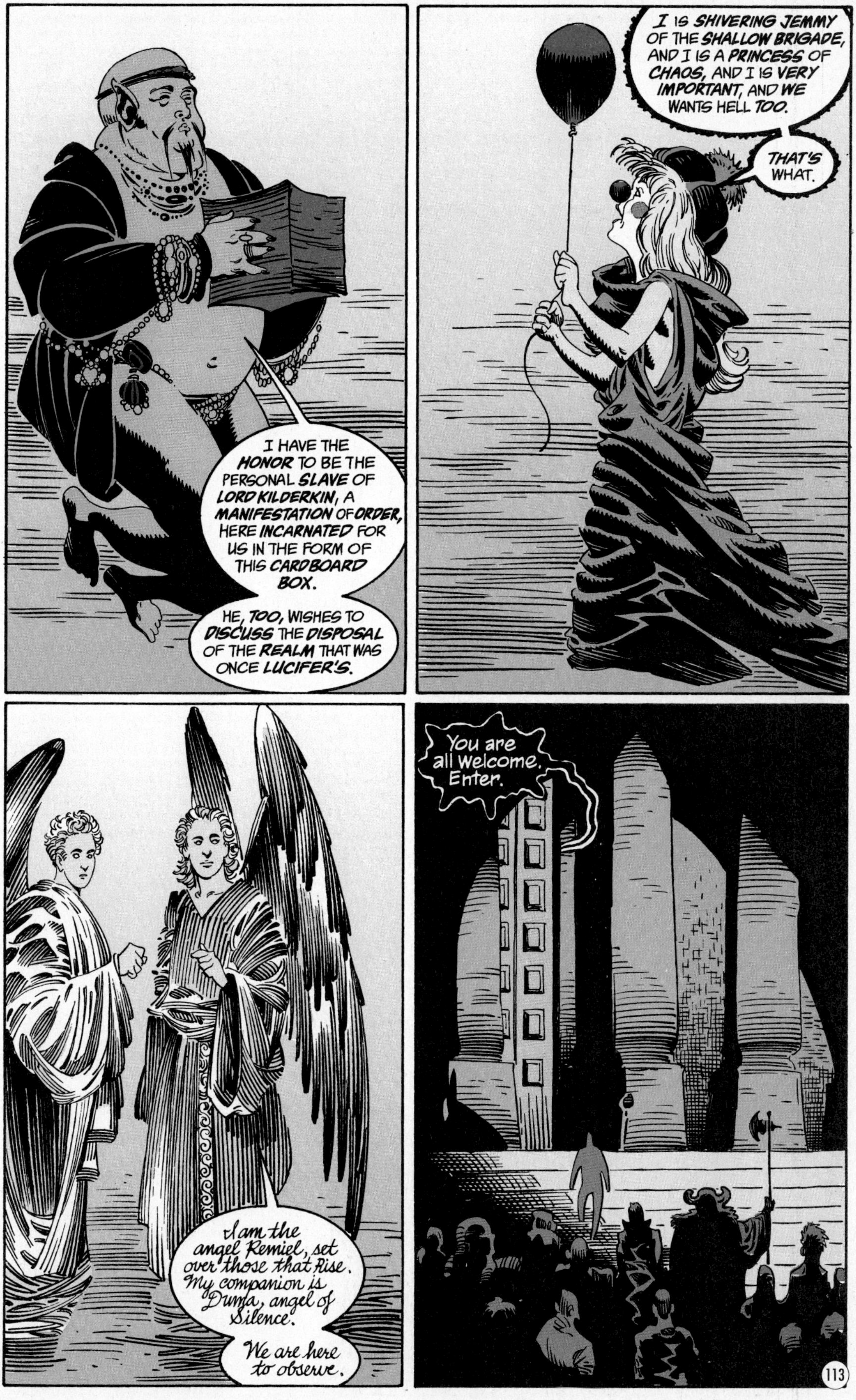
I HAVE THE HONOR TO BE THE PERSONAL SLAVE OF LORD KILDERKIN, A MANIFESTATION OF ORDER, HERE INCARNATED FOR US IN THE FORM OF THIS CARDBOARD BOX.
HE, TOO, WISHES TO DISCUSS THE DISPOSAL OF THE REALM THAT WAS ONCE LUCIFER'S.
I IS SHIVERING JEMMY OF THE SHALLOW BRIGADE, AND I IS A PRINCESS OF CHAOS, AND I IS VERY IMPORTANT, AND WE WANTS HELL TOO.
THAT'S WHAT.
I am the angel Remiel, set over those that Rise. My companion is Duma, angel of Silence.
We are here to observe.
You are all Welcome. Enter.

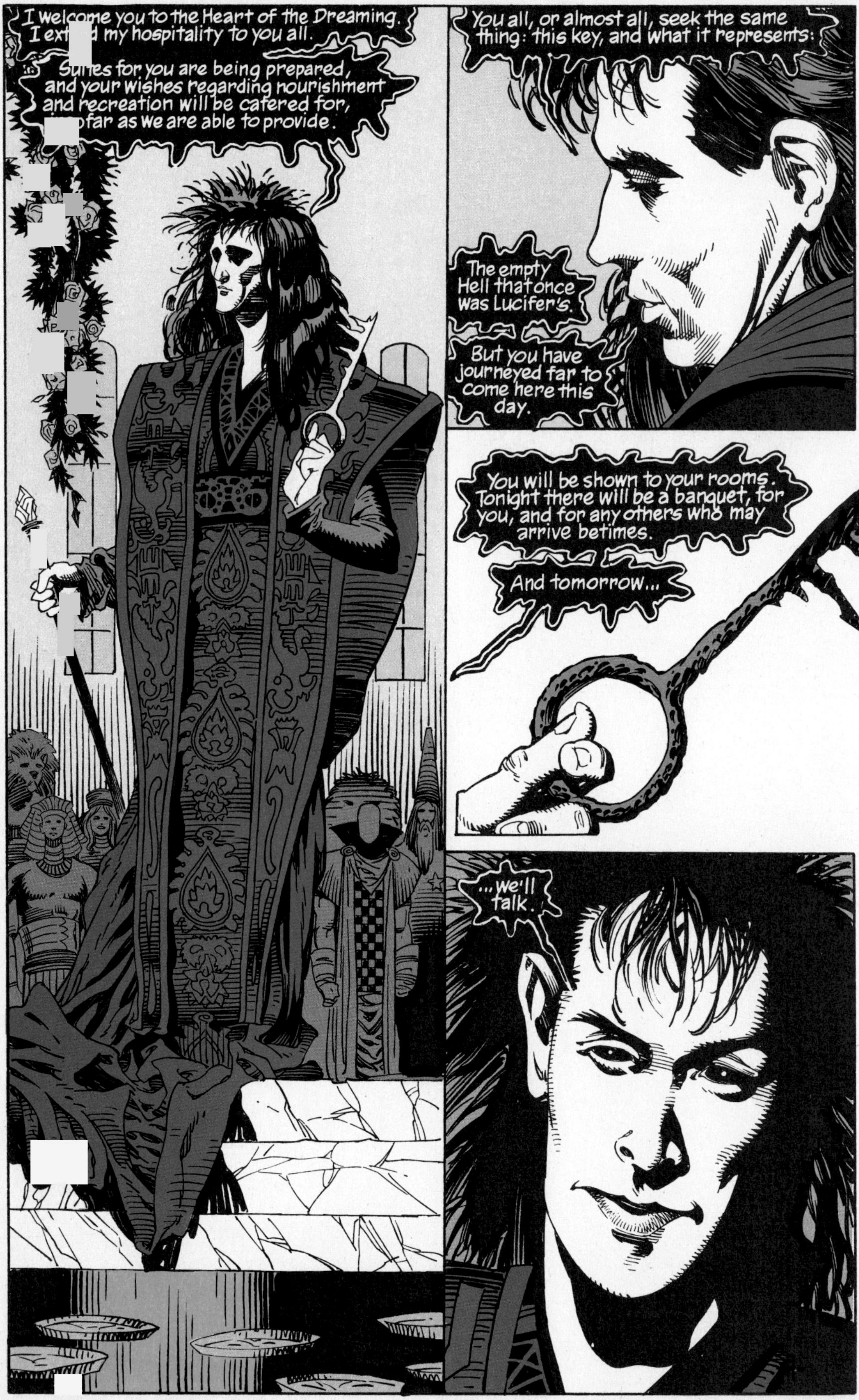
I welcome you to the Heart of the Dreaming. I ext d my hospitality to you all.
Suites for you are being prepared, and your wishes regarding nourishment and recreation will be catered for, sofar as we are able to provide.
You all, or almost all, seek the same thing: this key, and what it represents:
The empty Hell that once was Lucifer's.
But you have journeyed far to come here this day.
You will be shown to your rooms. Tonight there will be a banquet, for you, and for any others who may arrive betimes.
And tomorrow...
...we'll talk.

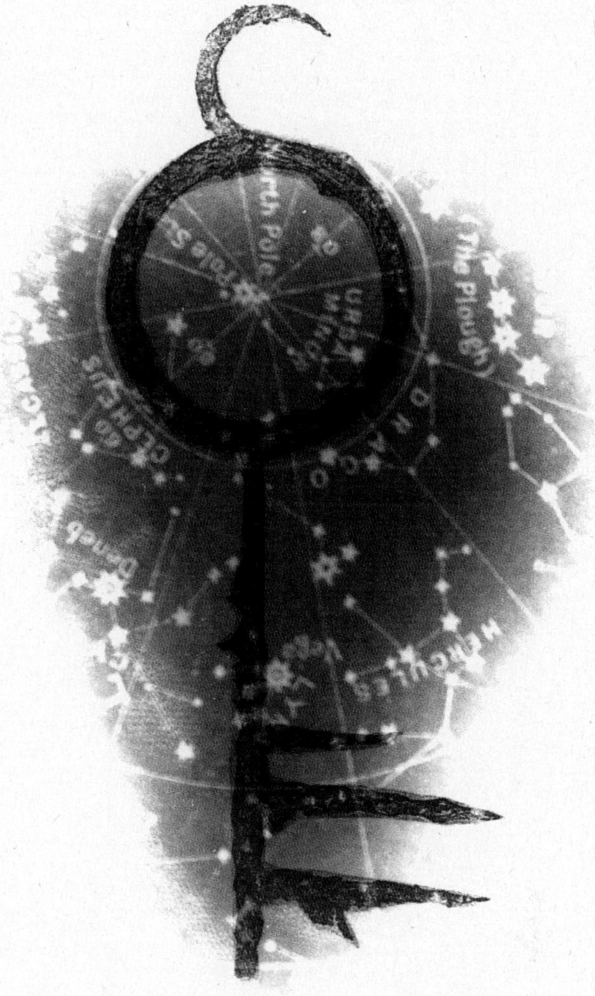
(The Plough)
DRACO
HERCULES
Deneb

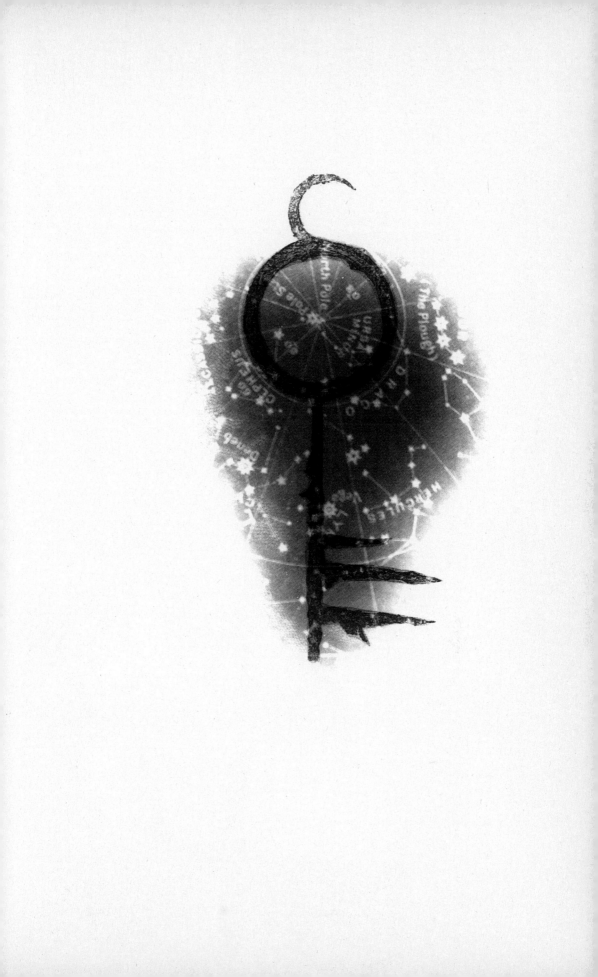

EPISODE 4

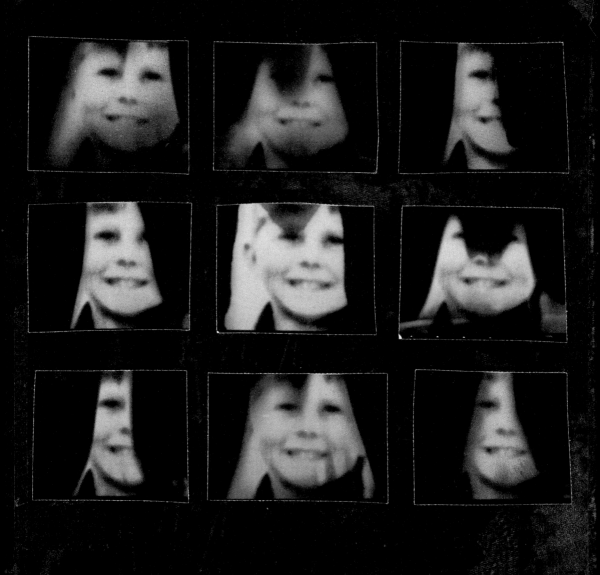

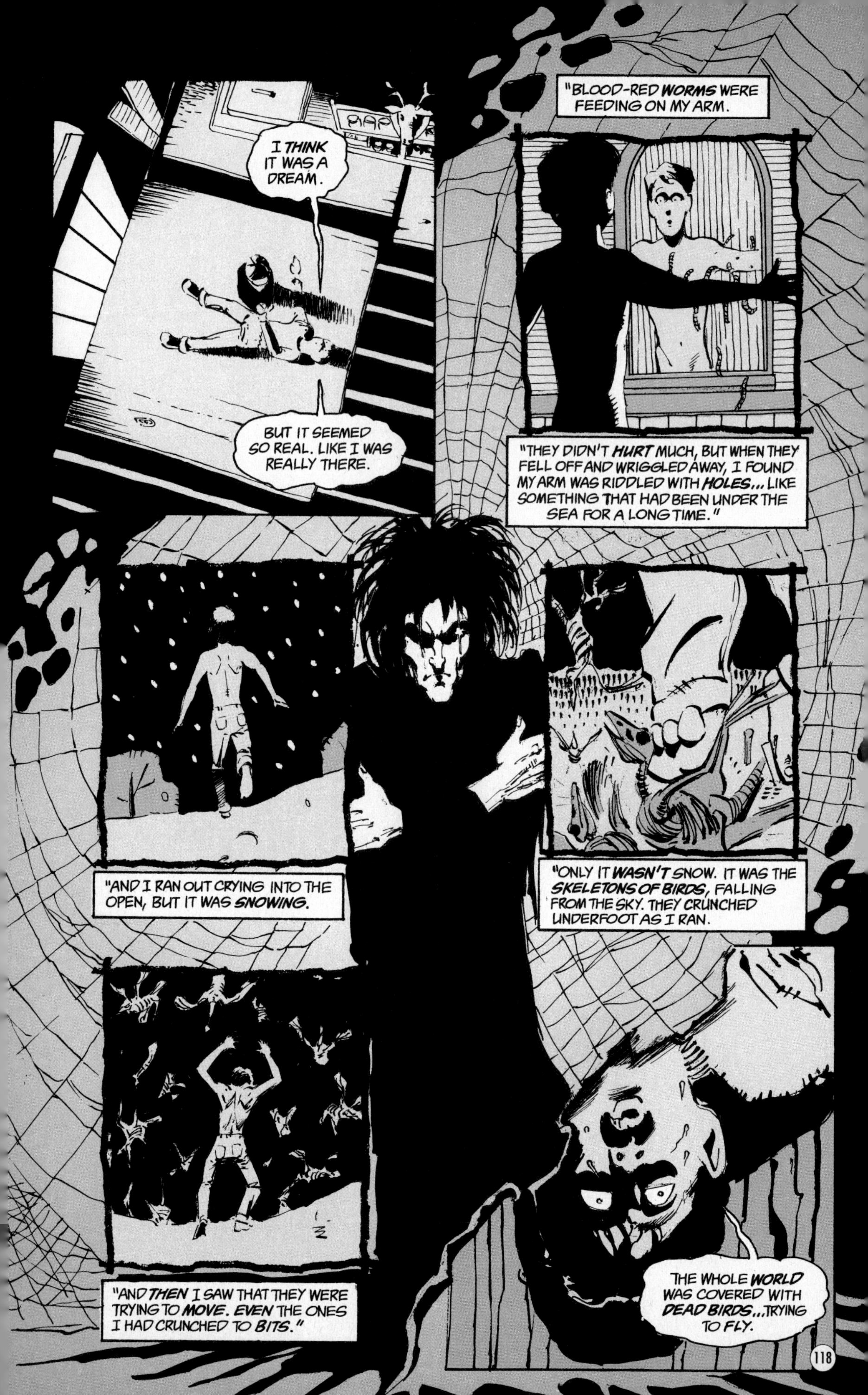
I THINK IT WAS A DREAM.
BUT IT SEEMED SO REAL. LIKE I WAS REALLY THERE.
"BLOOD-RED WORMS WERE FEEDING ON MY ARM.
"THEY DIDN'T HURT MUCH, BUT WHEN THEY FELL OFF AND WRIGGLED AWAY, I FOUND MY ARM WAS RIDDLED WITH HOLES... LIKE SOMETHING THAT HAD BEEN UNDER THE SEA FOR A LONG TIME."
"AND I RAN OUT CRYING INTO THE OPEN, BUT IT WAS SNOWING.
"ONLY IT WASN'T SNOW. IT WAS THE SKELETONS OF BIRDS, FALLING FROM THE SKY. THEY CRUNCHED UNDERFOOT AS I RAN.
"AND THEN I SAW THAT THEY WERE TRYING TO MOVE. EVEN THE ONES I HAD CRUNCHED TO BITS."
THE WHOLE WORLD WAS COVERED WITH DEAD BIRDS...TRYING TO FLY.

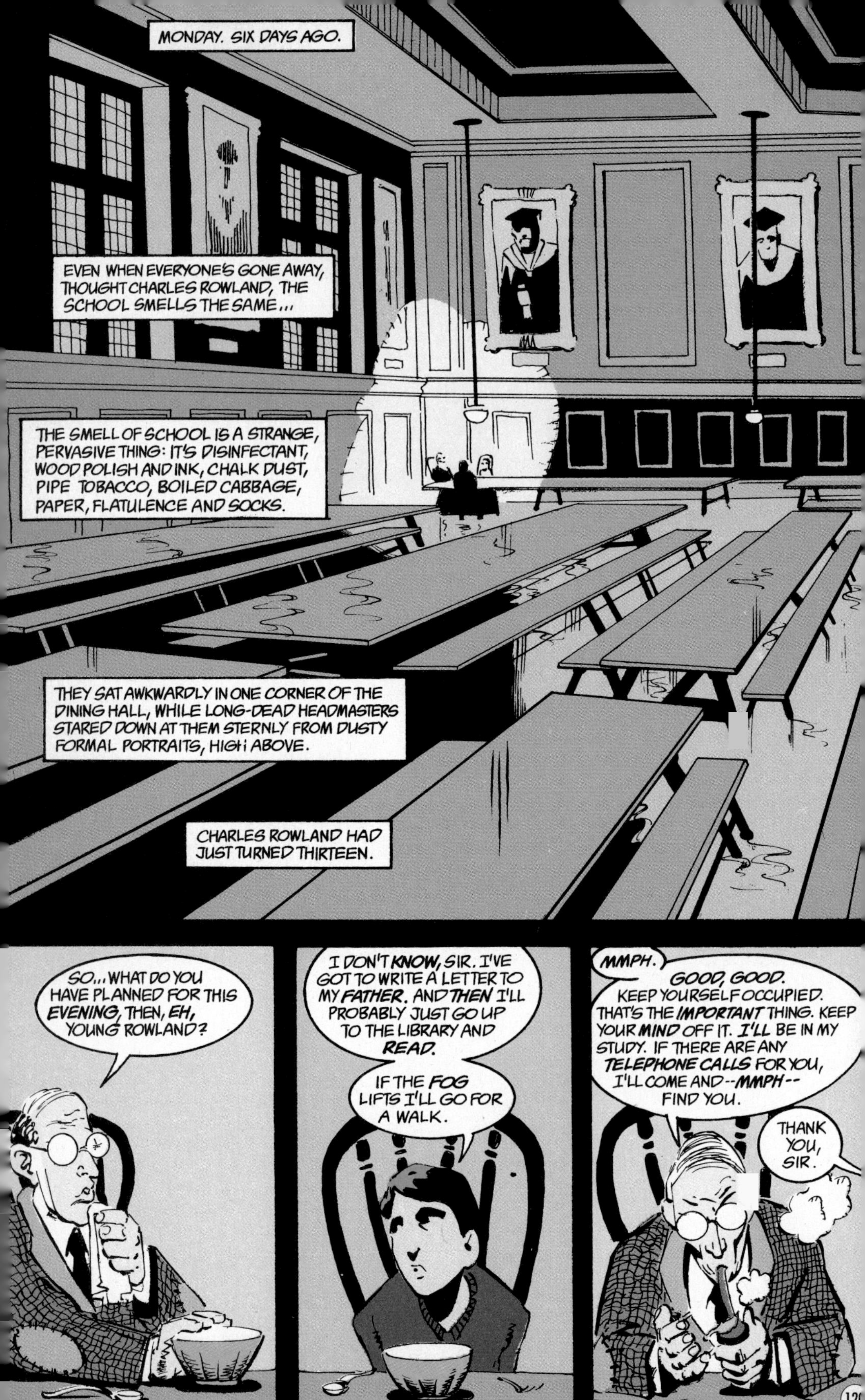
MONDAY. SIX DAYS AGO.
EVEN WHEN EVERYONE'S GONE AWAY, THOUGHT CHARLES ROWLAND, THE SCHOOL SMELLS THE SAME...
THE SMELL OF SCHOOL IS A STRANGE, PERVASIVE THING: IT'S DISINFECTANT, WOOD POLISH AND INK, CHALK DUST, PIPE TOBACCO, BOILED CABBAGE, PAPER, FLATULENCE AND SOCKS.
THEY SAT AWKWARDLY IN ONE CORNER OF THE DINING HALL, WHILE LONG-DEAD HEADMASTERS STARED DOWN AT THEM STERNLY FROM DUSTY FORMAL PORTRAITS, HIGH ABOVE.
CHARLES ROWLAND HAD JUST TURNED THIRTEEN.
SO... WHAT DO YOU HAVE PLANNED FOR THIS EVENING, THEN, EH, YOUNG ROWLAND?
I DON'T KNOW, SIR. I'VE GOT TO WRITE A LETTER TO MY FATHER. AND THEN I'LL PROBABLY JUST GO UP TO THE LIBRARY AND READ.
IF THE FOG LIFTS I'LL GO FOR A WALK.
MMPH.
GOOD, GOOD. KEEP YOURSELF OCCUPIED. THAT'S THE IMPORTANT THING. KEEP YOUR MIND OFF IT. I'LL BE IN MY STUDY. IF THERE ARE ANY TELEPHONE CALLS FOR YOU, I'LL COME AND--MMPH-- FIND YOU.
THANK YOU, SIR.

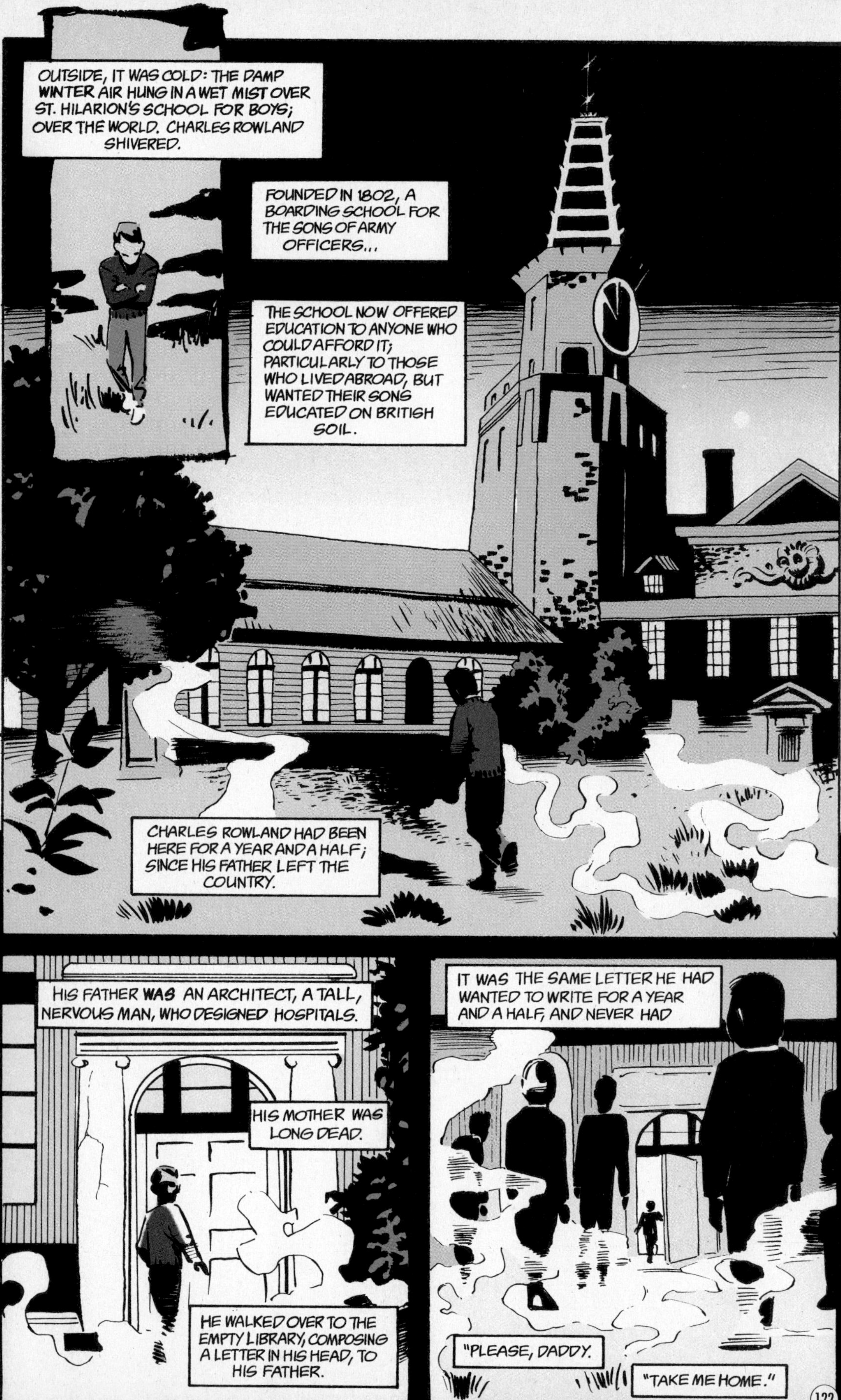
OUTSIDE, IT WAS COLD: THE DAMP WINTER AIR HUNG IN A WET MIST OVER ST. HILARION'S SCHOOL FOR BOYS; OVER THE WORLD. CHARLES ROWLAND SHIVERED.
FOUNDED IN 1802, A BOARDING SCHOOL FOR THE SONS OF ARMY OFFICERS...
THE SCHOOL NOW OFFERED EDUCATION TO ANYONE WHO COULD AFFORD IT; PARTICULARLY TO THOSE WHO LIVED ABROAD, BUT WANTED THEIR SONS EDUCATED ON BRITISH SOIL.
CHARLES ROWLAND HAD BEEN HERE FOR A YEAR AND A HALF; SINCE HIS FATHER LEFT THE COUNTRY.
HIS FATHER WAS AN ARCHITECT, A TALL, NERVOUS MAN, WHO DESIGNED HOSPITALS.
HIS MOTHER WAS LONG DEAD.
HE WALKED OVER TO THE EMPTY LIBRARY, COMPOSING A LETTER IN HIS HEAD, TO HIS FATHER.
IT WAS THE SAME LETTER HE HAD WANTED TO WRITE FOR A YEAR AND A HALF, AND NEVER HAD
"PLEASE, DADDY.
"TAKE ME HOME."

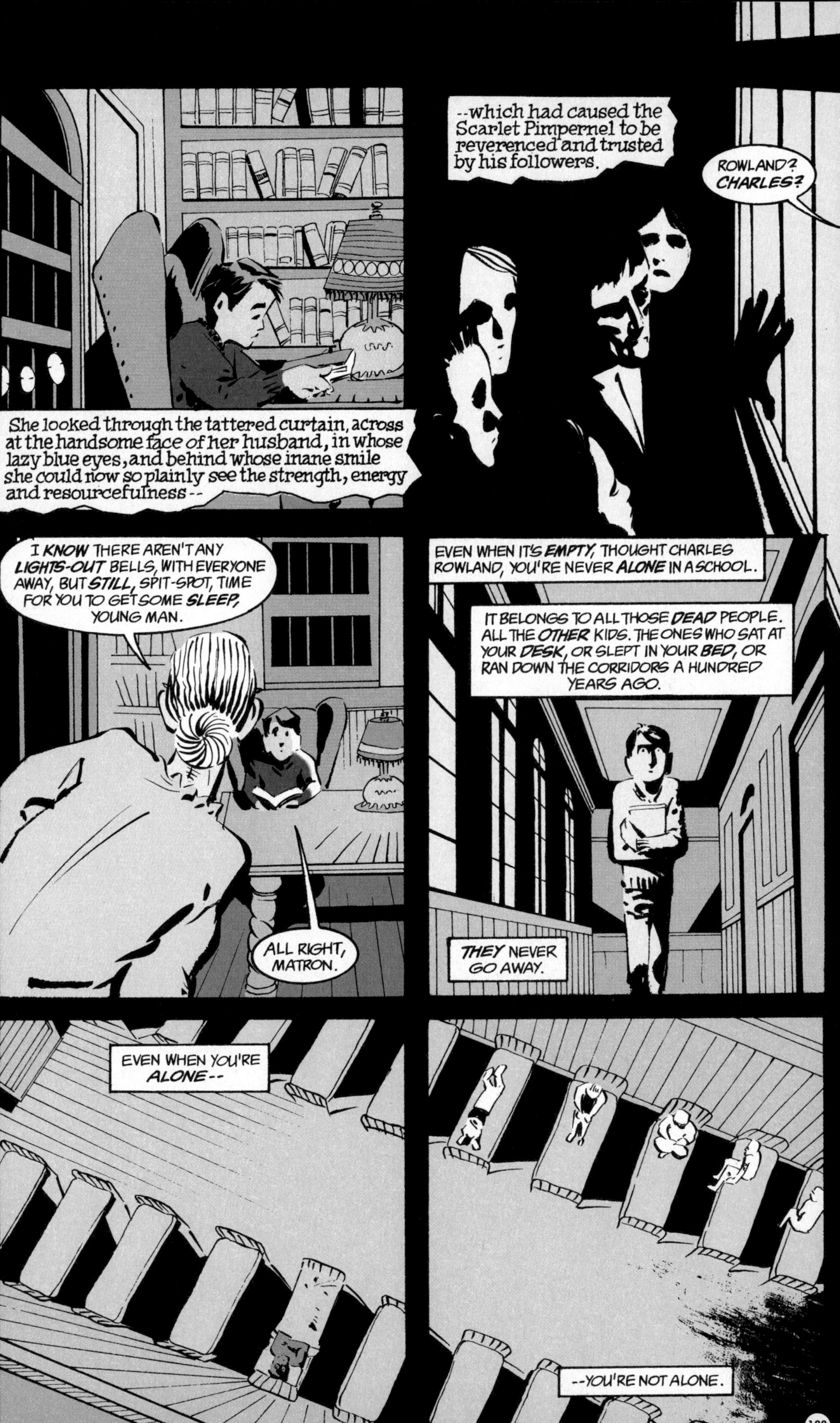
She looked through the tattered curtain, across at the handsome face of her husband, in whose lazy blue eyes, and behind whose inane smile she could now so plainly see the strength, energy and resourcefulness--
--which had caused the Scarlet Pimpernel to be reverenced and trusted by his followers.
ROWLAND? CHARLES?
I KNOW THERE AREN'T ANY LIGHTS-OUT BELLS, WITH EVERYONE AWAY, BUT STILL, SPIT-SPOT, TIME FOR YOU TO GET SOME SLEEP, YOUNG MAN.
ALL RIGHT, MATRON.
EVEN WHEN IT'S EMPTY, THOUGHT CHARLES ROWLAND, YOU'RE NEVER ALONE IN A SCHOOL.
IT BELONGS TO ALL THOSE DEAD PEOPLE. ALL THE OTHER KIDS. THE ONES WHO SAT AT YOUR DESK, OR SLEPT IN YOUR BED, OR RAN DOWN THE CORRIDORS A HUNDRED YEARS AGO.
THEY NEVER GO AWAY.
EVEN WHEN YOU'RE ALONE--
--YOU'RE NOT ALONE.

TUESDAY. FIVE DAYS AGO.

PUZZLED AND HUNGRY, HE WENT TO HIS LOCKER, AND GOT OUT HIS LAST PACKET OF CHOCOLATE DIGESTIVE BISCUITS.

THEN HE WALKED OUTSIDE, AND SAT ON THE WAR MEMORIAL, AND ATE THE WHOLE PACKET.

CHARLES ROWLAND WENT DOWN FOR BREAKFAST, BUT THERE WAS NOBODY THERE, AND NO BREAKFAST IN SIGHT.

AT LUNCHTIME, WHEN NO ONE APPEARED IN THE DINING HALL, HE WENT UP TO THE HEADMASTER'S STUDY.

KNOCK KNOCK

COME!

HMMPH. *THEODORE,* WHO'S YOUR LITTLE *FRIEND?*

AH. *ROWLAND.* YES. ROWLAND, THIS IS MY *MOTHER.* MOTHER, THIS IS *ROWLAND.*

ER....HELLO.

HOW DO YOU DO, YOUNG MAN?

THE *MISTS* STILL HUNG LOW AROUND THE SCHOOL; THEY HAD SWALLOWED THE PLAYING FIELDS, AND THE PAVILION, AND THE ART ROOMS.

IN MEMORY OF THOSE BOYS FROM · ST. HILARION'S · WHO LAID DOWN THEIR LIVES IN THE GREAT WAR (1914–1918)

ANDREWS, R.M.
AWCOCK, G.C.
BARROW, L.T.
BEETLE, J.
BLEEK, T.L.
BRUNT-SMITH, K.W.
CHEESEMAN, N.K.
COOK, S.
CROTTY, R.R.
CUTHBERTSON, S.M.L.W.
DAVIES, P.
DEVILLE, H.R.

ROWLAND WAS COLD, AND HIS HAIR AND SKIN FELT DAMP.

VERY WELL, THANKS.

UM, HOW ARE *YOU?*

CHARLES ROWLAND RETURNED TO THE DORMITORY, HUNGRY AND SCARED. THAT EVENING HE STARED AT THE MIST, AS NIGHT FELL.

HE SAT UP IN BED THAT NIGHT, HUNGRY AND FRIGHTENED; NOBODY CAME TO TURN OFF THE LIGHTS.

AND EVENTUALLY, CHARLES ROWLAND FELL ASLEEP.

HE WATCHED AS ALFRED, THE SCHOOL GROUNDS-MAN, RAN PAST, WAILING SOFTLY, PURSUED BY A WOMAN AND A CHILD. THE MISTS SWALLOWED THE THREE OF THEM; HE SAW NONE OF THEM AGAIN.

HE LET THEM BURN.

WHY ARE YOU...UP HERE? I MEAN, WHY DID YOU HIDE IN THE *ATTIC?*

BECAUSE MY *BONES* ARE UP HERE. IN THAT TRUNK. *SEE?* THIS IS WHERE I *DIED.*

THEY HID IT HERE. NO ONE *EVER* FOUND OUT.

HONESTLY-- I DON'T THINK THEY COULD HAVE *LOOKED* VERY HARD!

ALL THEIR STUFF IS STILL HERE. THEY *HARDLY* EVEN COVERED THEIR *TRACKS.* YOU CAN STILL SEE THE *CIRCLE* THEY DREW ON THE *FLOOR* OVER THERE...

THIS WAS WHERE THEY USED TO *COME,* YOU SEE.

AT *NIGHT.* TRYING TO RAISE *DEVILS* THAT *NEVER* CAME.

THEY'D DRESS UP, AND THEY'D *DO* STUFF. THEY'D KILL *FROGS* AND *RABBITS* AND *CATS...*

AND YOU.

AND ME.

WEDNESDAY. FOUR DAYS AGO.

WAKE THE BUG *UP*, CHEESEY.

GOD, IT'S A *BUG!*

YUCK! A BUG.

WHAT'S YOUR PATHETIC *NAME*, BUG?

GOD, WHAT A *SUB-HUMAN MORON.* COME ON, *SCUMBUG.* WHAT'S YOUR *NAME?*

OW!

OWWW! PLEASE! IT'S CHARLES ROWLAND.

THAT'S *BETTER*, BUG. I'M CHEESEMAN.

I'M BARROW.

I'M *SKINNER.* WE'RE *OLD BOYS.*

VERY OLD. HEE HEE HEE.

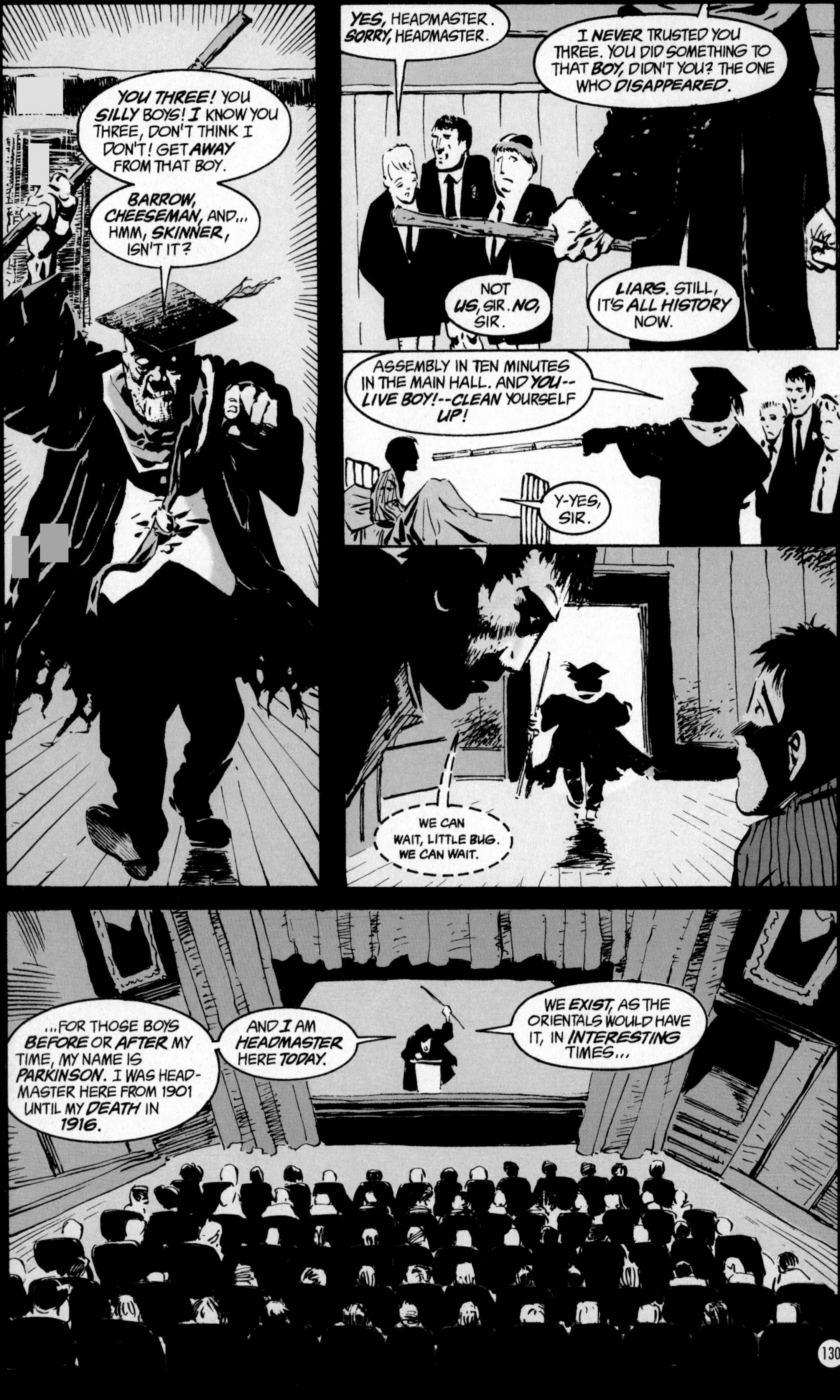

YOU THREE! YOU SILLY BOYS! I KNOW YOU THREE, DON'T THINK I DON'T! GET AWAY FROM THAT BOY.
BARROW, CHEESEMAN, AND... HMM, SKINNER, ISN'T IT?
YES, HEADMASTER. SORRY, HEADMASTER.
I NEVER TRUSTED YOU THREE. YOU DID SOMETHING TO THAT BOY, DIDN'T YOU? THE ONE WHO DISAPPEARED.
NOT US, SIR. NO, SIR.
LIARS. STILL, IT'S ALL HISTORY NOW.
ASSEMBLY IN TEN MINUTES IN THE MAIN HALL. AND YOU-- LIVE BOY!--CLEAN YOURSELF UP!
Y-YES, SIR.
WE CAN WAIT, LITTLE BUG. WE CAN WAIT.
...FOR THOSE BOYS BEFORE OR AFTER MY TIME, MY NAME IS PARKINSON. I WAS HEAD-MASTER HERE FROM 1901 UNTIL MY DEATH IN 1916.
AND I AM HEADMASTER HERE TODAY.
WE EXIST, AS THE ORIENTALS WOULD HAVE IT, IN INTERESTING TIMES...

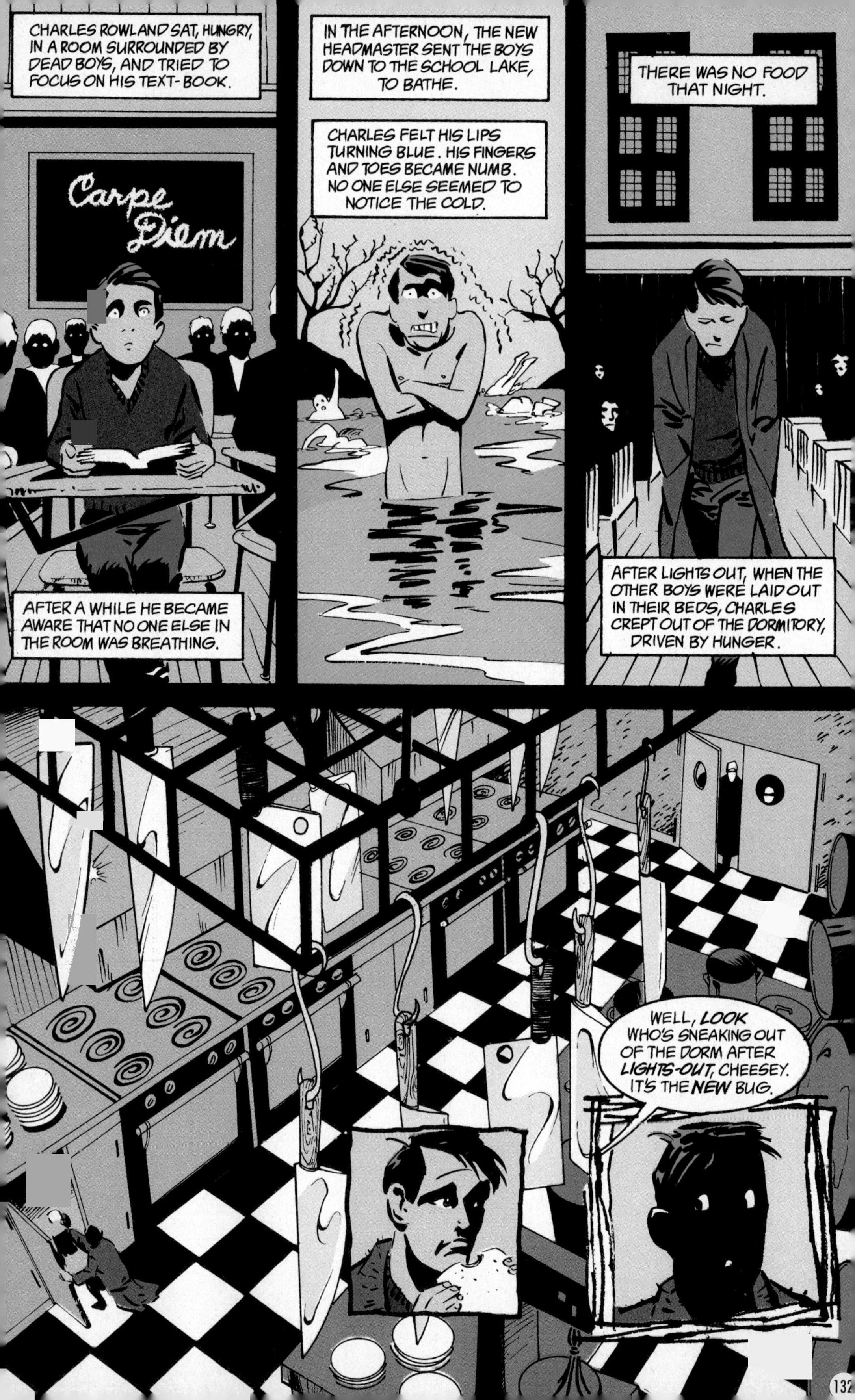

CHARLES ROWLAND SAT, HUNGRY, IN A ROOM SURROUNDED BY DEAD BOYS, AND TRIED TO FOCUS ON HIS TEXT-BOOK.
Carpe Diem
AFTER A WHILE HE BECAME AWARE THAT NO ONE ELSE IN THE ROOM WAS BREATHING.
IN THE AFTERNOON, THE NEW HEADMASTER SENT THE BOYS DOWN TO THE SCHOOL LAKE, TO BATHE.
CHARLES FELT HIS LIPS TURNING BLUE. HIS FINGERS AND TOES BECAME NUMB. NO ONE ELSE SEEMED TO NOTICE THE COLD.
THERE WAS NO FOOD THAT NIGHT.
AFTER LIGHTS OUT, WHEN THE OTHER BOYS WERE LAID OUT IN THEIR BEDS, CHARLES CREPT OUT OF THE DORMITORY, DRIVEN BY HUNGER.
WELL, LOOK WHO'S SNEAKING OUT OF THE DORM AFTER LIGHTS-OUT, CHEESEY. IT'S THE NEW BUG.

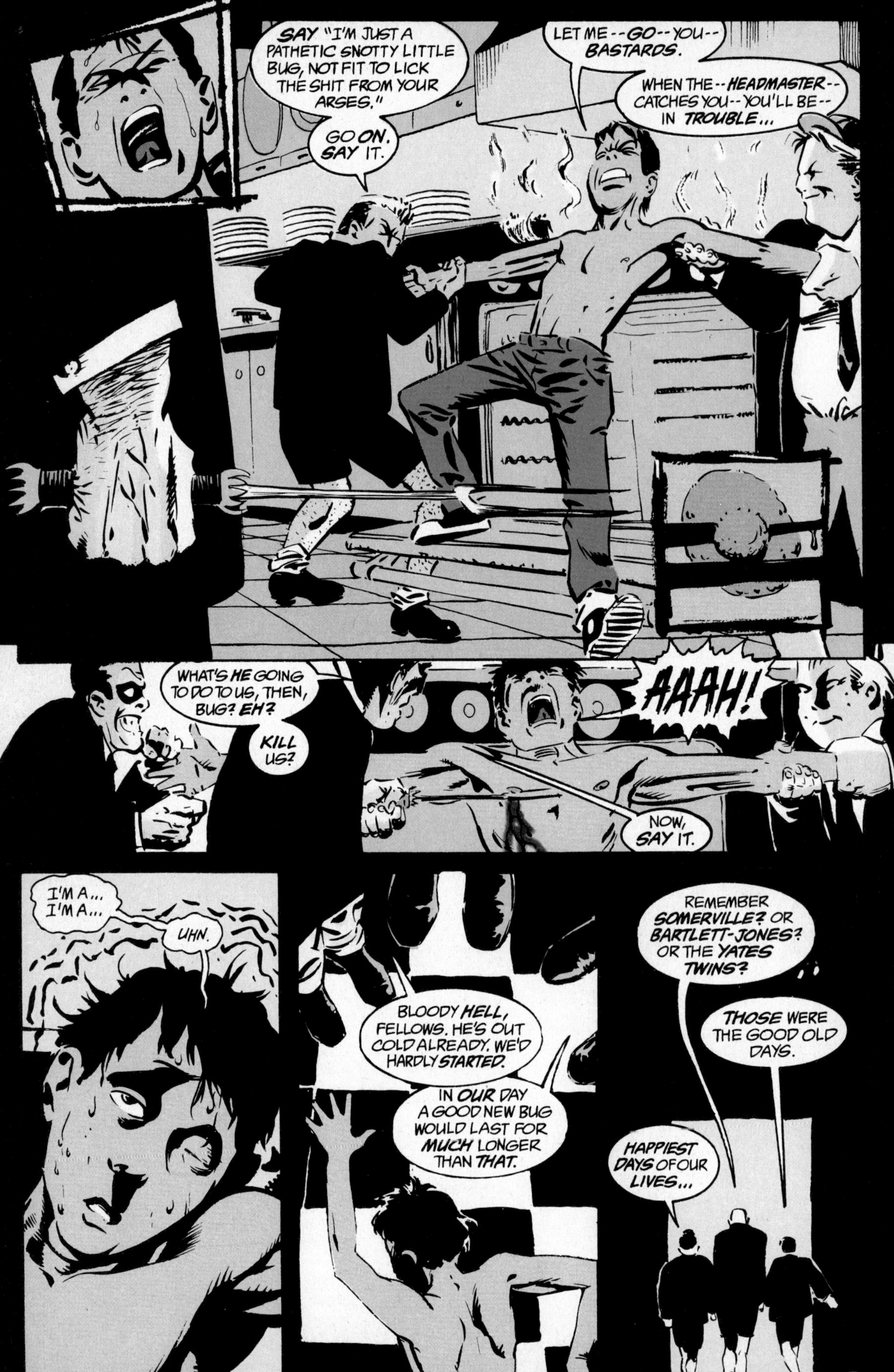

SAY "I'M JUST A PATHETIC SNOTTY LITTLE BUG, NOT FIT TO LICK THE SHIT FROM YOUR ARSES."
GO ON. SAY IT.
LET ME--GO--YOU--BASTARDS.
WHEN THE--HEADMASTER--CATCHES YOU--YOU'LL BE--IN TROUBLE...
WHAT'S HE GOING TO DO TO US, THEN, BUG? EH?
KILL US?
AAAH!
NOW, SAY IT.
I'M A... I'M A...
UHN.
BLOODY HELL, FELLOWS. HE'S OUT COLD ALREADY. WE'D HARDLY STARTED.
IN OUR DAY A GOOD NEW BUG WOULD LAST FOR MUCH LONGER THAN THAT.
REMEMBER SOMERVILLE? OR BARTLETT-JONES? OR THE YATES TWINS?
THOSE WERE THE GOOD OLD DAYS.
HAPPIEST DAYS OF OUR LIVES...

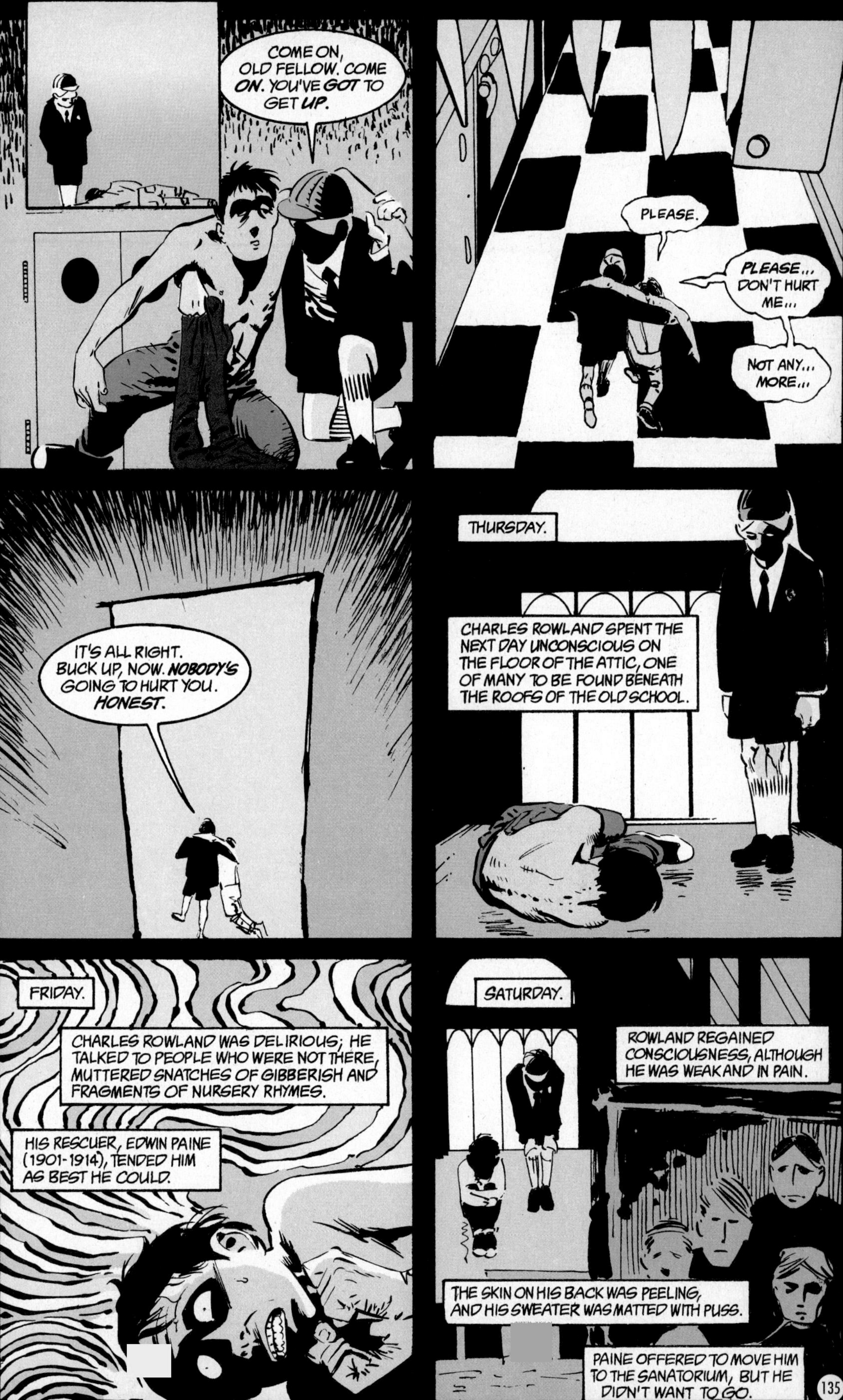

COME ON, OLD FELLOW. COME ON. YOU'VE GOT TO GET UP.
PLEASE.
PLEASE... DON'T HURT ME...
NOT ANY... MORE...
IT'S ALL RIGHT. BUCK UP, NOW. NOBODY'S GOING TO HURT YOU. HONEST.
THURSDAY.
CHARLES ROWLAND SPENT THE NEXT DAY UNCONSCIOUS ON THE FLOOR OF THE ATTIC, ONE OF MANY TO BE FOUND BENEATH THE ROOFS OF THE OLD SCHOOL.
FRIDAY.
CHARLES ROWLAND WAS DELIRIOUS; HE TALKED TO PEOPLE WHO WERE NOT THERE, MUTTERED SNATCHES OF GIBBERISH AND FRAGMENTS OF NURSERY RHYMES.
HIS RESCUER, EDWIN PAINE (1901-1914), TENDED HIM AS BEST HE COULD.
SATURDAY.
ROWLAND REGAINED CONSCIOUSNESS, ALTHOUGH HE WAS WEAK AND IN PAIN.
THE SKIN ON HIS BACK WAS PEELING, AND HIS SWEATER WAS MATTED WITH PUSS.
PAINE OFFERED TO MOVE HIM TO THE SANATORIUM, BUT HE DIDN'T WANT TO GO.

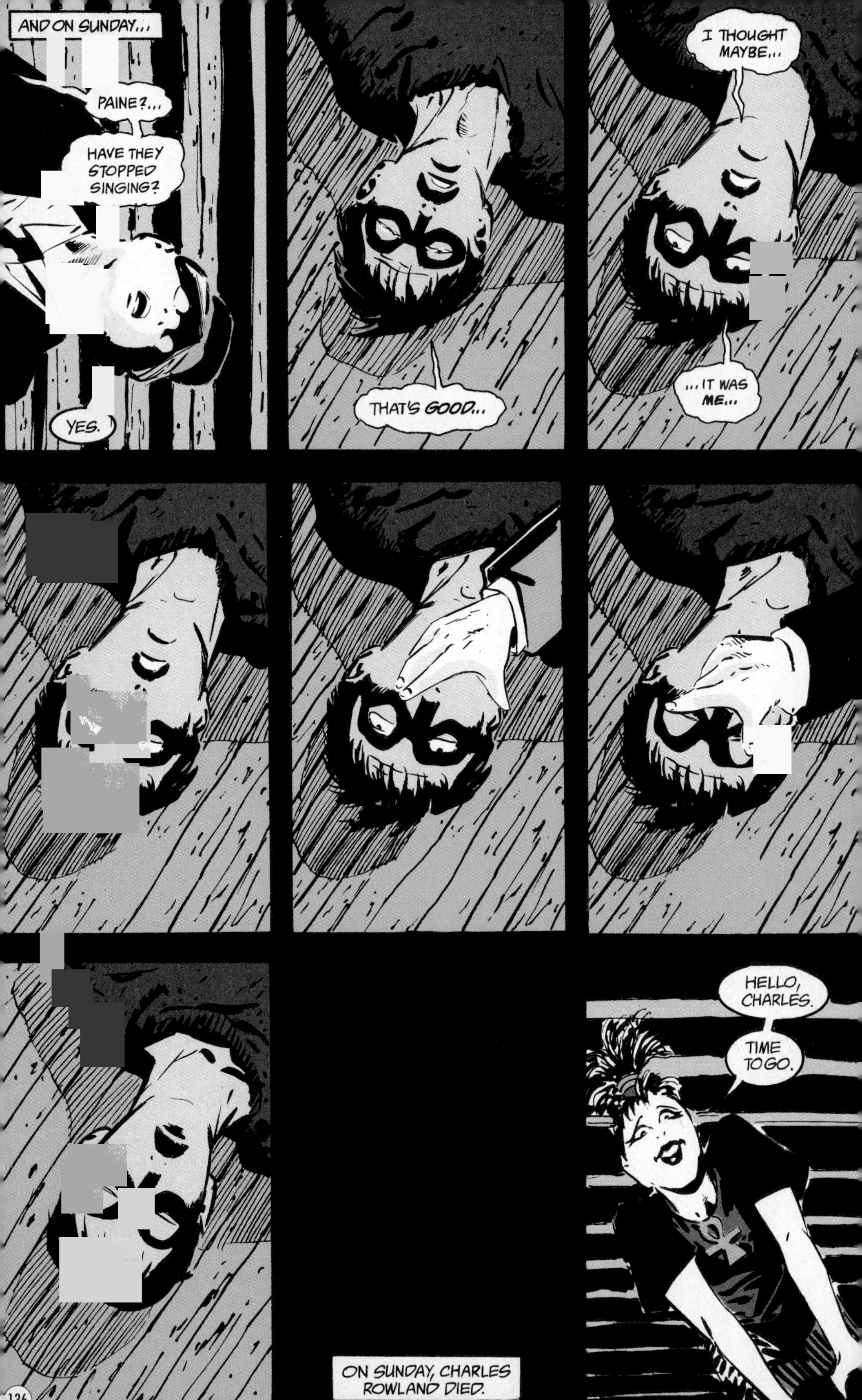
AND ON SUNDAY...
PAINE?...
HAVE THEY STOPPED SINGING?
YES.
THAT'S GOOD...
I THOUGHT MAYBE...
...IT WAS ME...
HELLO, CHARLES.
TIME TO GO.
ON SUNDAY, CHARLES ROWLAND DIED.

In which a banquet is held, and of what comes after; concerning diplomacy and bedrooms, blackmail and threats; and an unusual recipe for sausages.

EPISODE 5

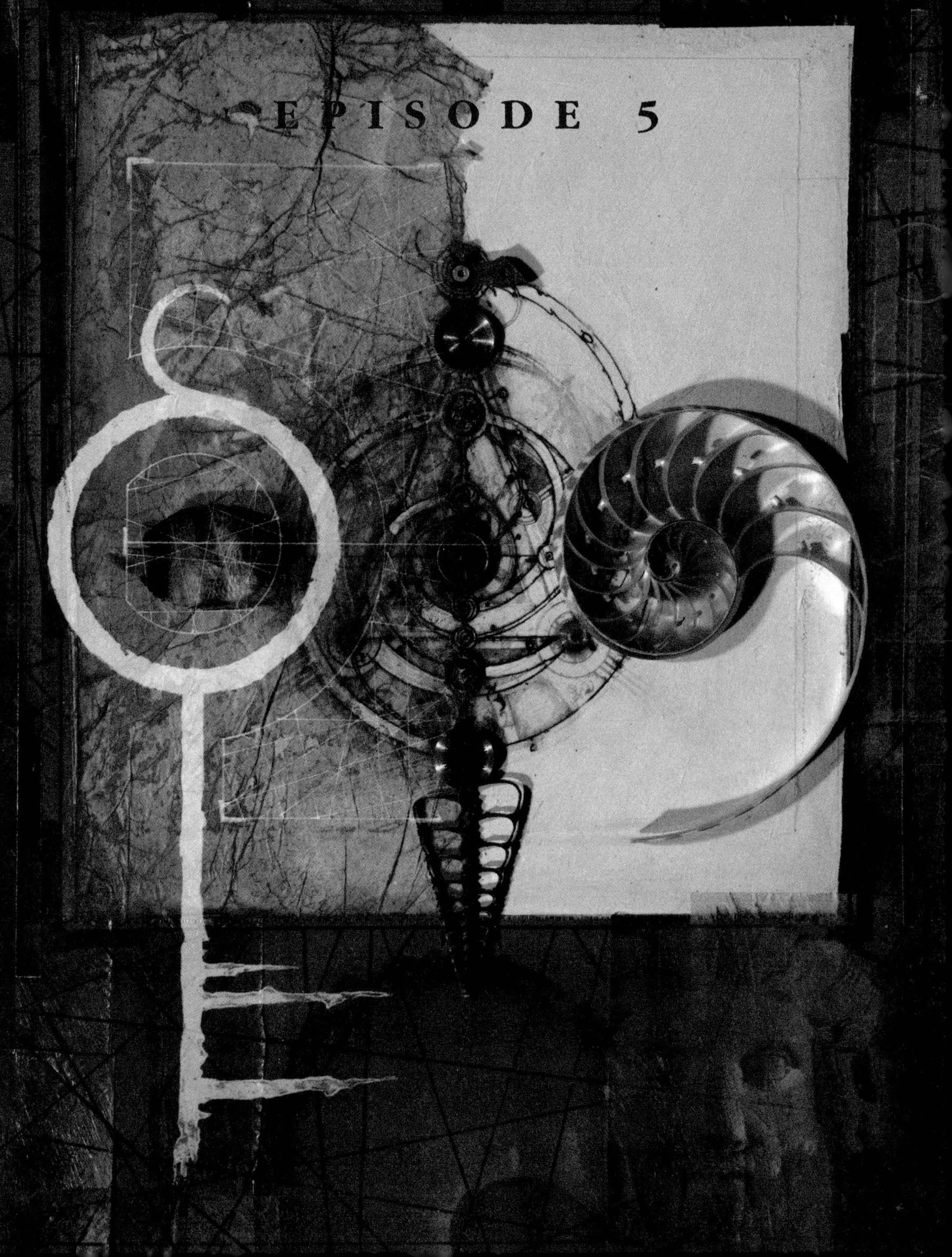

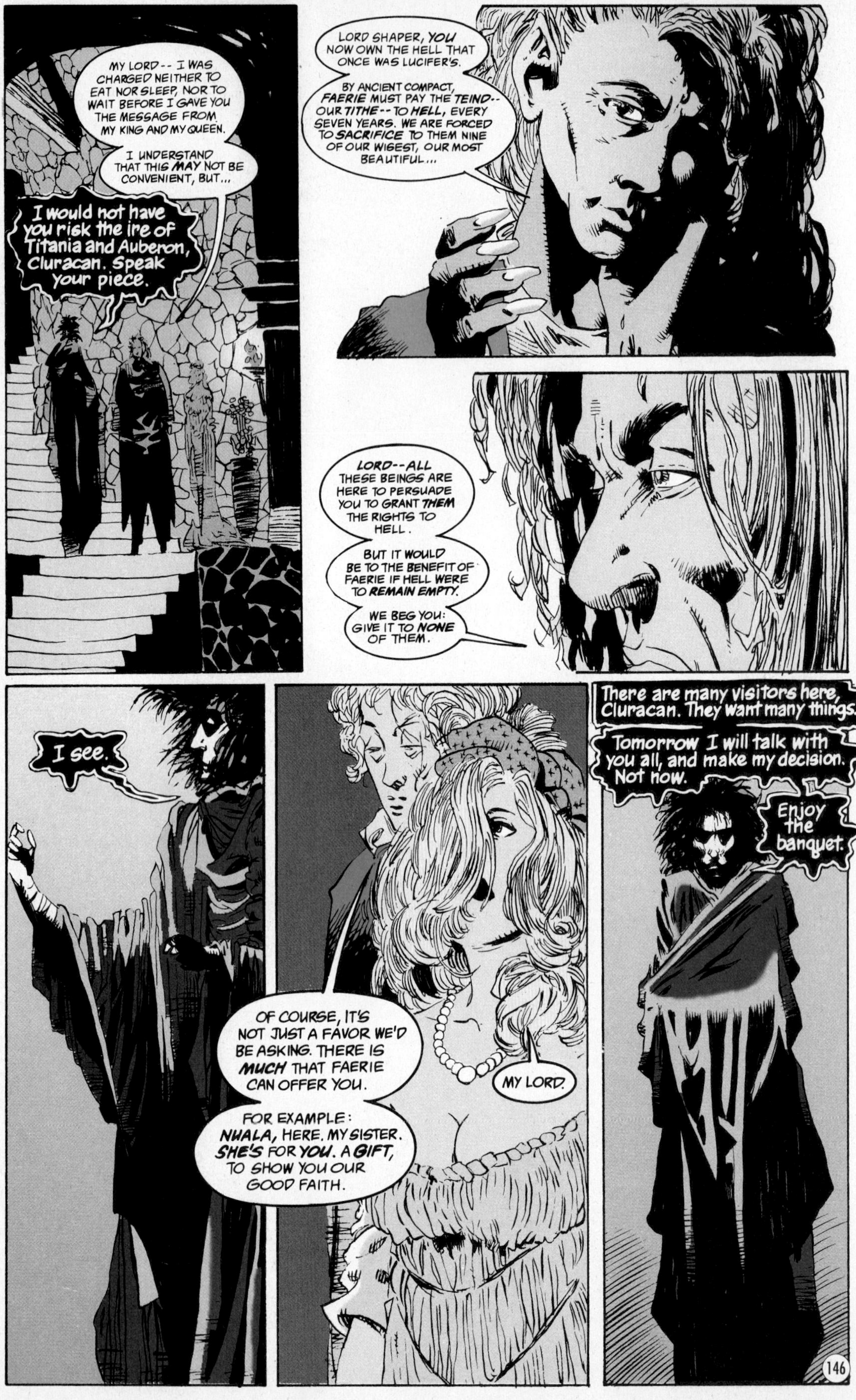

MY LORD -- I WAS CHARGED NEITHER TO EAT NOR SLEEP, NOR TO WAIT BEFORE I GAVE YOU THE MESSAGE FROM MY KING AND MY QUEEN.
I UNDERSTAND THAT THIS MAY NOT BE CONVENIENT, BUT...
I would not have you risk the ire of Titania and Auberon, Cluracan. Speak your piece.
LORD SHAPER, YOU NOW OWN THE HELL THAT ONCE WAS LUCIFER'S.
BY ANCIENT COMPACT, FAERIE MUST PAY THE TEIND -- OUR TITHE -- TO HELL, EVERY SEVEN YEARS. WE ARE FORCED TO SACRIFICE TO THEM NINE OF OUR WISEST, OUR MOST BEAUTIFUL...
LORD -- ALL THESE BEINGS ARE HERE TO PERSUADE YOU TO GRANT THEM THE RIGHTS TO HELL.
BUT IT WOULD BE TO THE BENEFIT OF FAERIE IF HELL WERE TO REMAIN EMPTY.
WE BEG YOU: GIVE IT TO NONE OF THEM.
I see.
OF COURSE, IT'S NOT JUST A FAVOR WE'D BE ASKING. THERE IS MUCH THAT FAERIE CAN OFFER YOU.
FOR EXAMPLE: NUALA, HERE. MY SISTER. SHE'S FOR YOU. A GIFT, TO SHOW YOU OUR GOOD FAITH.
MY LORD.
There are many visitors here, Cluracan. They want many things.
Tomorrow I will talk with you all, and make my decision. Not now.
Enjoy the banquet.

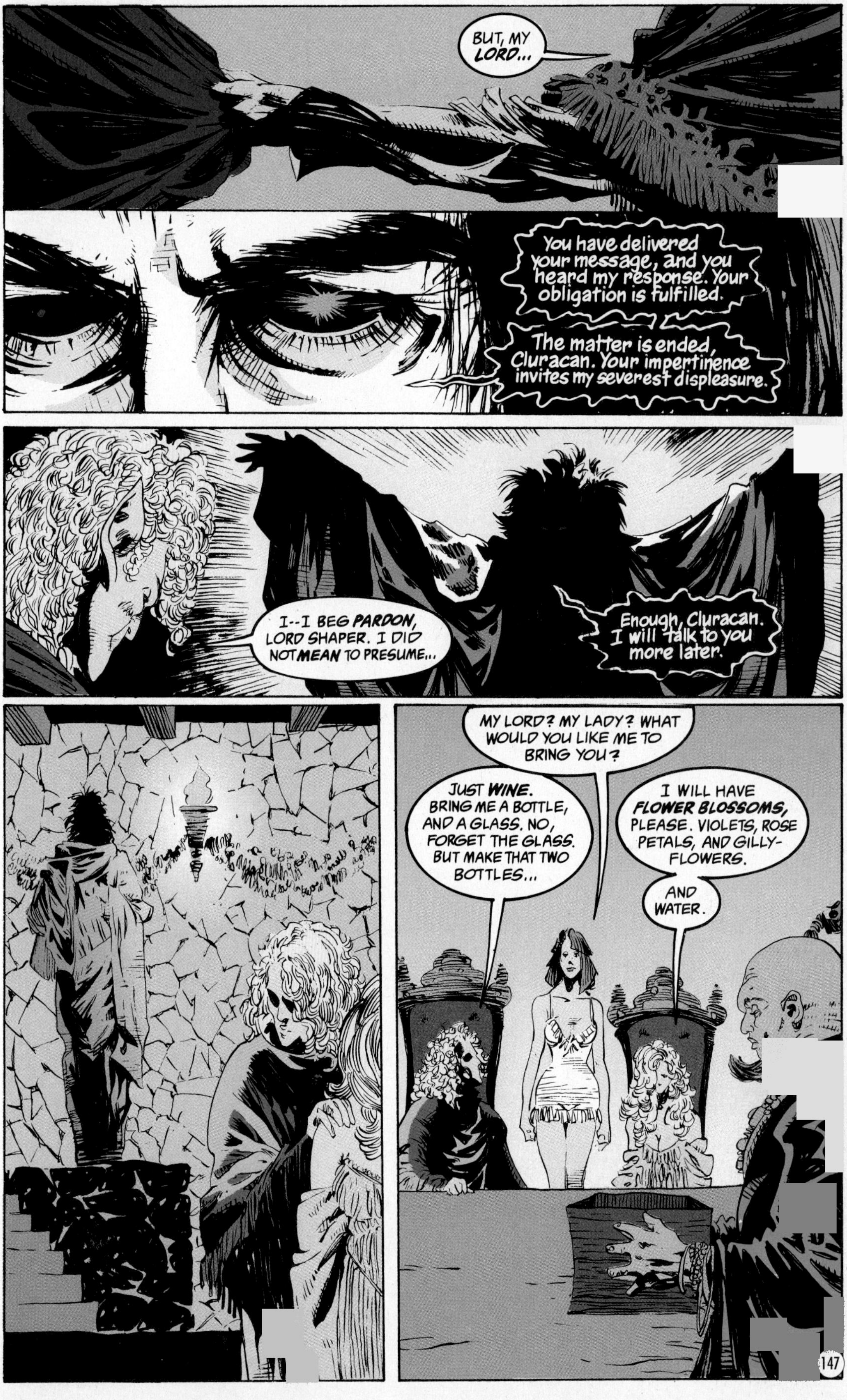
BUT, MY LORD...
You have delivered your message, and you heard my response. Your obligation is fulfilled.
The matter is ended, Cluracan. Your impertinence invites my severest displeasure.
I--I BEG PARDON, LORD SHAPER. I DID NOT MEAN TO PRESUME...
Enough, Cluracan. I will talk to you more later.
MY LORD? MY LADY? WHAT WOULD YOU LIKE ME TO BRING YOU?
JUST WINE. BRING ME A BOTTLE, AND A GLASS. NO, FORGET THE GLASS. BUT MAKE THAT TWO BOTTLES...
I WILL HAVE FLOWER BLOSSOMS, PLEASE. VIOLETS, ROSE PETALS, AND GILLY-FLOWERS.
AND WATER.

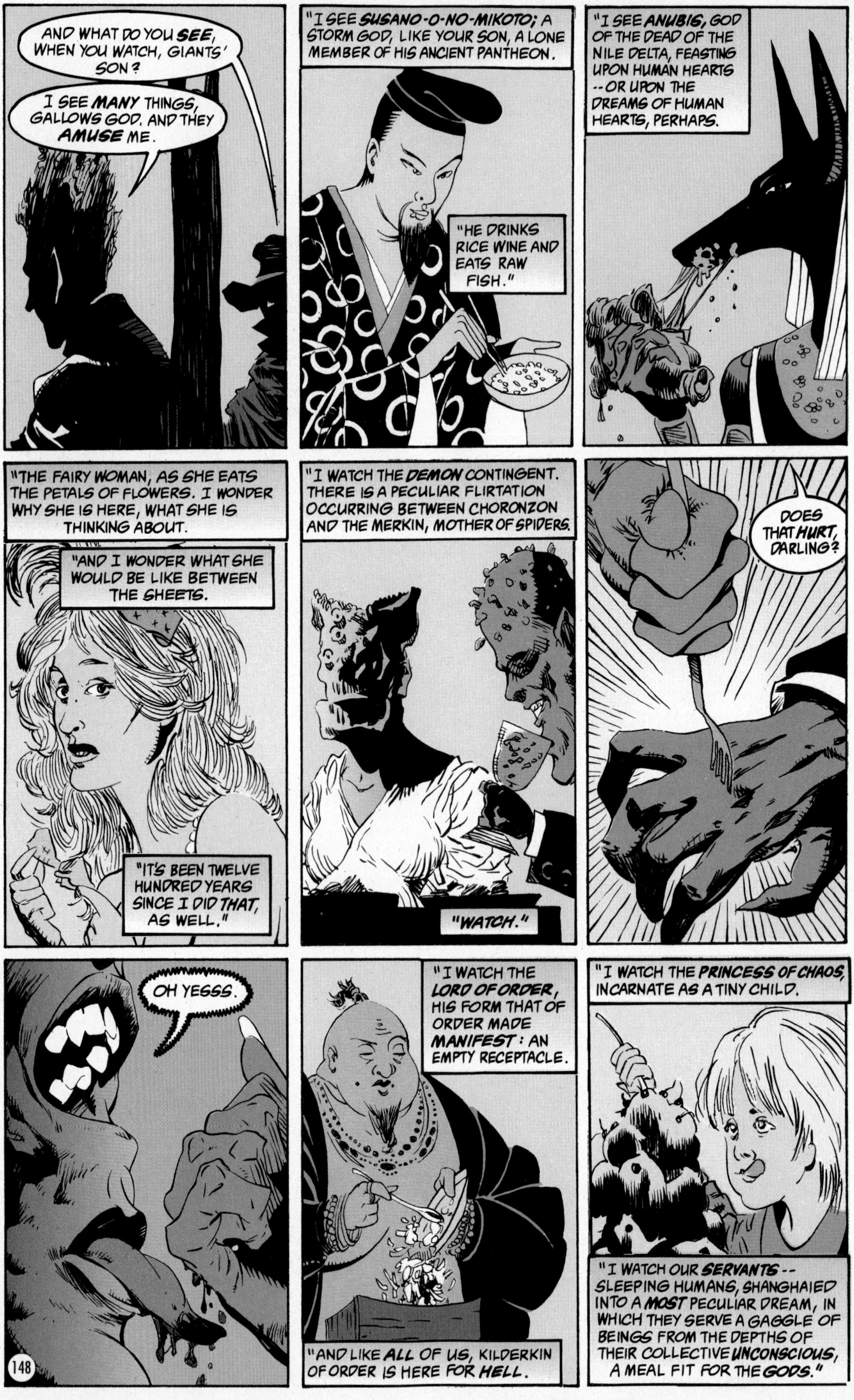
AND WHAT DO YOU SEE, WHEN YOU WATCH, GIANTS' SON?
I SEE MANY THINGS, GALLOWS GOD. AND THEY AMUSE ME.
"I SEE SUSANO-O-NO-MIKOTO; A STORM GOD, LIKE YOUR SON, A LONE MEMBER OF HIS ANCIENT PANTHEON.
"HE DRINKS RICE WINE AND EATS RAW FISH."
"I SEE ANUBIS, GOD OF THE DEAD OF THE NILE DELTA, FEASTING UPON HUMAN HEARTS --OR UPON THE DREAMS OF HUMAN HEARTS, PERHAPS.
"THE FAIRY WOMAN, AS SHE EATS THE PETALS OF FLOWERS. I WONDER WHY SHE IS HERE, WHAT SHE IS THINKING ABOUT.
"AND I WONDER WHAT SHE WOULD BE LIKE BETWEEN THE SHEETS.
"IT'S BEEN TWELVE HUNDRED YEARS SINCE I DID THAT, AS WELL."
"I WATCH THE DEMON CONTINGENT. THERE IS A PECULIAR FLIRTATION OCCURRING BETWEEN CHORONZON AND THE MERKIN, MOTHER OF SPIDERS.
"WATCH."
DOES THAT HURT, DARLING?
OH YESSS.
"I WATCH THE LORD OF ORDER, HIS FORM THAT OF ORDER MADE MANIFEST: AN EMPTY RECEPTACLE.
"AND LIKE ALL OF US, KILDERKIN OF ORDER IS HERE FOR HELL.
"I WATCH THE PRINCESS OF CHAOS, INCARNATE AS A TINY CHILD.
"I WATCH OUR SERVANTS -- SLEEPING HUMANS, SHANGHAIED INTO A MOST PECULIAR DREAM, IN WHICH THEY SERVE A GAGGLE OF BEINGS FROM THE DEPTHS OF THEIR COLLECTIVE UNCONSCIOUS, A MEAL FIT FOR THE GODS."

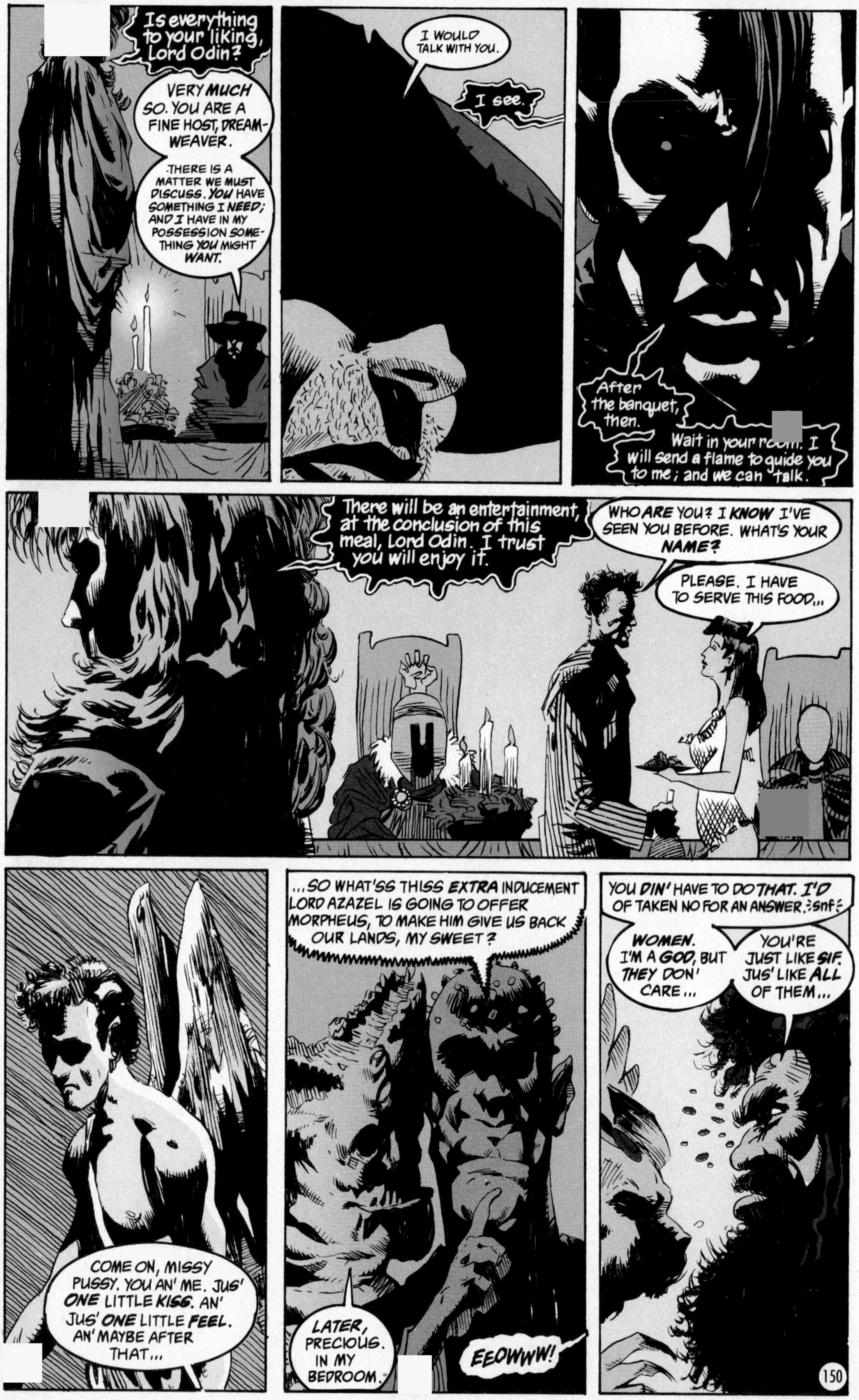
Is everything to your liking, Lord Odin?
VERY MUCH SO. YOU ARE A FINE HOST, DREAM-WEAVER.
THERE IS A MATTER WE MUST DISCUSS. YOU HAVE SOMETHING I NEED; AND I HAVE IN MY POSSESSION SOMETHING YOU MIGHT WANT.
I WOULD TALK WITH YOU.
I see.
After the banquet, then.
Wait in your room. I will send a flame to guide you to me; and we can talk.
There will be an entertainment, at the conclusion of this meal, Lord Odin. I trust you will enjoy it.
WHO ARE YOU? I KNOW I'VE SEEN YOU BEFORE. WHAT'S YOUR NAME?
PLEASE. I HAVE TO SERVE THIS FOOD...
COME ON, MISSY PUSSY. YOU AN' ME. JUS' ONE LITTLE KISS. AN' JUS' ONE LITTLE FEEL. AN' MAYBE AFTER THAT...
...SO WHAT'SS THISS EXTRA INDUCEMENT LORD AZAZEL IS GOING TO OFFER MORPHEUS, TO MAKE HIM GIVE US BACK OUR LANDS, MY SWEET?
LATER, PRECIOUS. IN MY BEDROOM.
EEOWWW!
YOU DIN' HAVE TO DO THAT. I'D OF TAKEN NO FOR AN ANSWER. snf
WOMEN. I'M A GOD, BUT THEY DON' CARE...
YOU'RE JUST LIKE SIF. JUS' LIKE ALL OF THEM...
150

TAA DAAH! NOW, MY LITTLE TROLLEY-OGGLER, CAN YOU WIGGLE YOUR RIGHT FOOT FOR THE NICE PEOPLE?

"I TELL YOU, THE DRUNKEN OAF PROPOSED TO MAKE LOVE TO ME!"

As host, I can but apologize, Lady Bast. You were obviously provoked, and I will speak to Lord Odin about it. Where is Thor NOW?

CUH-CAIN, YOU, ERM, YOU RUHREALLY CAN PUH-P-PUT ME BACK TOGETHER AGAIN. UHN, C-CAN'T YOU?

I LEFT HIM LAYING UNDER THE TABLE, CHANTING SOME SONG TO HIMSELF.

IT BEGAN: "MY HAMMER HAS A HUGE HARD HANDLE."

THE SOT WAS ALSO TRYING TO WIPE HIS VOMIT FROM THE CARPET WITH HIS BEARD.

Again, lady, I apologize.

IT IS NO MATTER, DREAM LORD. THAT WAS NOT WHY I WISHED TO TALK WITH YOU.

No? Then, why?

"WE MUST TALK IN PRIVATE. YOU HAVE SOMETHING THAT WE WANT. VERY BADLY. AND WE HAVE SOMETHING YOU DESIRE."

"Very well. Later. I will send for you, Lady Bast."

AND WHAT'S IN THE EMPTY BOX? BLESS MY SOUL! IT ISN'T EMPTY!

CUH-CUH-CAIN. YUH-YOU BUHBUHBUH...

SHUT UP, YOU CRETIN. YOU SAID YOU WANTED TO BE IN SHOW BUSINESS, DIDN'T YOU?

CLAP CLAP CLAP

LOOK! IT MISTER SHOUTY. HE'S A POOEY MAN.

AND FOR MY NEXT TRICK...

GREGORY, THE MINCING MACHINE, PLEASE.

152

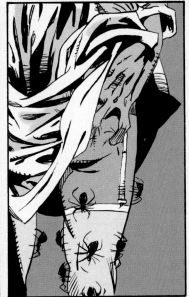

YOU ASKED WHAT THE *OTHER* PRIZE WAS, *DIDN'T* YOU? WHAT *ELSE* OUR LORD AZAZEL WAS GOING TO OFFER THE DREAM KING, IN EXCHANGE FOR HELL.

WELL, IT *MUST* BE OBVIOUS NOW, MY DARLING.

IT'S *YOU.*

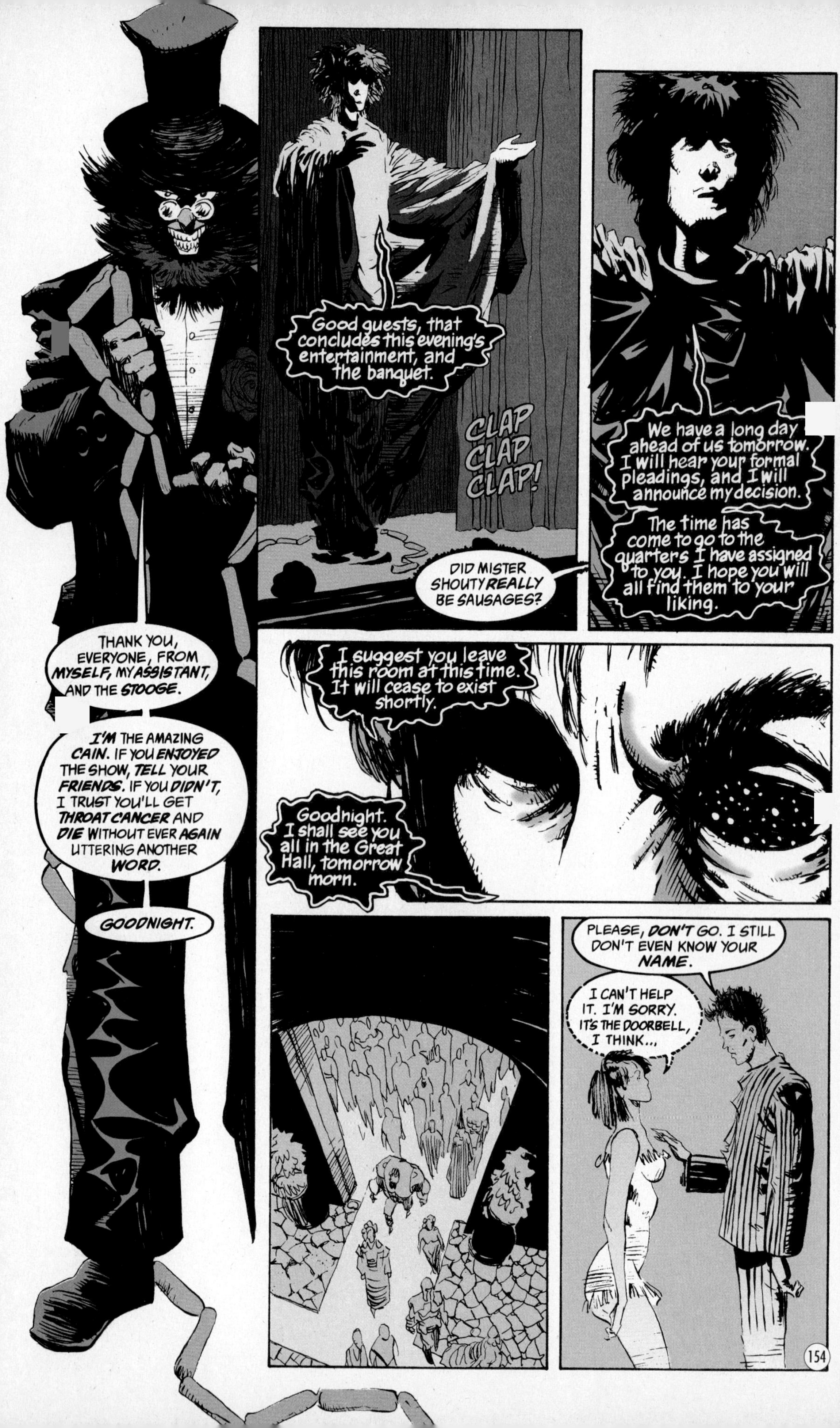

Good guests, that concludes this evening's entertainment, and the banquet.
CLAP CLAP CLAP!
DID MISTER SHOUTY REALLY BE SAUSAGES?
We have a long day ahead of us tomorrow. I will hear your formal pleadings, and I will announce my decision.
The time has come to go to the quarters I have assigned to you. I hope you will all find them to your liking.
THANK YOU, EVERYONE, FROM MYSELF, MY ASSISTANT, AND THE STOOGE.
I'M THE AMAZING CAIN. IF YOU ENJOYED THE SHOW, TELL YOUR FRIENDS. IF YOU DIDN'T, I TRUST YOU'LL GET THROAT CANCER AND DIE WITHOUT EVER AGAIN UTTERING ANOTHER WORD.
GOODNIGHT.
I suggest you leave this room at this time. It will cease to exist shortly.
Goodnight. I shall see you all in the Great Hall, tomorrow morn.
PLEASE, DON'T GO. I STILL DON'T EVEN KNOW YOUR NAME.
I CAN'T HELP IT. I'M SORRY. IT'S THE DOORBELL, I THINK...

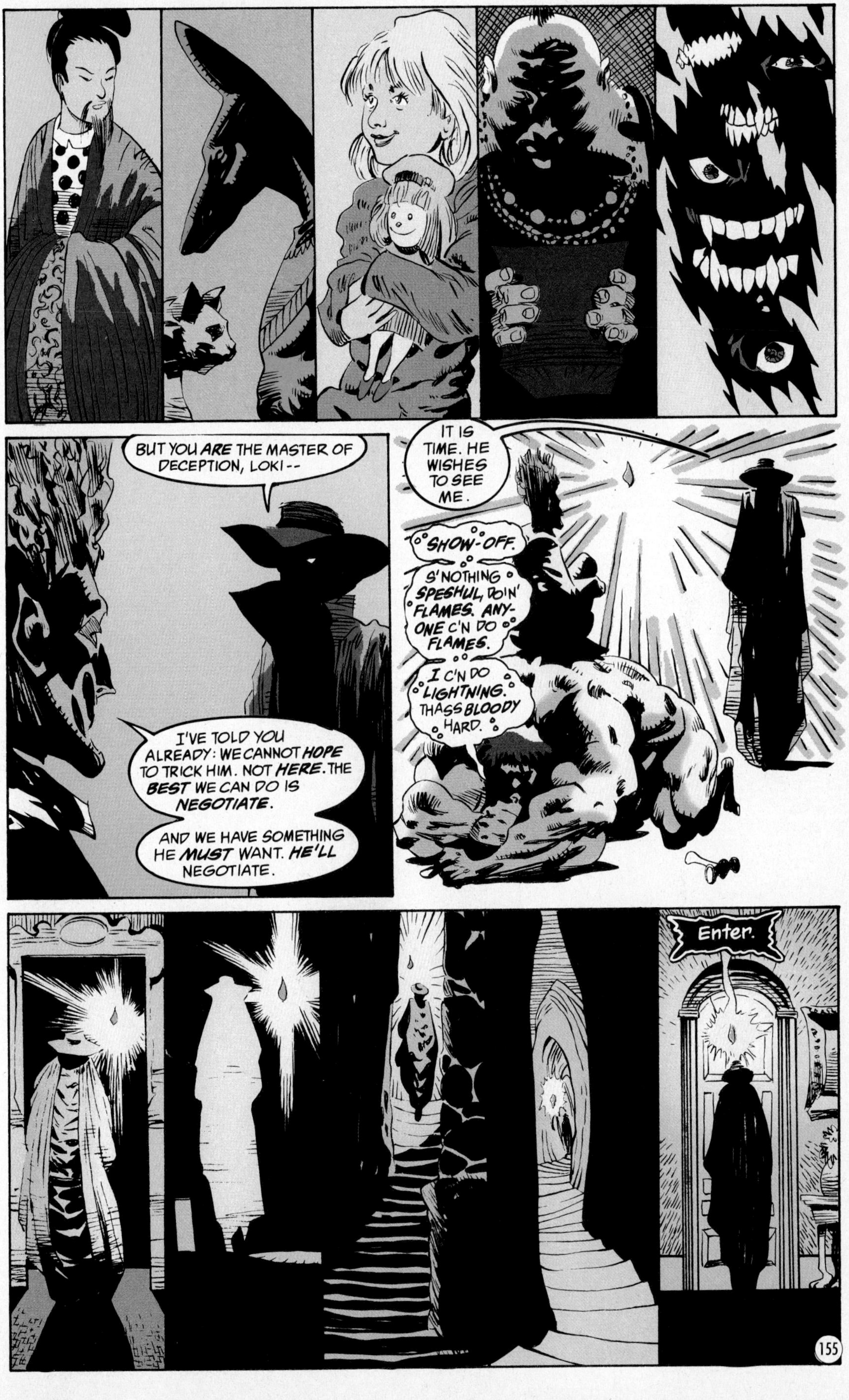
BUT YOU ARE THE MASTER OF DECEPTION, LOKI--
I'VE TOLD YOU ALREADY: WE CANNOT HOPE TO TRICK HIM. NOT HERE. THE BEST WE CAN DO IS NEGOTIATE.
AND WE HAVE SOMETHING HE MUST WANT. HE'LL NEGOTIATE.
IT IS TIME. HE WISHES TO SEE ME.
SHOW-OFF.
S'NOTHING SPESHUL, DOIN' FLAMES. ANY-ONE C'N DO FLAMES.
I C'N DO LIGHTNING. THASS BLOODY HARD.
Enter.

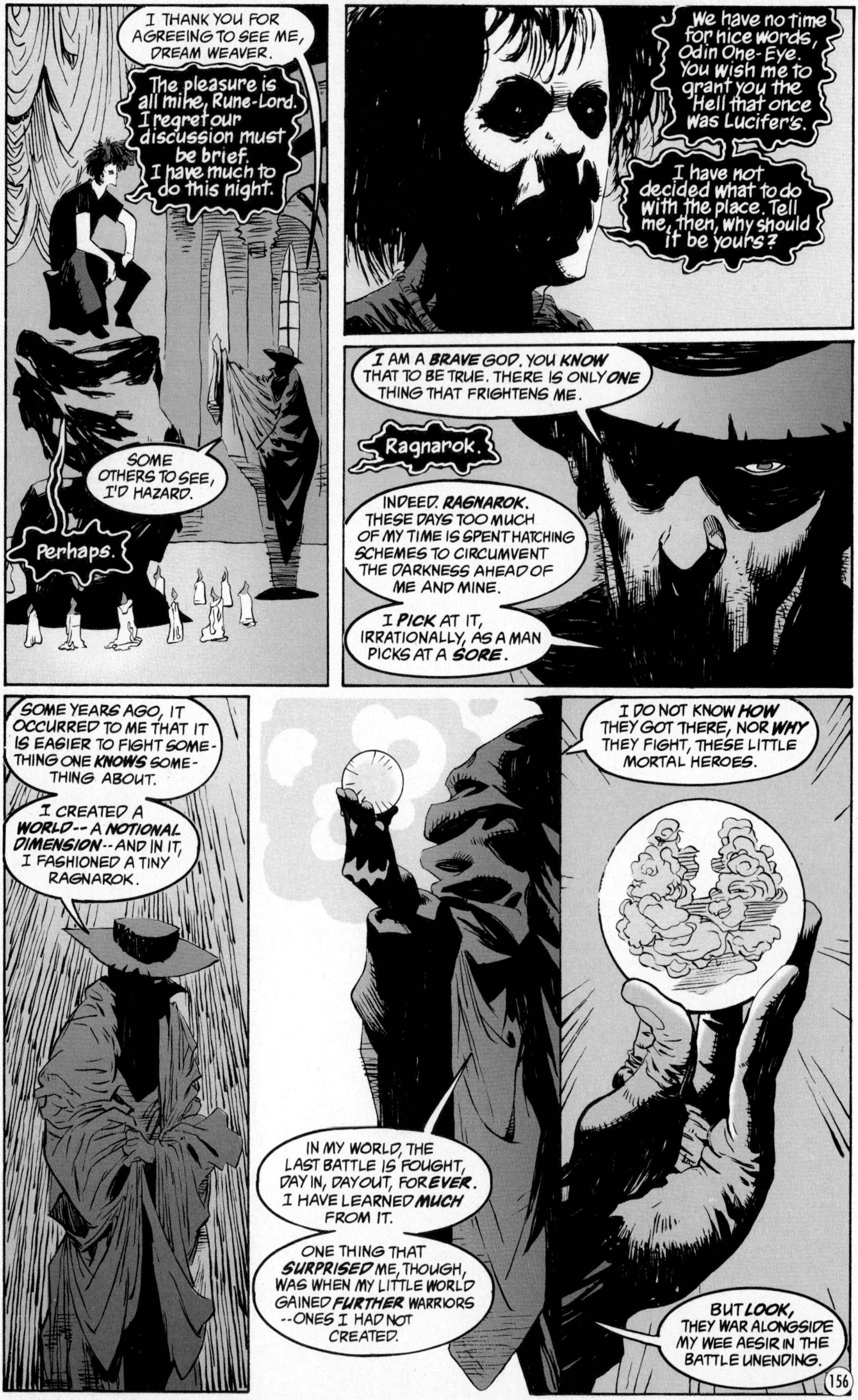
I THANK YOU FOR AGREEING TO SEE ME, DREAM WEAVER.
The pleasure is all mine, Rune-Lord. I regret our discussion must be brief. I have much to do this night.
SOME OTHERS TO SEE, I'D HAZARD.
Perhaps.
We have no time for nice words, Odin One-Eye. You wish me to grant you the Hell that once was Lucifer's.
I have not decided what to do with the place. Tell me, then, why should it be yours?
I AM A BRAVE GOD. YOU KNOW THAT TO BE TRUE. THERE IS ONLY ONE THING THAT FRIGHTENS ME.
Ragnarok.
INDEED. RAGNAROK. THESE DAYS TOO MUCH OF MY TIME IS SPENT HATCHING SCHEMES TO CIRCUMVENT THE DARKNESS AHEAD OF ME AND MINE.
I PICK AT IT, IRRATIONALLY, AS A MAN PICKS AT A SORE.
SOME YEARS AGO, IT OCCURRED TO ME THAT IT IS EASIER TO FIGHT SOMETHING ONE KNOWS SOMETHING ABOUT.
I CREATED A WORLD-- A NOTIONAL DIMENSION--AND IN IT, I FASHIONED A TINY RAGNAROK.
IN MY WORLD, THE LAST BATTLE IS FOUGHT, DAY IN, DAY OUT, FOREVER. I HAVE LEARNED MUCH FROM IT.
ONE THING THAT SURPRISED ME, THOUGH, WAS WHEN MY LITTLE WORLD GAINED FURTHER WARRIORS --ONES I HAD NOT CREATED.
I DO NOT KNOW HOW THEY GOT THERE, NOR WHY THEY FIGHT, THESE LITTLE MORTAL HEROES.
BUT LOOK, THEY WAR ALONGSIDE MY WEE AESIR IN THE BATTLE UNENDING.

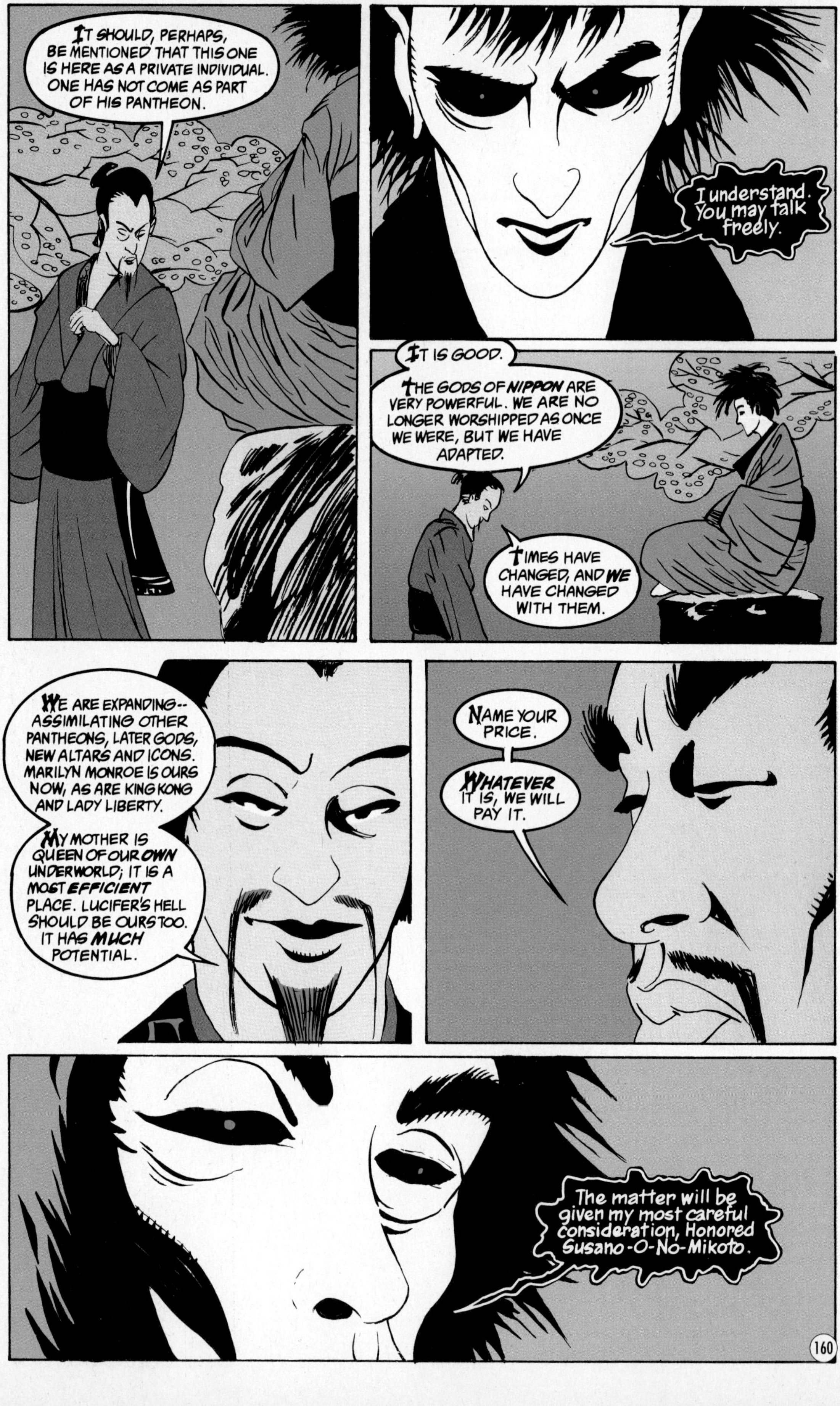

IT SHOULD, PERHAPS, BE MENTIONED THAT THIS ONE IS HERE AS A PRIVATE INDIVIDUAL. ONE HAS NOT COME AS PART OF HIS PANTHEON.
I understand. You may talk freely.
IT IS GOOD.
THE GODS OF NIPPON ARE VERY POWERFUL. WE ARE NO LONGER WORSHIPPED AS ONCE WE WERE, BUT WE HAVE ADAPTED.
TIMES HAVE CHANGED, AND WE HAVE CHANGED WITH THEM.
WE ARE EXPANDING-- ASSIMILATING OTHER PANTHEONS, LATER GODS, NEW ALTARS AND ICONS. MARILYN MONROE IS OURS NOW, AS ARE KING KONG AND LADY LIBERTY.
MY MOTHER IS QUEEN OF OUR OWN UNDERWORLD; IT IS A MOST EFFICIENT PLACE. LUCIFER'S HELL SHOULD BE OURS TOO. IT HAS MUCH POTENTIAL.
NAME YOUR PRICE.
WHATEVER IT IS, WE WILL PAY IT.
The matter will be given my most careful consideration, Honored Susano-O-No-Mikoto.

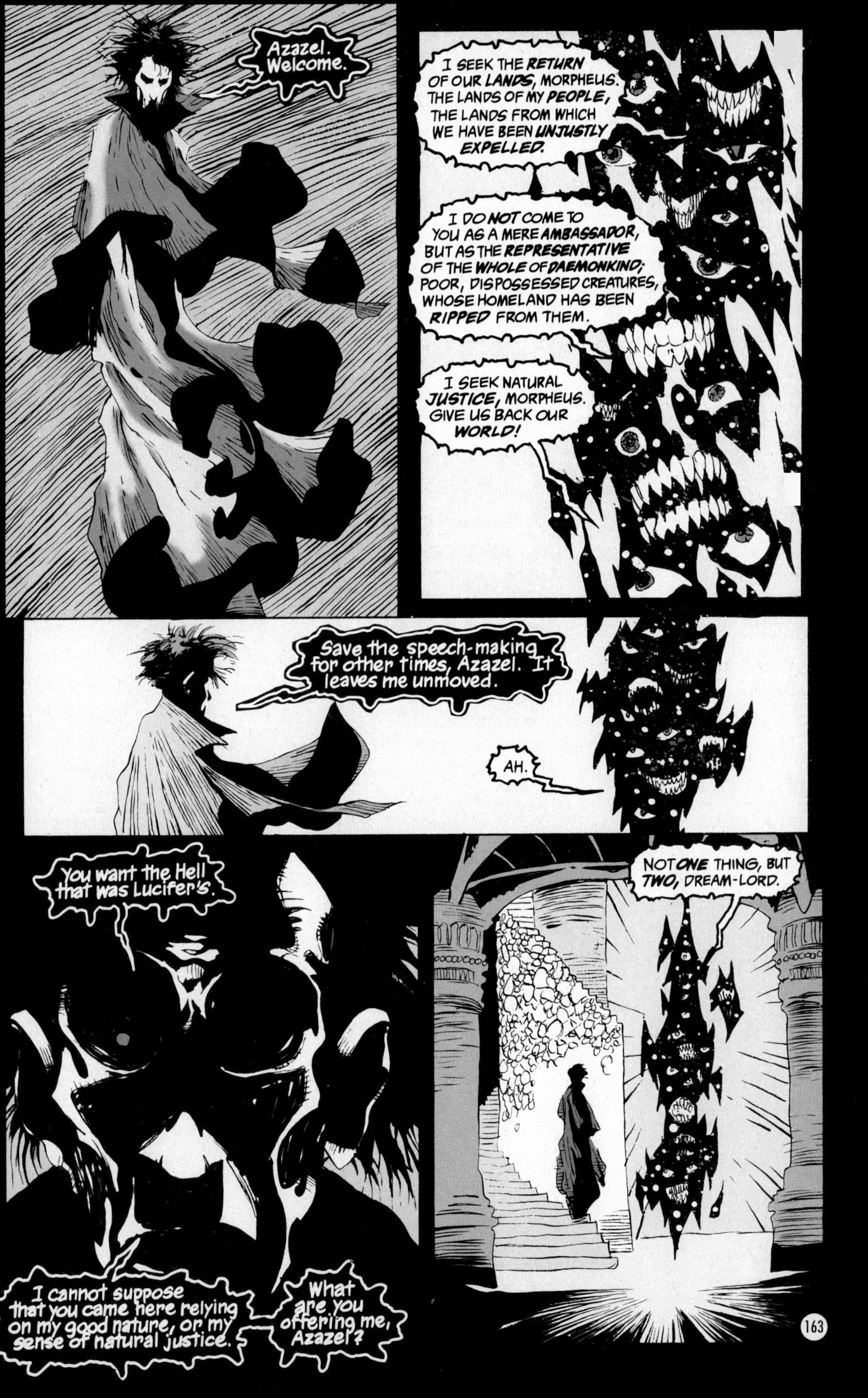
Azazel. Welcome.
I SEEK THE RETURN OF OUR LANDS, MORPHEUS. THE LANDS OF MY PEOPLE, THE LANDS FROM WHICH WE HAVE BEEN UNJUSTLY EXPELLED.
I DO NOT COME TO YOU AS A MERE AMBASSADOR, BUT AS THE REPRESENTATIVE OF THE WHOLE OF DAEMONKIND; POOR, DISPOSSESSED CREATURES, WHOSE HOMELAND HAS BEEN RIPPED FROM THEM.
I SEEK NATURAL JUSTICE, MORPHEUS. GIVE US BACK OUR WORLD!
Save the speech-making for other times, Azazel. It leaves me unmoved.
AH.
You want the Hell that was Lucifer's.
I cannot suppose that you came here relying on my good nature, or my sense of natural justice.
What are you offering me, Azazel?
NOT ONE THING, BUT TWO, DREAM-LORD.

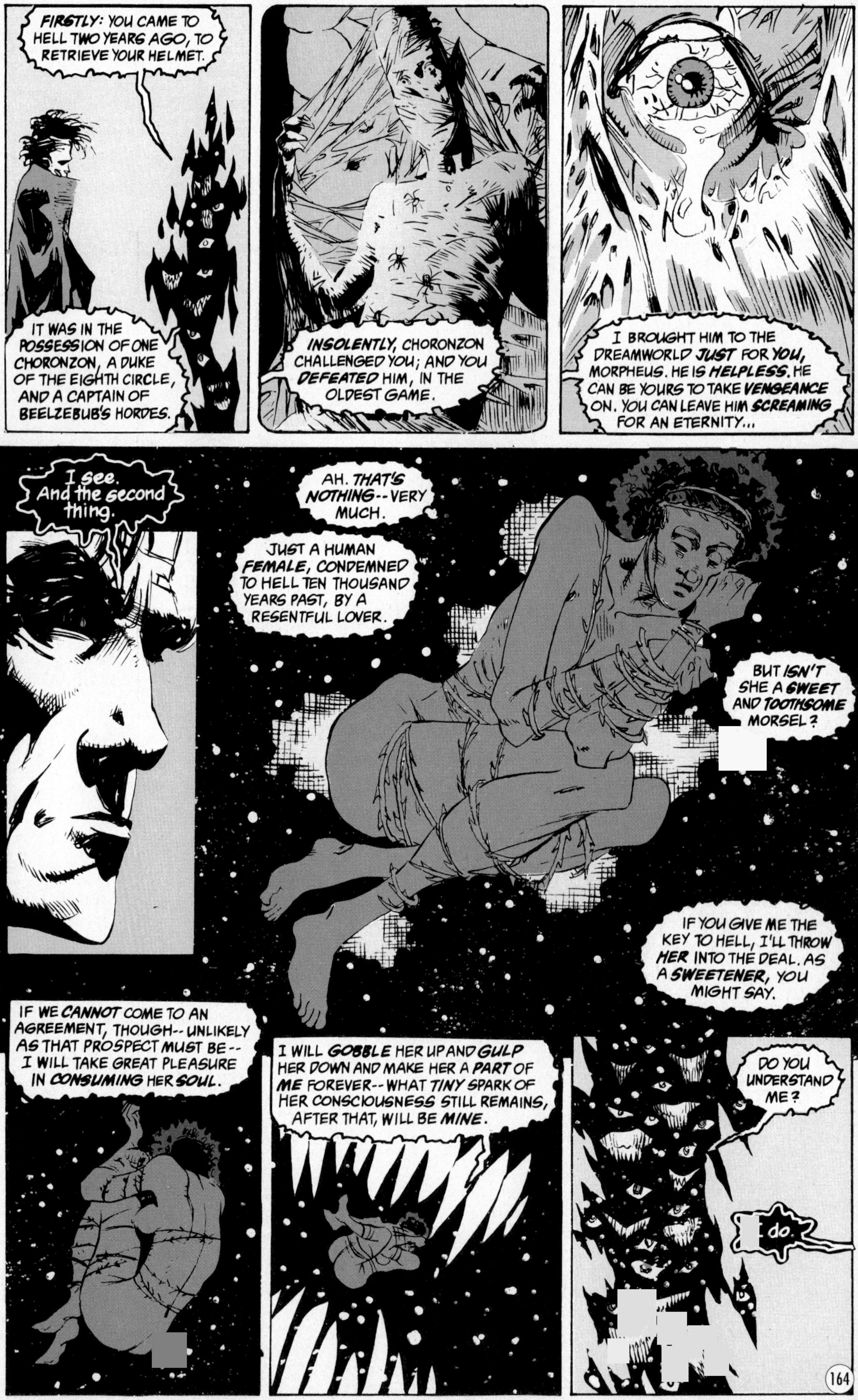
FIRSTLY: YOU CAME TO HELL TWO YEARS AGO, TO RETRIEVE YOUR HELMET.
IT WAS IN THE POSSESSION OF ONE CHORONZON, A DUKE OF THE EIGHTH CIRCLE, AND A CAPTAIN OF BEELZEBUB'S HORDES.
INSOLENTLY, CHORONZON CHALLENGED YOU; AND YOU DEFEATED HIM, IN THE OLDEST GAME.
I BROUGHT HIM TO THE DREAMWORLD JUST FOR YOU, MORPHEUS. HE IS HELPLESS. HE CAN BE YOURS TO TAKE VENGEANCE ON. YOU CAN LEAVE HIM SCREAMING FOR AN ETERNITY...
I see. And the second thing.
AH. THAT'S NOTHING--VERY MUCH.
JUST A HUMAN FEMALE, CONDEMNED TO HELL TEN THOUSAND YEARS PAST, BY A RESENTFUL LOVER.
BUT ISN'T SHE A SWEET AND TOOTHSOME MORSEL?
IF YOU GIVE ME THE KEY TO HELL, I'LL THROW HER INTO THE DEAL. AS A SWEETENER, YOU MIGHT SAY.
IF WE CANNOT COME TO AN AGREEMENT, THOUGH-- UNLIKELY AS THAT PROSPECT MUST BE-- I WILL TAKE GREAT PLEASURE IN CONSUMING HER SOUL.
I WILL GOBBLE HER UP AND GULP HER DOWN AND MAKE HER A PART OF ME FOREVER--WHAT TINY SPARK OF HER CONSCIOUSNESS STILL REMAINS, AFTER THAT, WILL BE MINE.
DO YOU UNDERSTAND ME?
do.

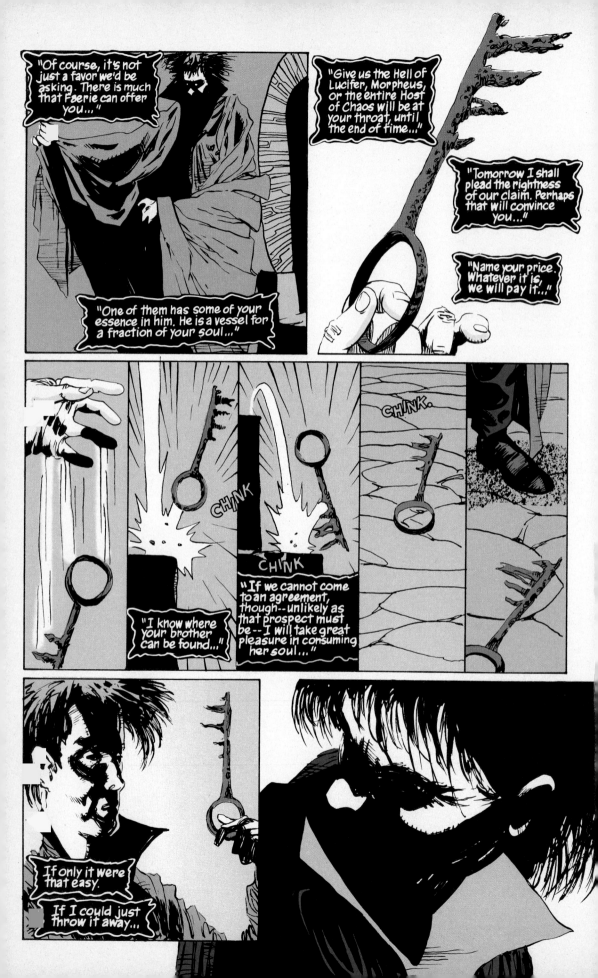

ON WHICH THE VEXING QUESTION
OF THE SOVEREIGNTY OF HELL
IS FINALLY SETTLED, TO THE
SATISFACTION OF SOME; THE
FINER POINTS OF HOSPITALITY;
AND IN WHICH IT IS DEMONSTRATED
THAT WHILE SOME MAY FALL,
OTHERS ARE PUSHED.

EPISODE 6

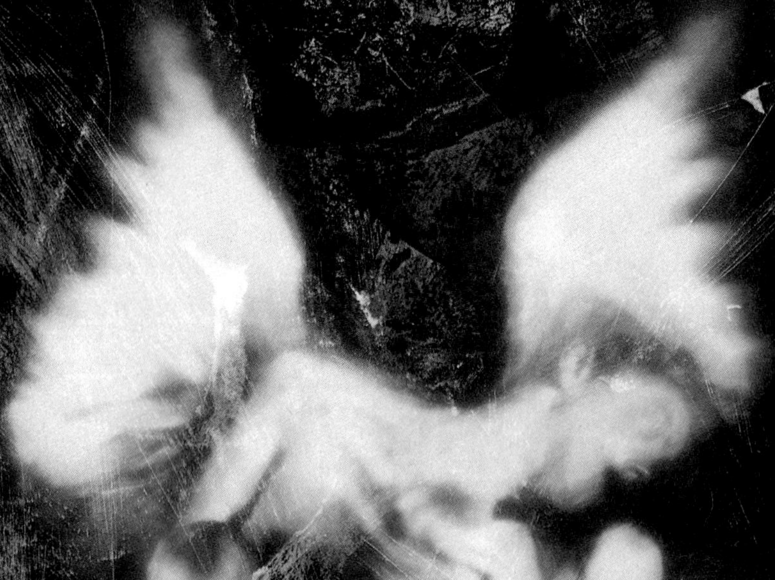

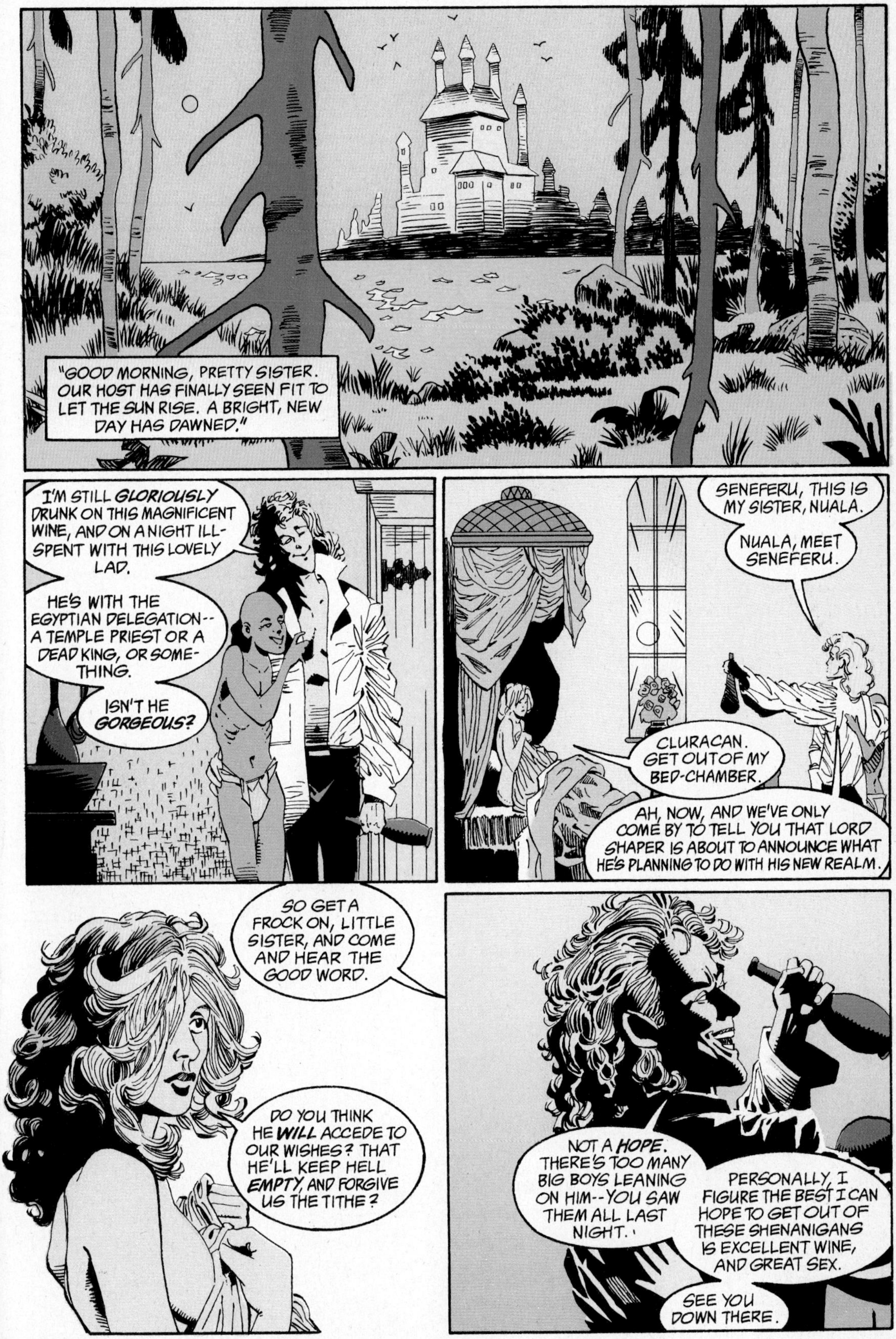
"GOOD MORNING, PRETTY SISTER. OUR HOST HAS FINALLY SEEN FIT TO LET THE SUN RISE. A BRIGHT, NEW DAY HAS DAWNED."
I'M STILL GLORIOUSLY DRUNK ON THIS MAGNIFICENT WINE, AND ON A NIGHT ILL-SPENT WITH THIS LOVELY LAD.
HE'S WITH THE EGYPTIAN DELEGATION--A TEMPLE PRIEST OR A DEAD KING, OR SOME-THING.
ISN'T HE GORGEOUS?
SENEFERU, THIS IS MY SISTER, NUALA.
NUALA, MEET SENEFERU.
CLURACAN. GET OUT OF MY BED-CHAMBER.
AH, NOW, AND WE'VE ONLY COME BY TO TELL YOU THAT LORD SHAPER IS ABOUT TO ANNOUNCE WHAT HE'S PLANNING TO DO WITH HIS NEW REALM.
SO GET A FROCK ON, LITTLE SISTER, AND COME AND HEAR THE GOOD WORD.
DO YOU THINK HE WILL ACCEDE TO OUR WISHES? THAT HE'LL KEEP HELL EMPTY, AND FORGIVE US THE TITHE?
NOT A HOPE. THERE'S TOO MANY BIG BOYS LEANING ON HIM--YOU SAW THEM ALL LAST NIGHT.
PERSONALLY, I FIGURE THE BEST I CAN HOPE TO GET OUT OF THESE SHENANIGANS IS EXCELLENT WINE, AND GREAT SEX.
SEE YOU DOWN THERE.

AND ALL *I* GET OUT OF IT IS A GOOD NIGHT'S SLEEP, I SUPPOSE.

OH WELL.

IF IT CAME TO *THAT*, I WOULD SIMPLY HAVE TO ADMIT THAT I DID NOT KNOW *EXACTLY* WHERE HIS BROTHER IS *NOW*. BUT I *DO* POSSESS CERTAIN FACTS...

WE MUST HOPE THEY ARE ENOUGH FOR THE DREAM LORD, OTHERWISE--

...SURPRISED NOT TO SEE A REPRESENTATIVE FROM THE GREEK GODS HERE. PERHAPS *THEY* KNOW SOMETHING MY PEOPLE DO NOT.

IT'S ALL INTERNAL POLITICS, OLD FRIEND. IT LEAVES NO ROOM FOR TRAVEL. BUT IF YOU ASK ME--

170

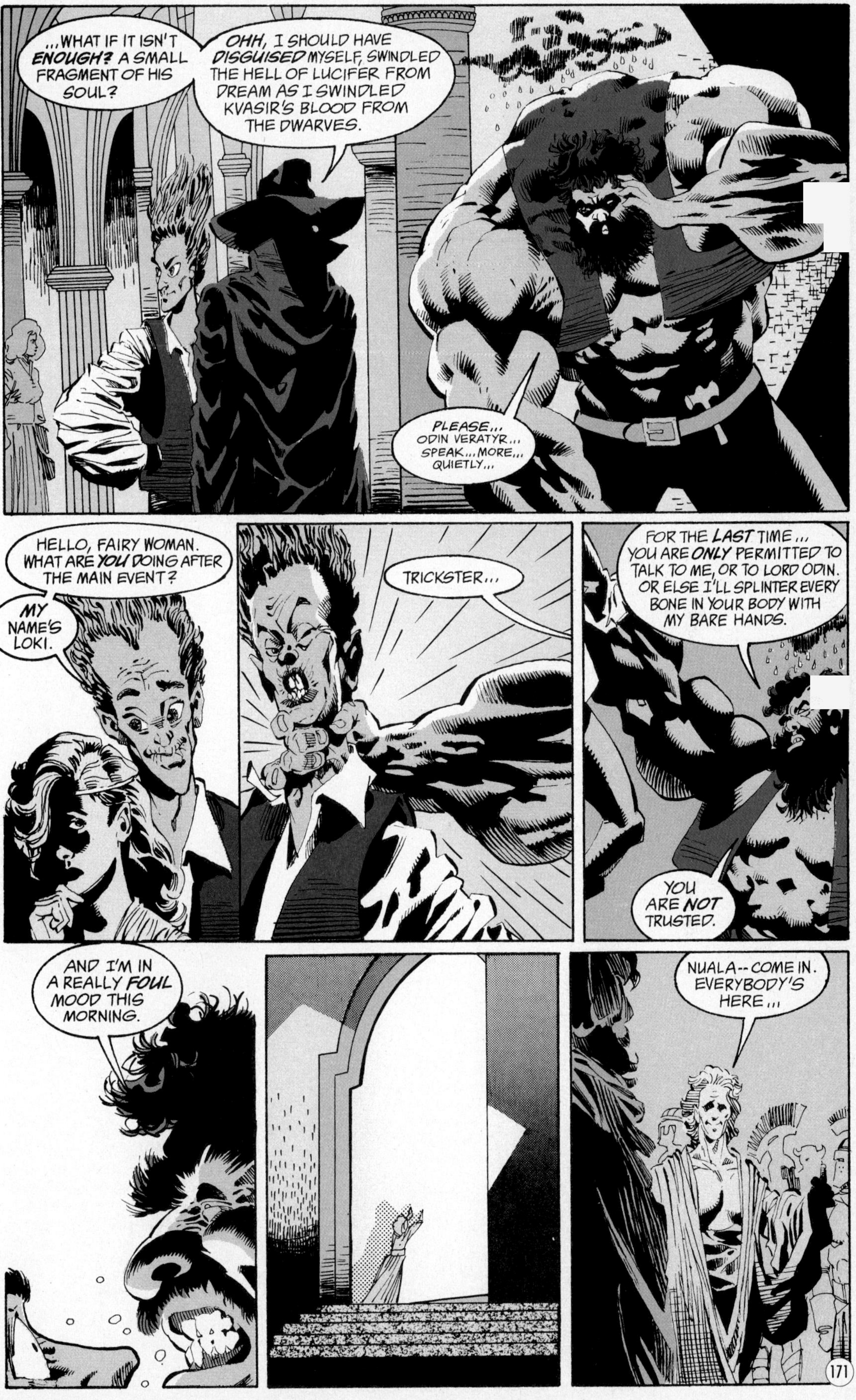
...WHAT IF IT ISN'T ENOUGH? A SMALL FRAGMENT OF HIS SOUL?
OHH, I SHOULD HAVE DISGUISED MYSELF, SWINDLED THE HELL OF LUCIFER FROM DREAM AS I SWINDLED KVASIR'S BLOOD FROM THE DWARVES.
PLEASE... ODIN VERATYR... SPEAK... MORE... QUIETLY...
HELLO, FAIRY WOMAN. WHAT ARE YOU DOING AFTER THE MAIN EVENT?
MY NAME'S LOKI.
TRICKSTER...
FOR THE LAST TIME... YOU ARE ONLY PERMITTED TO TALK TO ME, OR TO LORD ODIN. OR ELSE I'LL SPLINTER EVERY BONE IN YOUR BODY WITH MY BARE HANDS.
YOU ARE NOT TRUSTED.
AND I'M IN A REALLY FOUL MOOD THIS MORNING.
NUALA--COME IN. EVERYBODY'S HERE...

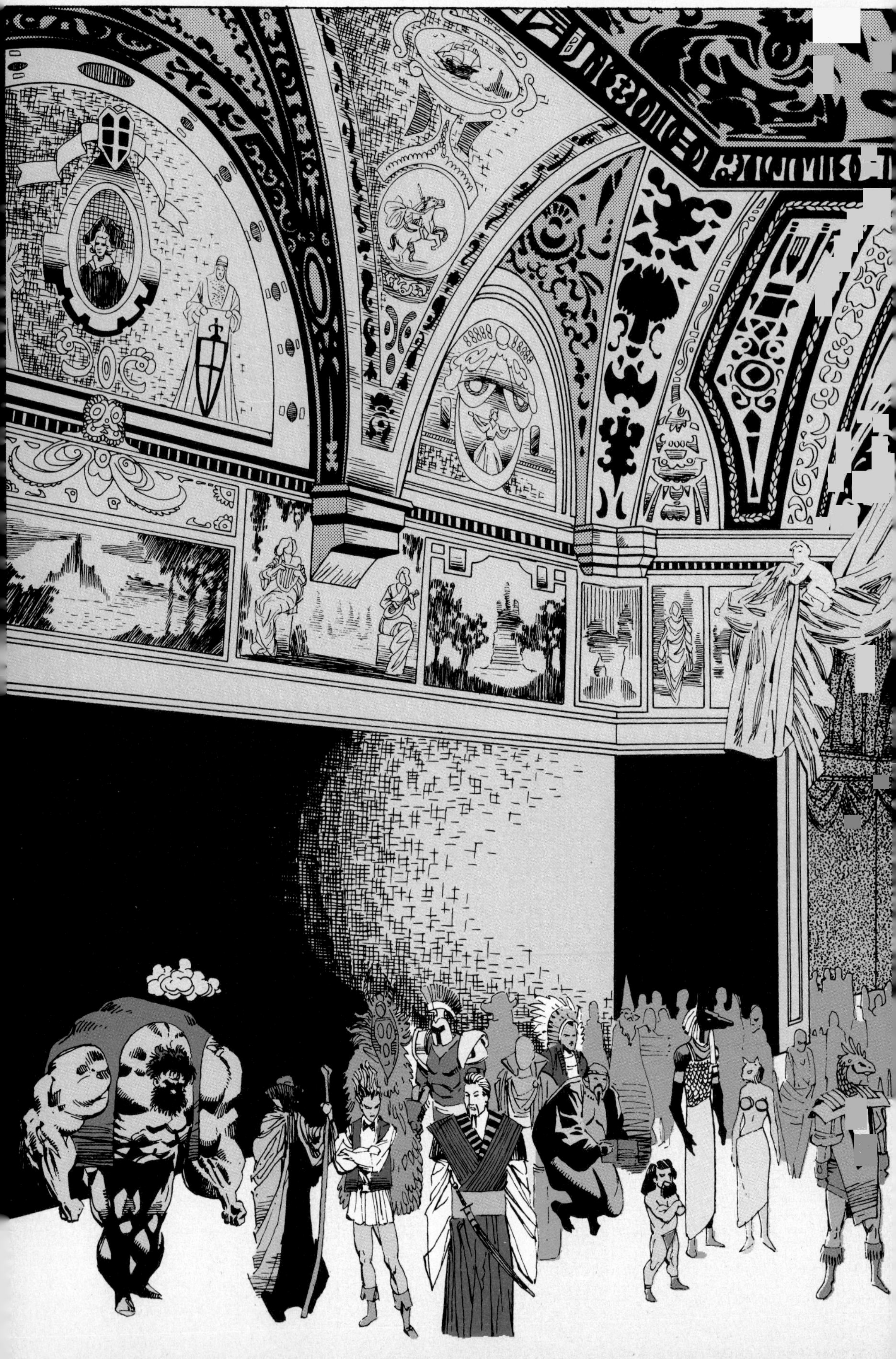

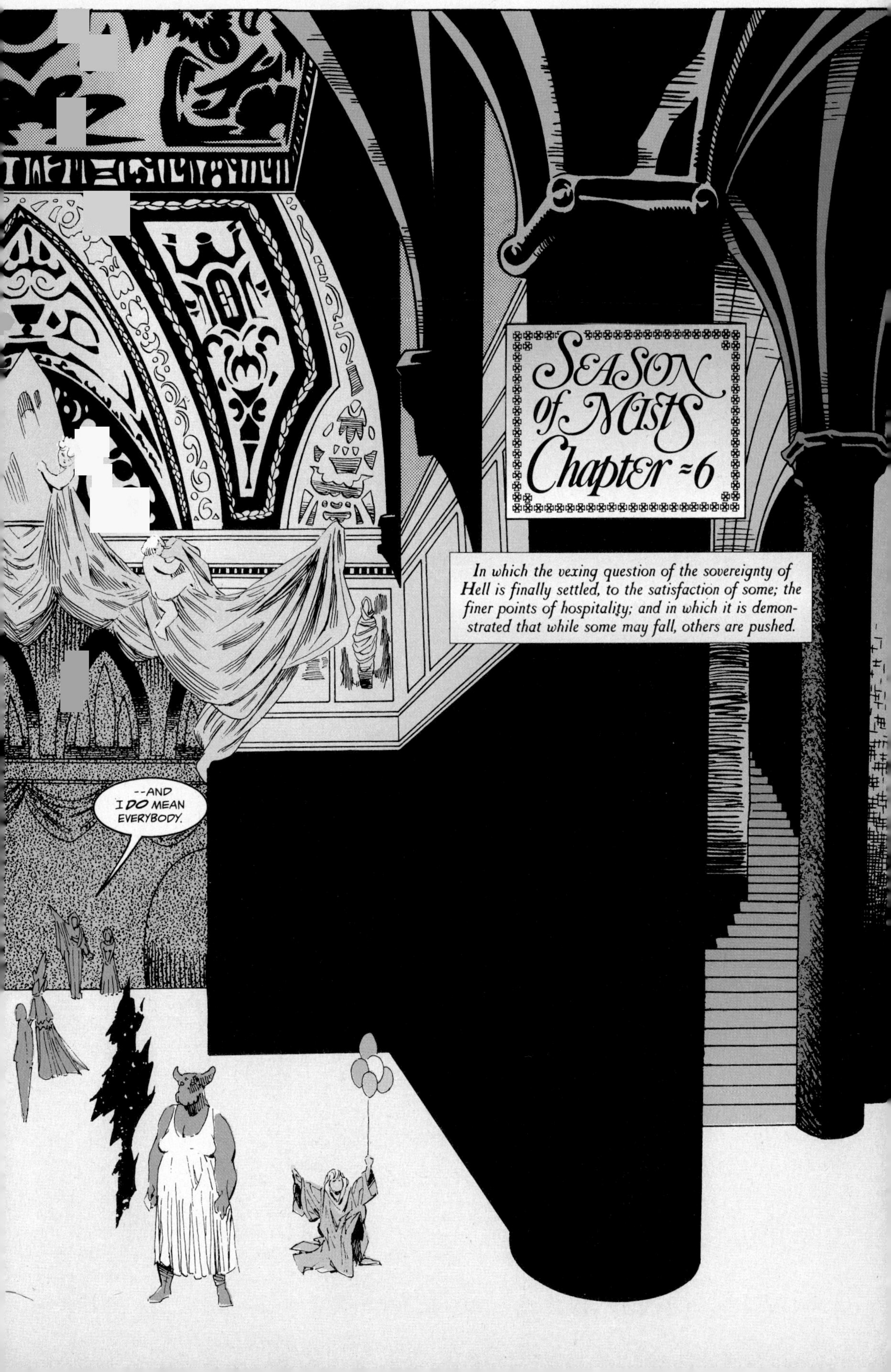
SEASON of MISTS Chapter ≈6
In which the vexing question of the sovereignty of Hell is finally settled, to the satisfaction of some; the finer points of hospitality; and in which it is demonstrated that while some may fall, others are pushed.
--AND I DO MEAN EVERYBODY.

MRR. WELL?

WHERE IS HE?

YOU LOOK LIKE YOU HAVEN'T SLEPT A WINK ALL NIGHT.

I don't sleep, Matthew.

I DIDN'T SAY YOU DID. I JUST SAID THAT WAS WHAT YOU LOOKED LIKE.

BUSY NIGHT, HUH?

Yes. I spent the first half of it talking with a few of our visitors.

I spent the second half... thinking.

They all want it; I don't. I never thought that disposing of the unwanted could be so hard.

Everything keeps shifting and changing, Matthew. It's like treading a path through mist.

Dream?

174

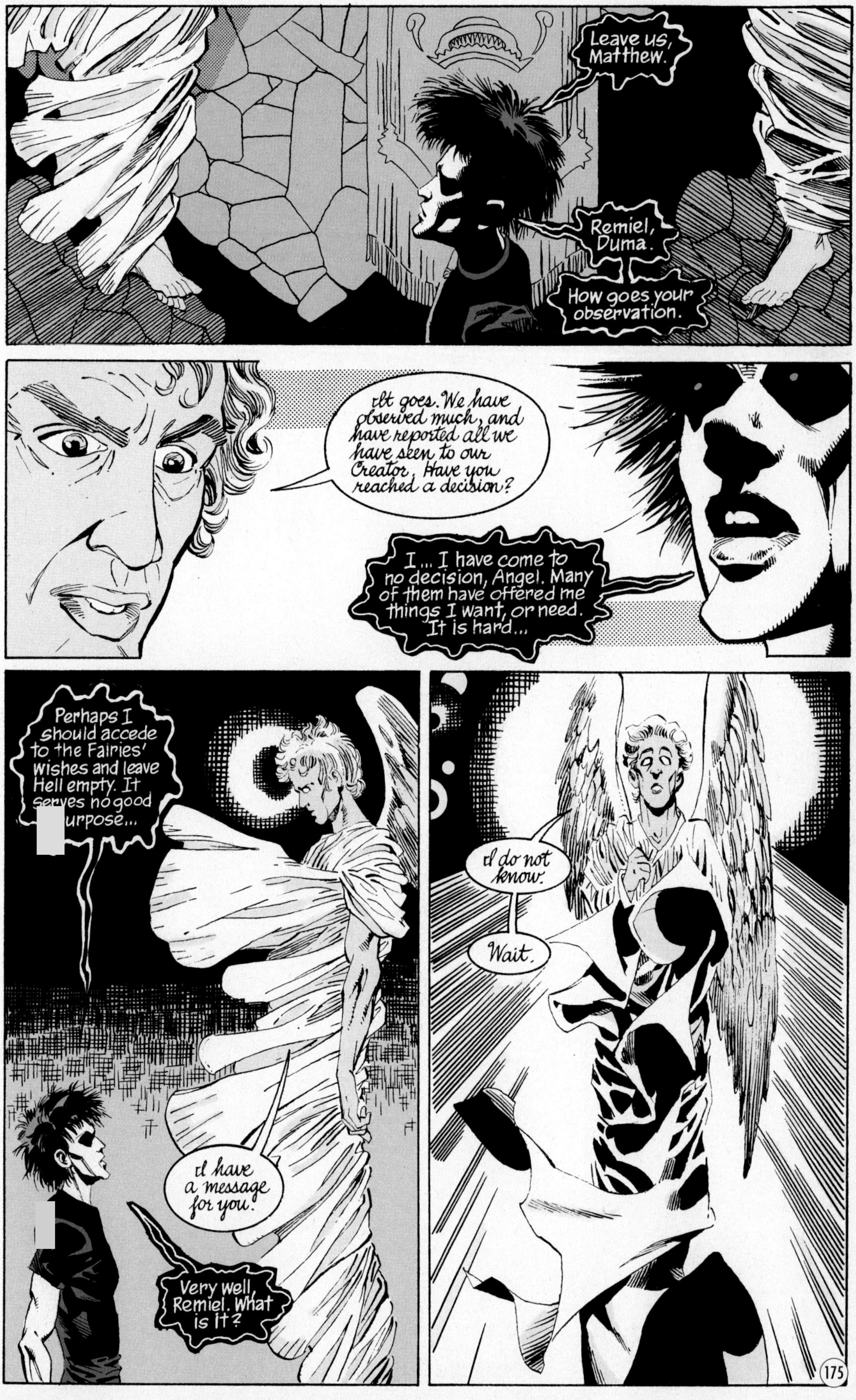
Leave us, Matthew.
Remiel, Duma.
How goes your observation.
It goes. We have observed much, and have reported all we have seen to our Creator. Have you reached a decision?
I... I have come to no decision, Angel. Many of them have offered me things I want, or need. It is hard...
Perhaps I should accede to the Fairies' wishes and leave Hell empty. It serves no good urpose...
I have a message for you.
Very well, Remiel. What is it?
I do not know.
Wait.

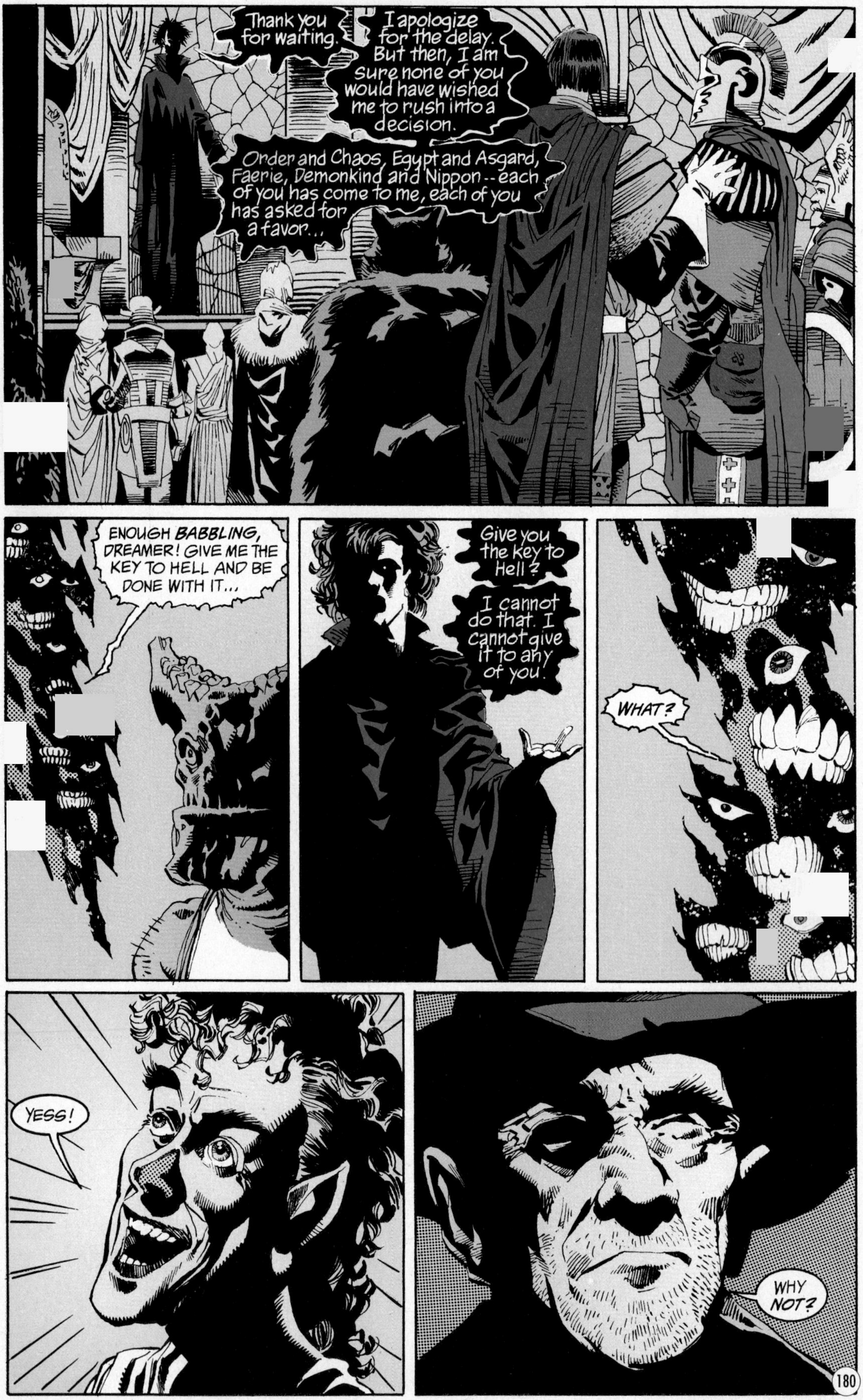
Thank you for waiting.
I apologize for the delay. But then, I am sure none of you would have wished me to rush into a decision.
Order and Chaos, Egypt and Asgard, Faerie, Demonkind and Nippon -- each of you has come to me, each of you has asked for a favor...
ENOUGH BABBLING, DREAMER! GIVE ME THE KEY TO HELL AND BE DONE WITH IT...
Give you the key to Hell?
I cannot do that. I cannot give it to any of you.
WHAT?
YESS!
WHY NOT?

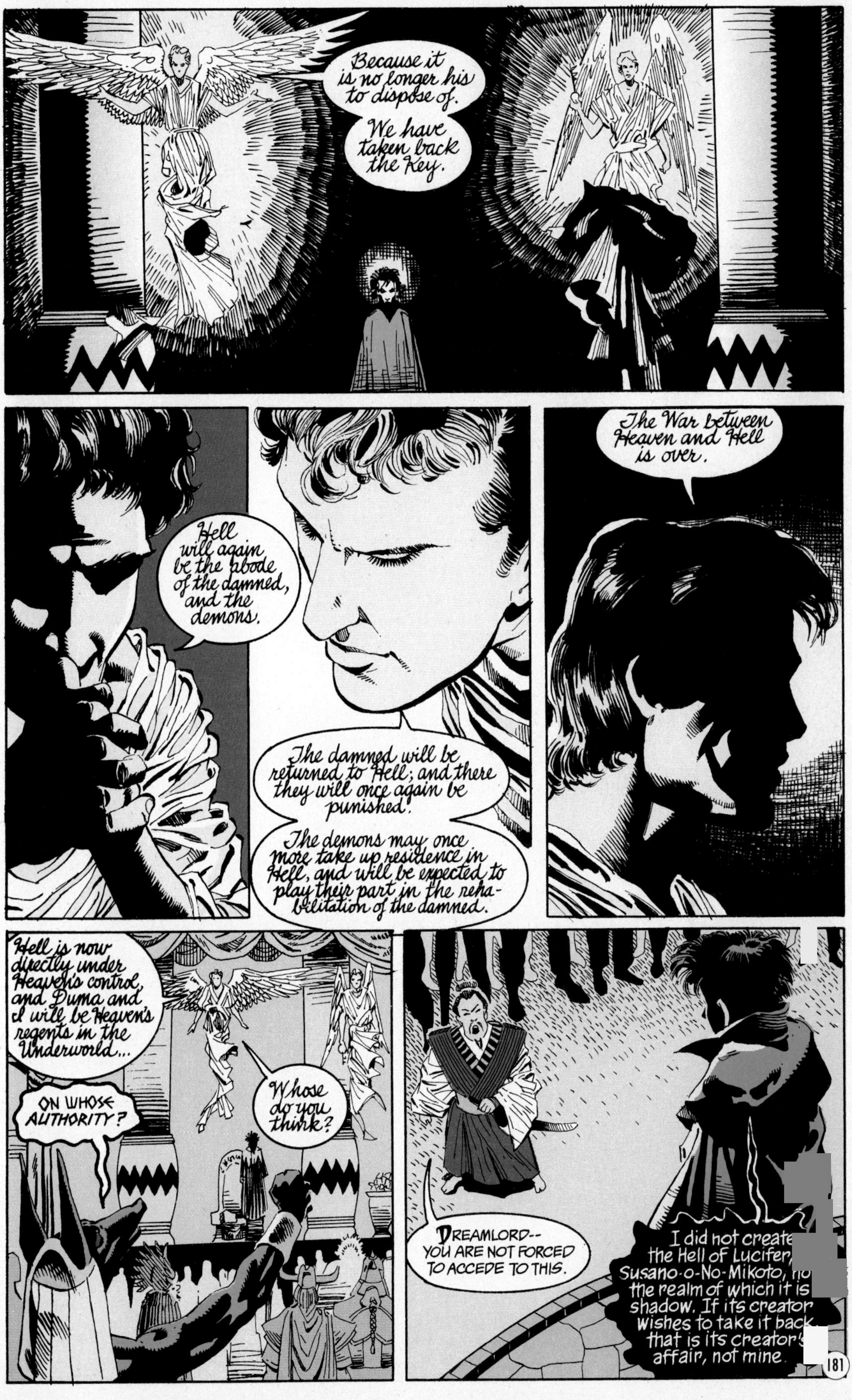
Because it is no longer his to dispose of.
We have taken back the Key.
Hell will again be the abode of the damned, and the demons.
The damned will be returned to Hell; and there they will once again be punished.
The demons may once more take up residence in Hell, and will be expected to play their part in the rehabilitation of the damned.
The War between Heaven and Hell is over.
Hell is now directly under Heaven's control, and Duma and I will be Heaven's regents in the Underworld...
ON WHOSE AUTHORITY?
Whose do you think?
DREAMLORD-- YOU ARE NOT FORCED TO ACCEDE TO THIS.
I did not create the Hell of Lucifer, Susano-o-No-Mikoto, no the realm of which it is shadow. If its creator wishes to take it back that is its creator's affair, not mine.

I thank you all for coming here, and I trust that, although you may be disappointed by my decision, you will understand it.

I hope it will cause none of you undue distress.

CAUSE US DISTRESS? OHH, THAT'S A FINE ONE, MORPHEUS. WHAT ABOUT THE DISTRESS IT'S GOING TO CAUSE YOU?

I KNOW YOUR RULES. YOU OFFERED US HOSPITALITY WHEN WE ARRIVED.

YOU CAN DO NOTHING NOW TO HARM ANY OF US.

I WILL LEAVE HERE AS I CAME... AND NADA, YOUR LITTLE HUMAN SWEETHEART, WILL LEAVE HERE WITH ME.

I SAID I WOULD DEVOUR HER SOUL. AND I WILL.

SLOWLY, THOUGH. A BITE AT A TIME. AND WITH EVERY BITE I WILL BE THINKING OF YOU.

Oh, Azazel.

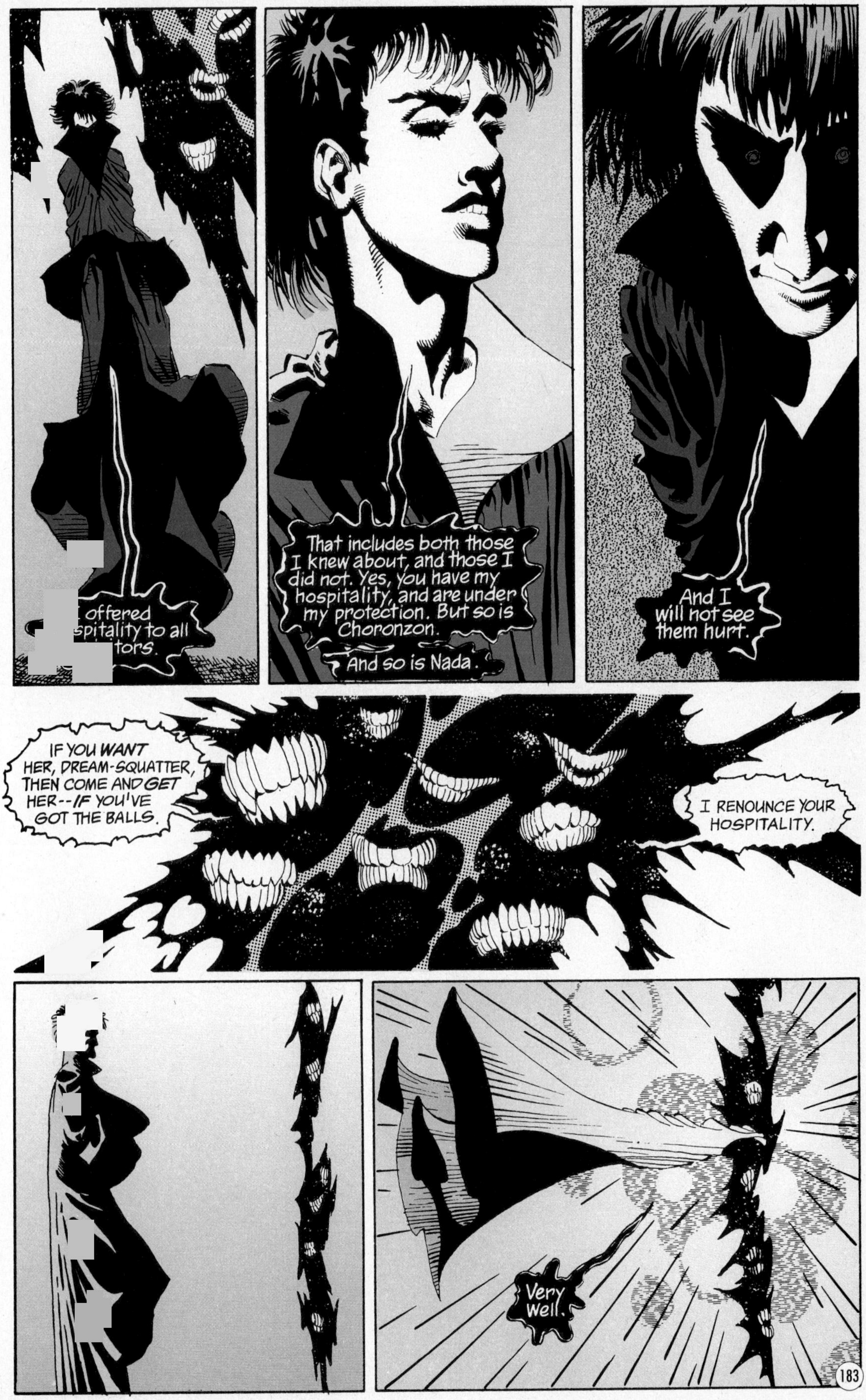
offered
spitality to all
tors.
That includes both those I knew about, and those I did not. Yes, you have my hospitality, and are under my protection. But so is Choronzon.
And so is Nada.
And I will not see them hurt.
IF YOU WANT HER, DREAM-SQUATTER, THEN COME AND GET HER--IF YOU'VE GOT THE BALLS.
I RENOUNCE YOUR HOSPITALITY.
Very Well.

I DID NOT... *BELIEVE*... YOU WOULD BE WILLING TO ENTER INTO US...DREAMER.

But I did, Azazel.

DO YOU? REALLY?

THEN FIND THEM, IF YOU CAN.

Very well.

YES. YES, YOU DID. VERY WELL. FIND THEM, AND RELEASE THEM, AND THEY ARE YOURS, AND YOU MAY LEAVE ME FREELY.

FAIL AND I WILL *FEAST* ON THEIR *SOULS*-- AND ON *YOURS*.

I understand.

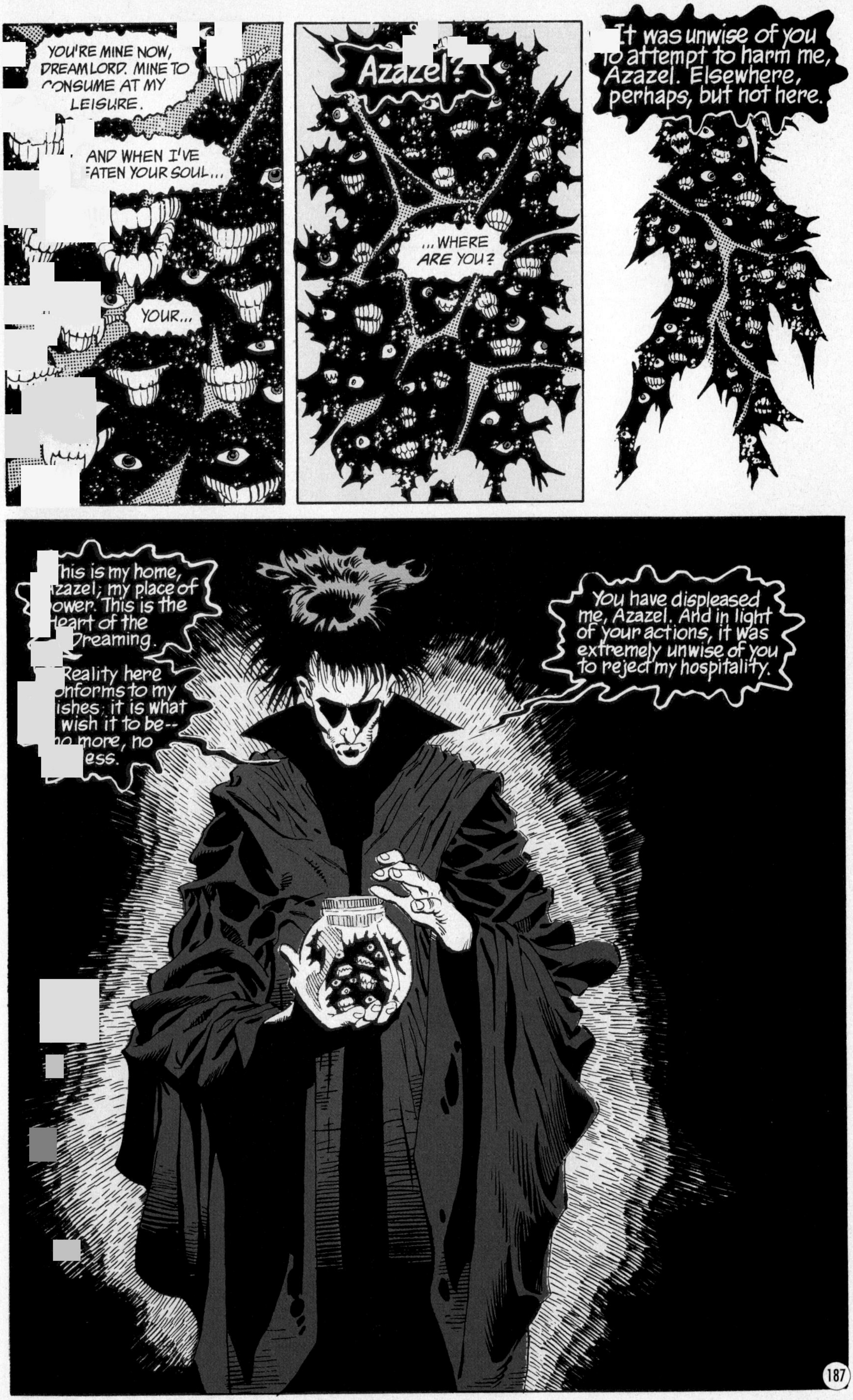
YOU'RE MINE NOW, DREAMLORD. MINE TO CONSUME AT MY LEISURE.
AND WHEN I'VE EATEN YOUR SOUL...
YOUR...
Azazel?
...WHERE ARE YOU?
It was unwise of you to attempt to harm me, Azazel. Elsewhere, perhaps, but not here.
This is my home, Azazel; my place of power. This is the Heart of the Dreaming.
Reality here conforms to my wishes; it is what I wish it to be-- no more, no less.
You have displeased me, Azazel. And in light of your actions, it was extremely unwise of you to reject my hospitality.

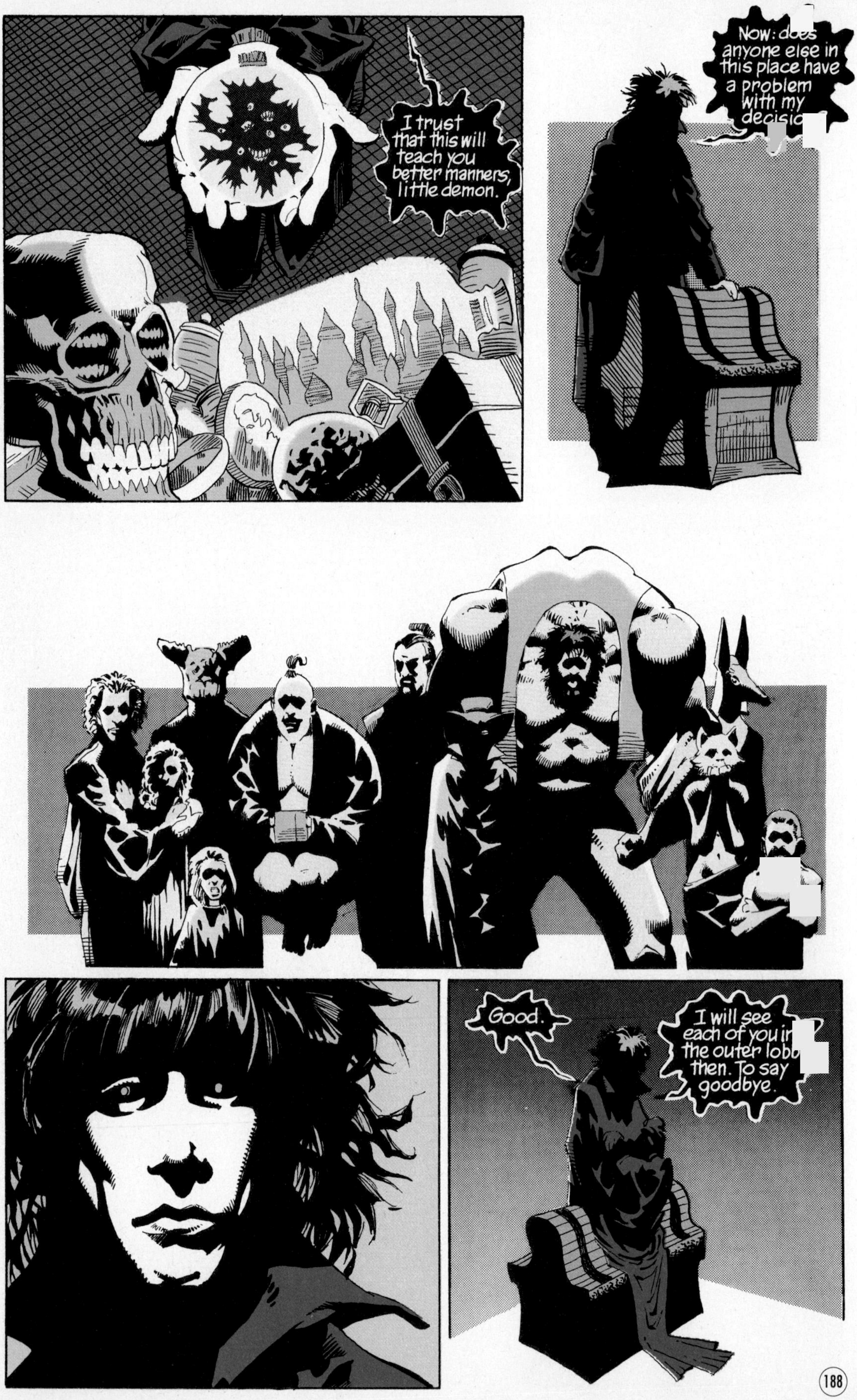
I trust that this will teach you better manners, little demon.
Now: d anyone else in this place have a problem with my decisi
Good.
I will see each of you i the outer lob then. To say goodbye.

DREAM,

YOUR DECISION WAS JUST AND ORDERLY. AS SUCH, THOUGH I REGRET IT, I CANNOT FAULT IT.

KILDERKIN

Thank you, Lord Kilderkin. Your understanding is appreciated. I wish you well.

HMMPH. WE IS ALWAYS MORE FUN THAN THE ORDER PEOPLE. CARDBOARD BOXES!

NOBODY CLEVER BE'S CARDBOARD BOXES.

"So: I take it that I have incurred the wrath of Chaos, from now until the end of time. From the Shivering Brigade to the Laughing Dancers."

RE-ALLY?

OH, THAT. I JUS' MADE THAT STUFF UP. WE DIN'T WANT IT, WE JUS' DIN'T WANT ANYONE ELSE TO GET IT.

ANYWAY, THANK-YOU-FOR-HAVING-ME-AT-YOUR-PARTY, MISTER DREAMY.

I HAD A LOVELY TIME.

Choronzon. Mother of Spiders. Where do you go now?

THERE IS A LINE ALREADY FORMING OUTSIDE THE GATES OF HELL. WE WILL JOIN IT. AND WHEN THE GATES ARE OPENED WE WILL ENTER.

MORPHEUS...

LORD AZAZEL... WHAT WILL YOU DO WITH HIM? WHAT WILL YOU DO TO HIM?

Do to him? Nothing. I shall merely give him time to reflect, and the opportunity to mend his manners. I expect I shall eventually let him out. Eventually.

189

WE WILL RETURN TO OUR OWN LAND, THEN, DREAM-KING.

NICE MEETING YOU.

I AM SORRY WE WERE UNABLE TO COME TO AN AGREEMENT, OLD FRIEND.

My brother desires privacy, Lady Bast, and I am prepared to respect that desire.

IT IS WELL.

BUT *IF* YOU CHANGE YOUR MIND, THEN COME TO ME, AND WE CAN TALK FURTHER.

Lord Odin. I regret that I was forced to reject your offer.

AYE-- *YOU'RE* SORRY. HMPH. WELL, YOU ARE *STILL* WELCOME IN MY HALL OF GLADSHEIM, SHAPER.

MY HOUSE IS YOURS, AND *MY* MEAD AND MEAT ARE AT YOUR DISPOSAL.

I appreciate that, Odin All-Father. Fare you well; and you, too, Thor. I trust you enjoyed yourself.

I... I HOPE I WAS NOT TOO *BOISTEROUS* LAST NIGHT, LORD. I AM A *BLUFF*, ROUGH-AND-READY, TAKE-ME-AS-YOU-FIND-ME DEITY, AND *NOT* ONE FOR *AIRS* AND *GRACES*.

I had noticed.

And Loki. Will you say goodbye?

THE TRICKSTER SEEMS UNWILLING TO RETURN TO ASGARD, SHAPER.

NO! YOU DO NOT *UNDERSTAND!* THIS IS WRONG--

190

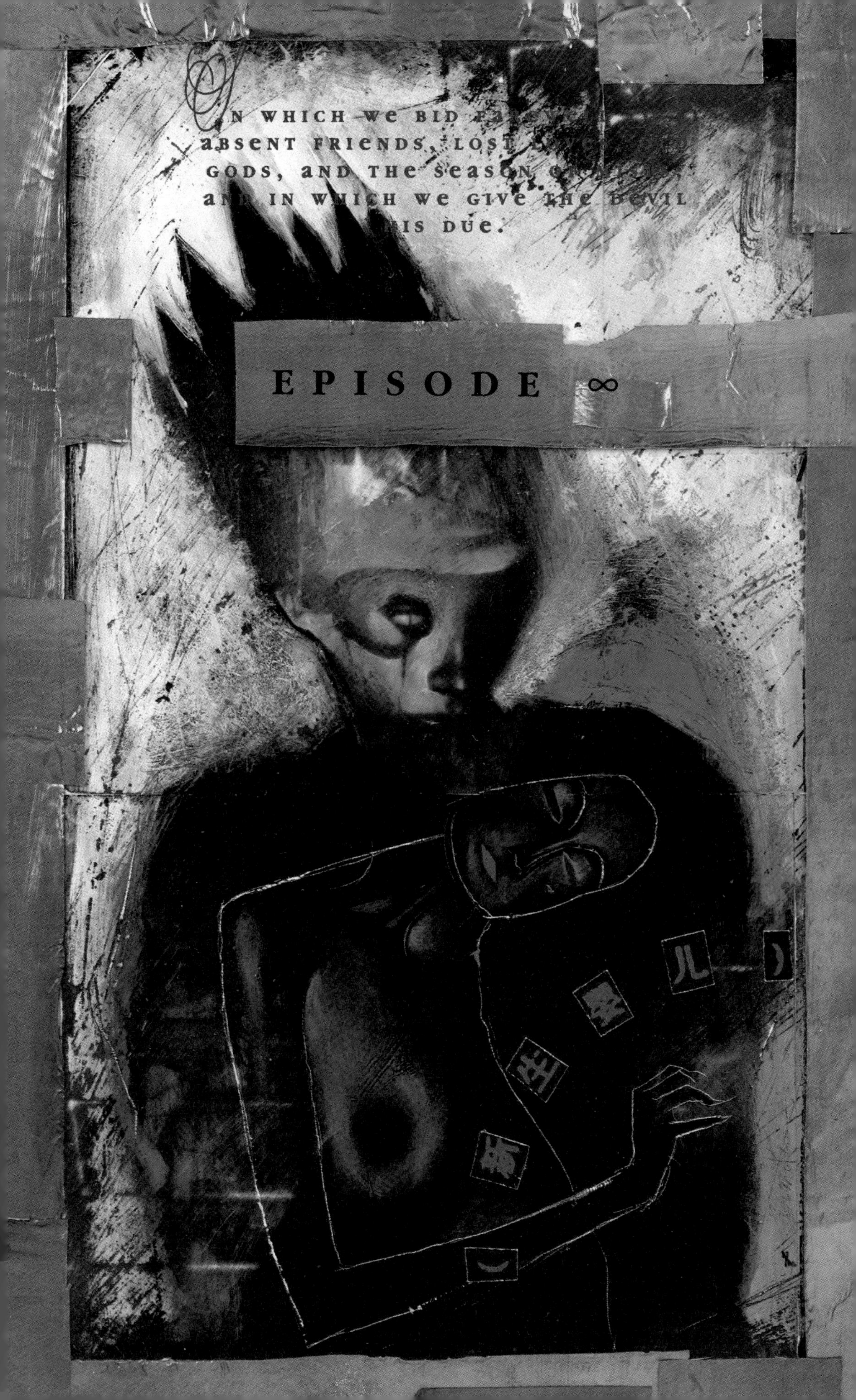
N WHICH WE BID
ABSENT FRIENDS, LOST
GODS, AND THE SEASON
AND IN WHICH WE GIVE THE DEVIL
IS DUE.
EPISODE ∞

And once the demons are here, the damned will also return. The tortured must have their torturers, after all. Soon the chimneys will smoke, and the ditches will run with blood and offal and tears.

Soon it will be difficult to tell that anything has changed, here in Hell.

Why do you not speak? Eh?

You are no longer the Angel of Silence. Even now another stands in your place in the Silver City...

Well? Say something.

No?

But it has, Duma. You cannot turn your back on that.

Ah me. I don't suppose it matters whether you look or no. You are down here, friend, until the end of time; and so am I.

Rulers of Hell, answerable only to our creator.

For good or ill...

...it's just the two of us.

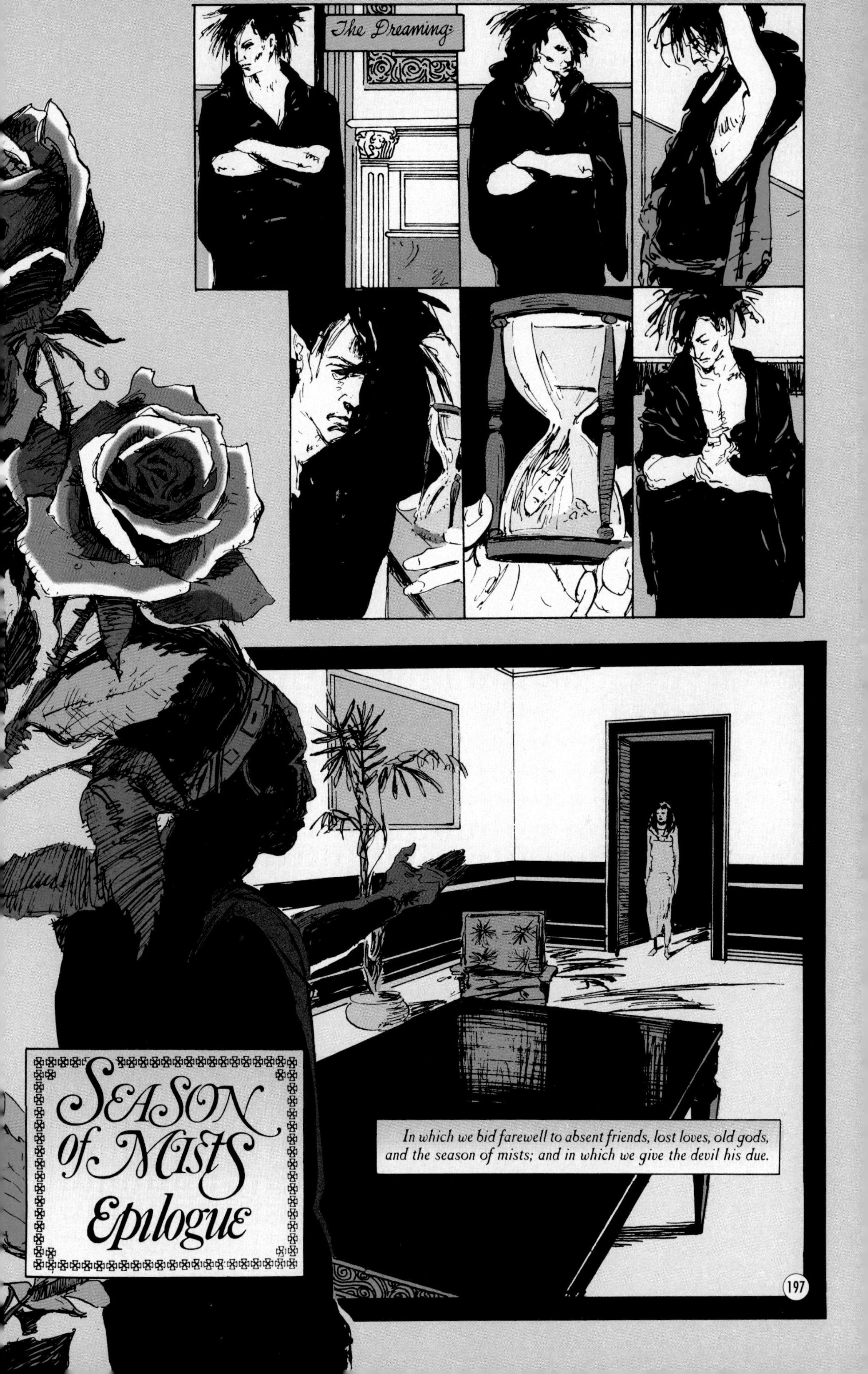

The Dreaming:
SEASON of MISTS
Epilogue
In which we bid farewell to absent friends, lost loves, old gods, and the season of mists; and in which we give the devil his due.

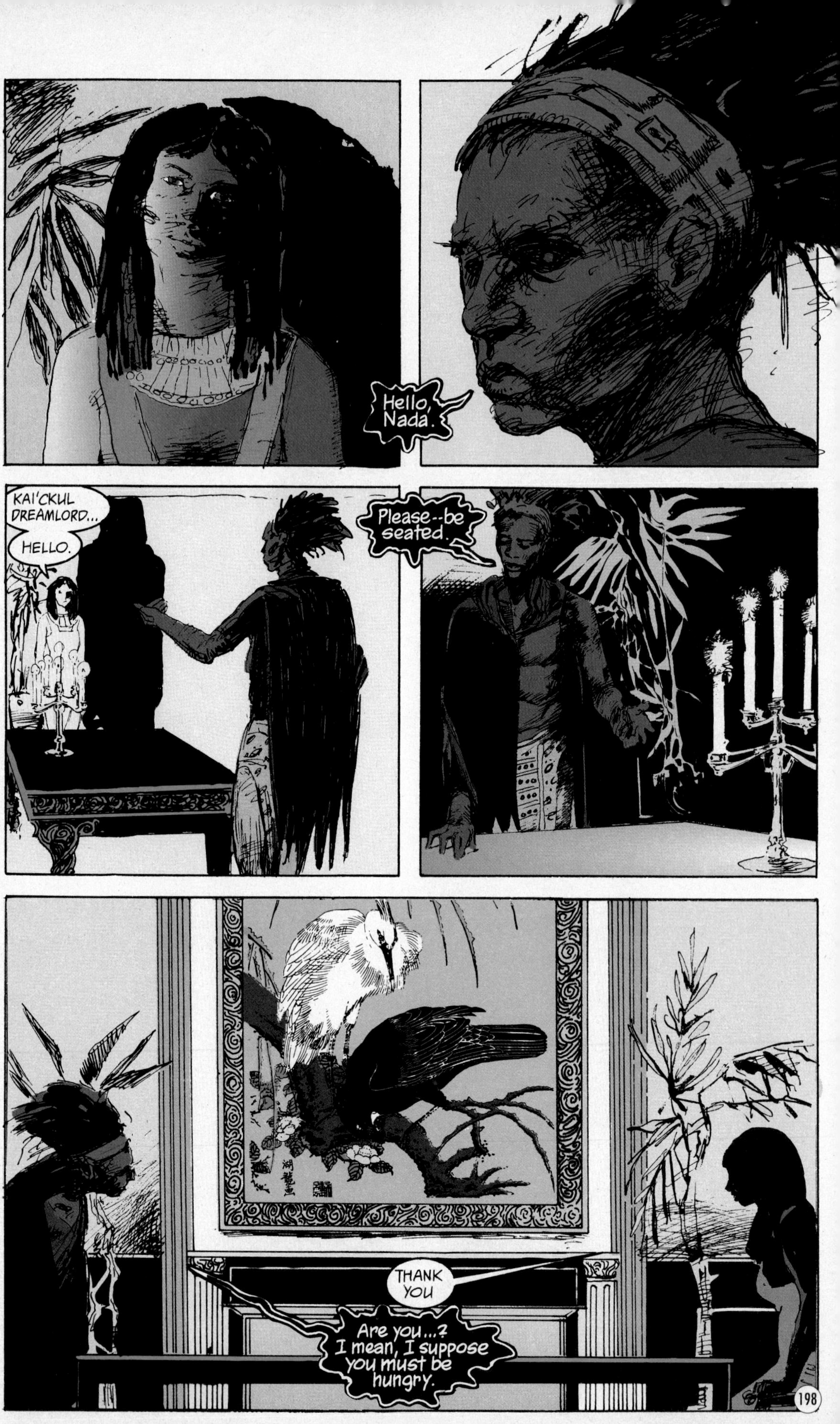

Hello, Nada.
KAI'CKUL DREAMLORD...
HELLO.
Please--be seated.
THANK YOU
Are you...? I mean, I suppose you must be hungry.

VERY WELL. I ACCEPT YOUR APOLOGY.

I SAID *NO* TO *THAT* OFFER TEN THOUSAND YEARS BACK, DREAM. I HAVE NOT CHANGED MY MIND.

If you wish, Nada... you could stay here with me. Be my queen.

BUT *YOU* COULD GIVE ALL *THIS* UP, YOU KNOW.

You suggested that once before, Nada. My answer has not changed. I have my responsibilities. I cannot abandon them.

SO YOU SAID, A *VERY* LONG TIME AGO.

Well, old love.

If you will not stay with me--and I, obviously, will not go with you--then perhaps it is time for us to discuss your future...

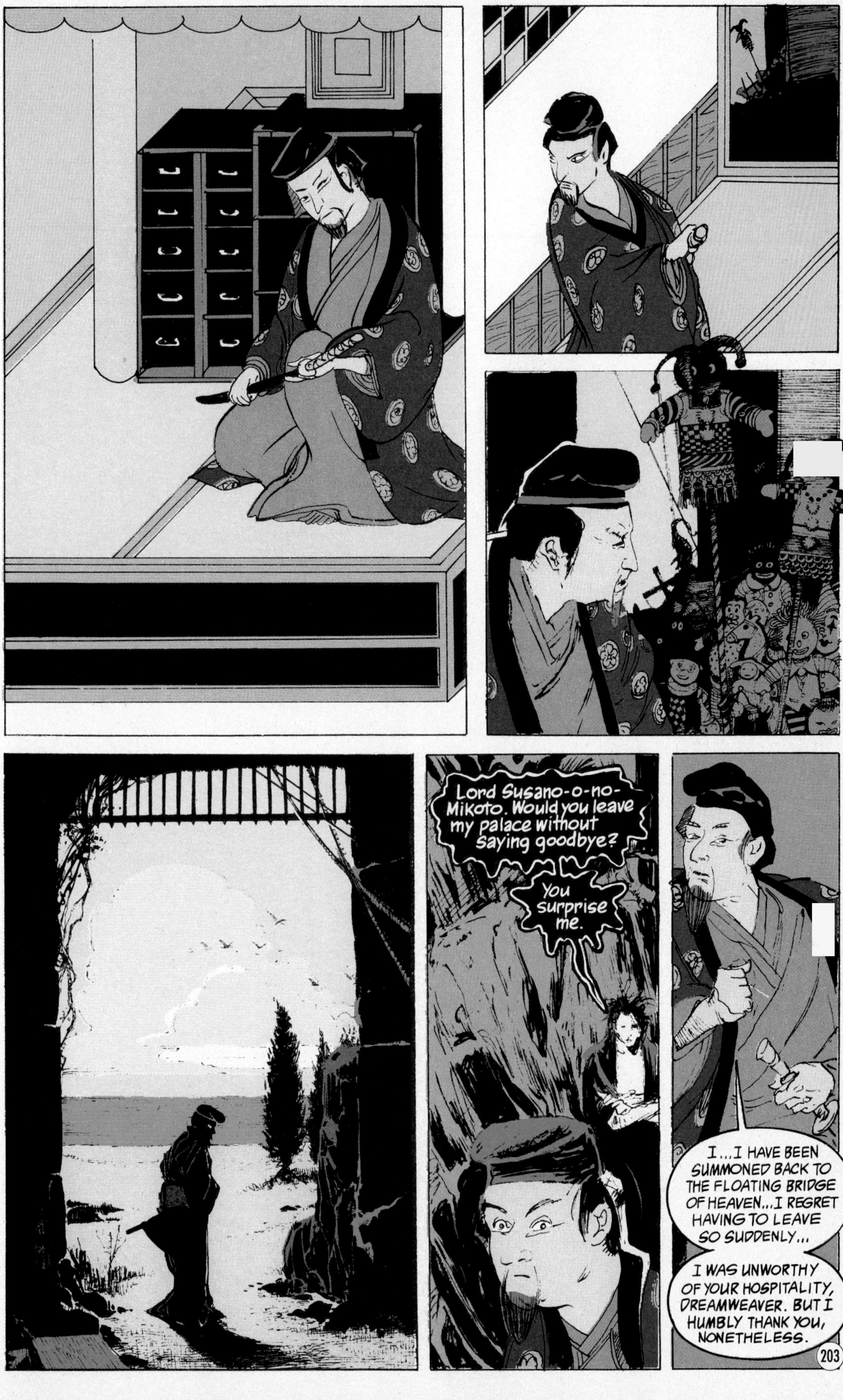
Lord Susano-o-no-Mikoto. Would you leave my palace without saying goodbye?
You surprise me.
I...I HAVE BEEN SUMMONED BACK TO THE FLOATING BRIDGE OF HEAVEN...I REGRET HAVING TO LEAVE SO SUDDENLY...
I WAS UNWORTHY OF YOUR HOSPITALITY, DREAMWEAVER. BUT I HUMBLY THANK YOU, NONETHELESS.

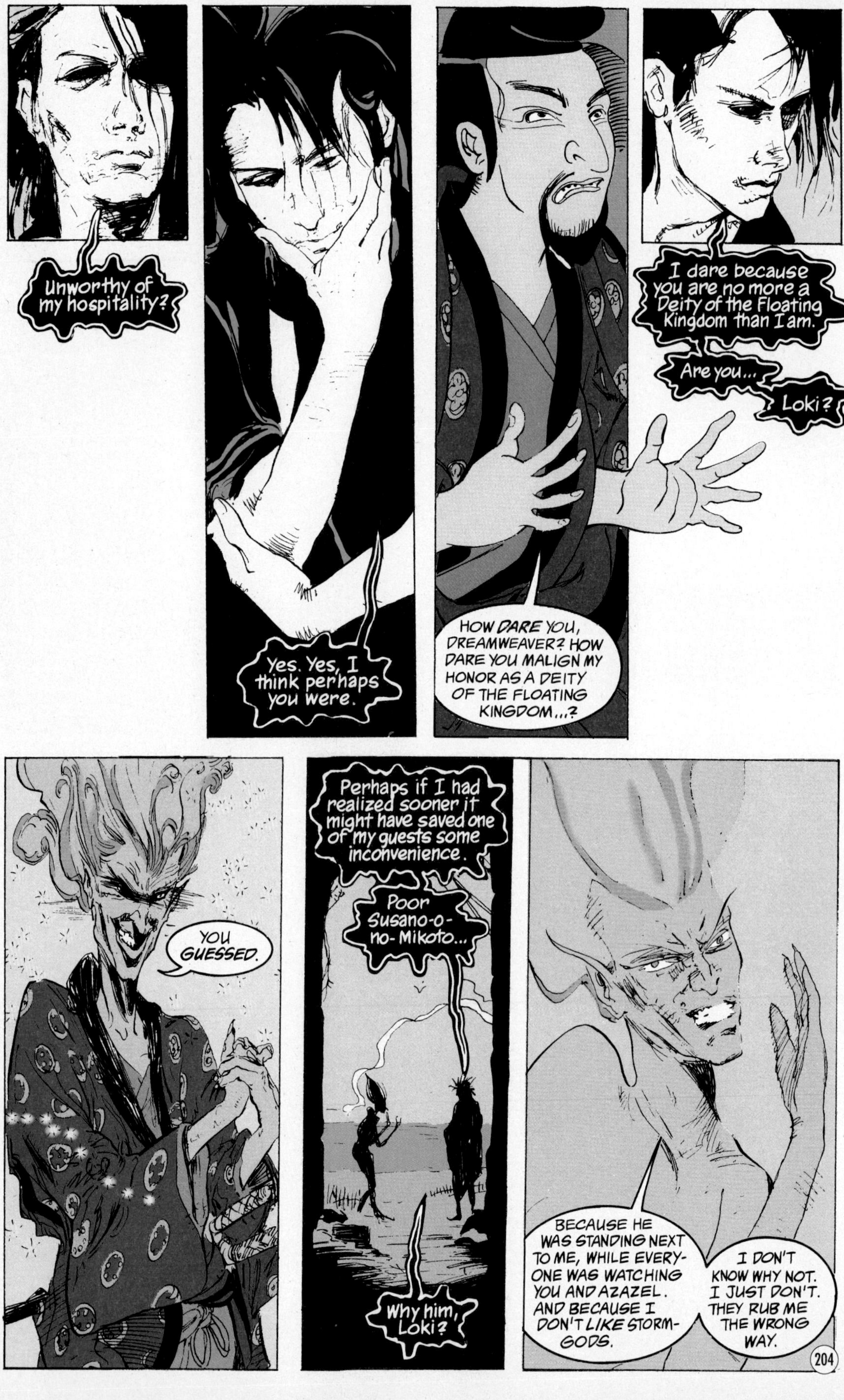
Unworthy of my hospitality?
Yes. Yes, I think perhaps you were.
HOW DARE YOU, DREAMWEAVER? HOW DARE YOU MALIGN MY HONOR AS A DEITY OF THE FLOATING KINGDOM...?
I dare because you are no more a Deity of the Floating Kingdom than I am.
Are you...
Loki?
YOU GUESSED.
Perhaps if I had realized sooner it might have saved one of my guests some inconvenience.
Poor Susano-o-no-Mikoto...
Why him, Loki?
BECAUSE HE WAS STANDING NEXT TO ME, WHILE EVERY-ONE WAS WATCHING YOU AND AZAZEL. AND BECAUSE I DON'T LIKE STORM-GODS.
I DON'T KNOW WHY NOT. I JUST DON'T. THEY RUB ME THE WRONG WAY.

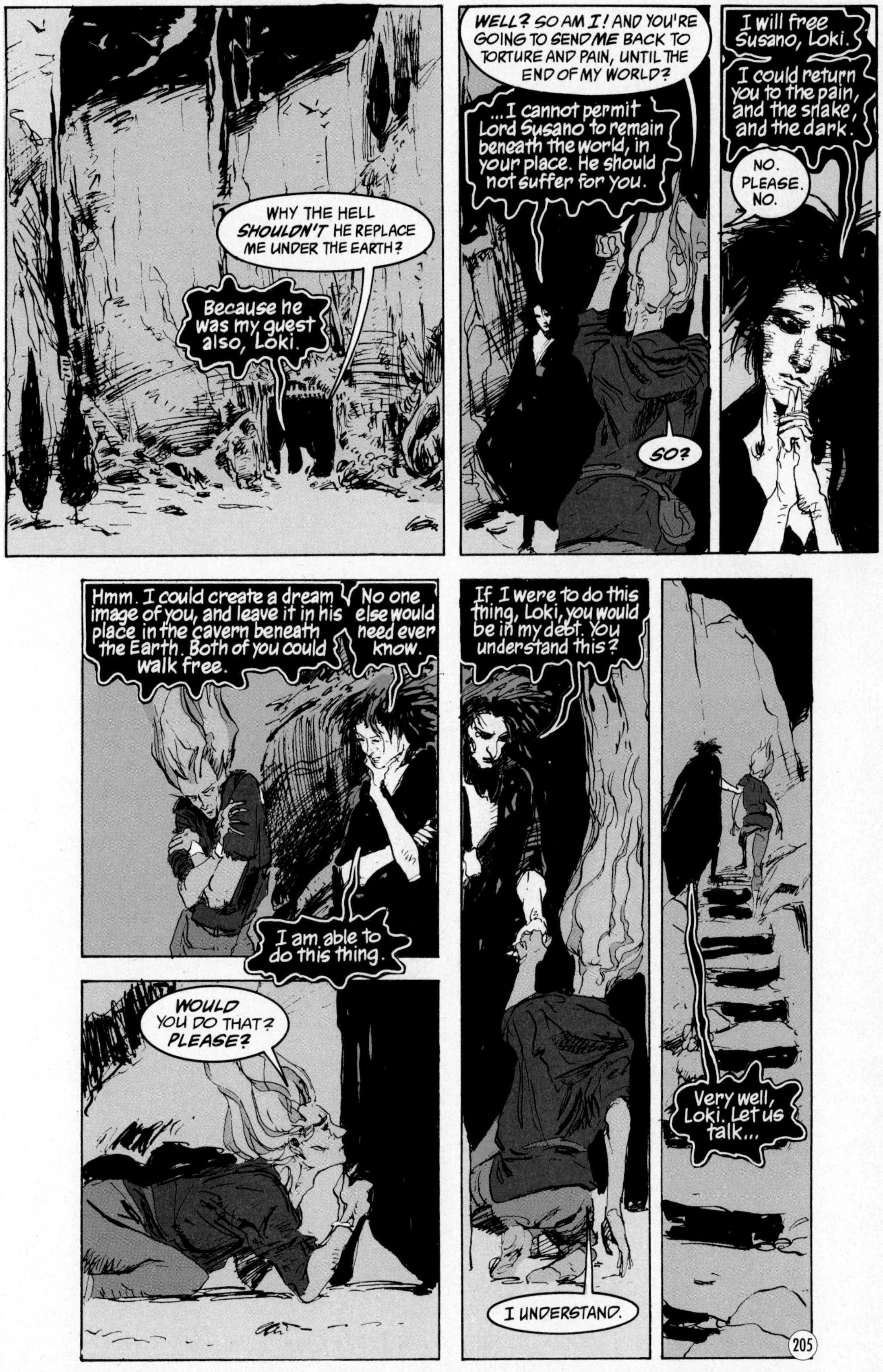
WHY THE HELL SHOULDN'T HE REPLACE ME UNDER THE EARTH?
Because he was my guest also, Loki.
WELL? SO AM I! AND YOU'RE GOING TO SEND ME BACK TO TORTURE AND PAIN, UNTIL THE END OF MY WORLD?
...I cannot permit Lord Susano to remain beneath the world, in your place. He should not suffer for you.
SO?
I will free Susano, Loki.
I could return you to the pain, and the snake, and the dark.
NO. PLEASE. NO.
Hmm. I could create a dream image of you, and leave it in his place in the cavern beneath the Earth. Both of you could walk free.
No one else would need ever know.
I am able to do this thing.
WOULD YOU DO THAT? PLEASE?
If I were to do this thing, Loki, you would be in my debt. You understand this?
I UNDERSTAND.
Very well, Loki. Let us talk...

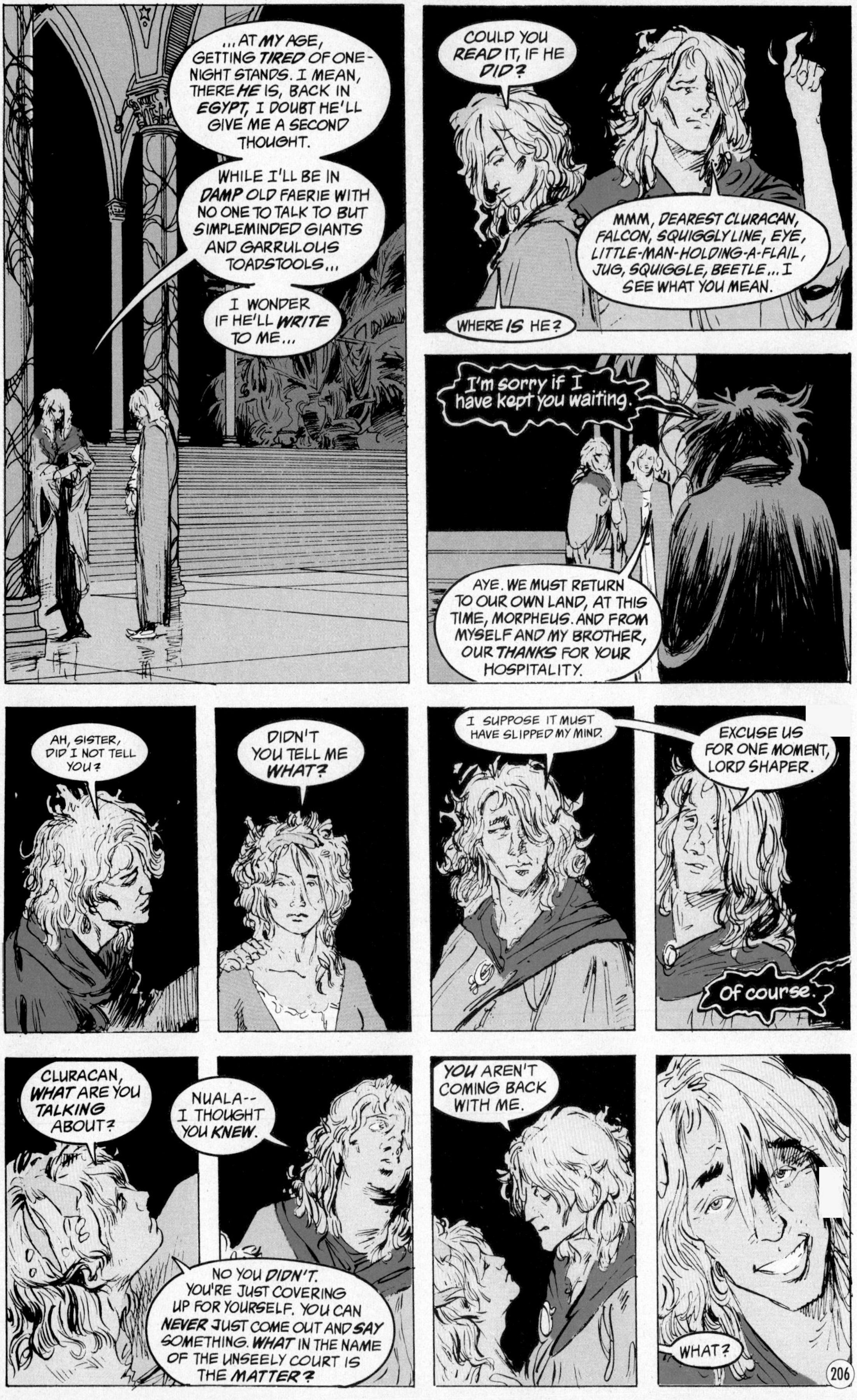
...AT MY AGE, GETTING TIRED OF ONE-NIGHT STANDS. I MEAN, THERE HE IS, BACK IN EGYPT, I DOUBT HE'LL GIVE ME A SECOND THOUGHT.
WHILE I'LL BE IN DAMP OLD FAERIE WITH NO ONE TO TALK TO BUT SIMPLEMINDED GIANTS AND GARRULOUS TOADSTOOLS...
I WONDER IF HE'LL WRITE TO ME...
COULD YOU READ IT, IF HE DID?
MMM, DEAREST CLURACAN, FALCON, SQUIGGLY LINE, EYE, LITTLE-MAN-HOLDING-A-FLAIL, JUG, SQUIGGLE, BEETLE... I SEE WHAT YOU MEAN.
WHERE IS HE?
I'm sorry if I have kept you waiting.
AYE. WE MUST RETURN TO OUR OWN LAND, AT THIS TIME, MORPHEUS. AND FROM MYSELF AND MY BROTHER, OUR THANKS FOR YOUR HOSPITALITY.
AH, SISTER, DID I NOT TELL YOU?
DIDN'T YOU TELL ME WHAT?
I SUPPOSE IT MUST HAVE SLIPPED MY MIND.
EXCUSE US FOR ONE MOMENT, LORD SHAPER.
Of course.
CLURACAN, WHAT ARE YOU TALKING ABOUT?
NUALA-- I THOUGHT YOU KNEW.
NO YOU DIDN'T. YOU'RE JUST COVERING UP FOR YOURSELF. YOU CAN NEVER JUST COME OUT AND SAY SOMETHING. WHAT IN THE NAME OF THE UNSEELY COURT IS THE MATTER?
YOU AREN'T COMING BACK WITH ME.
WHAT?

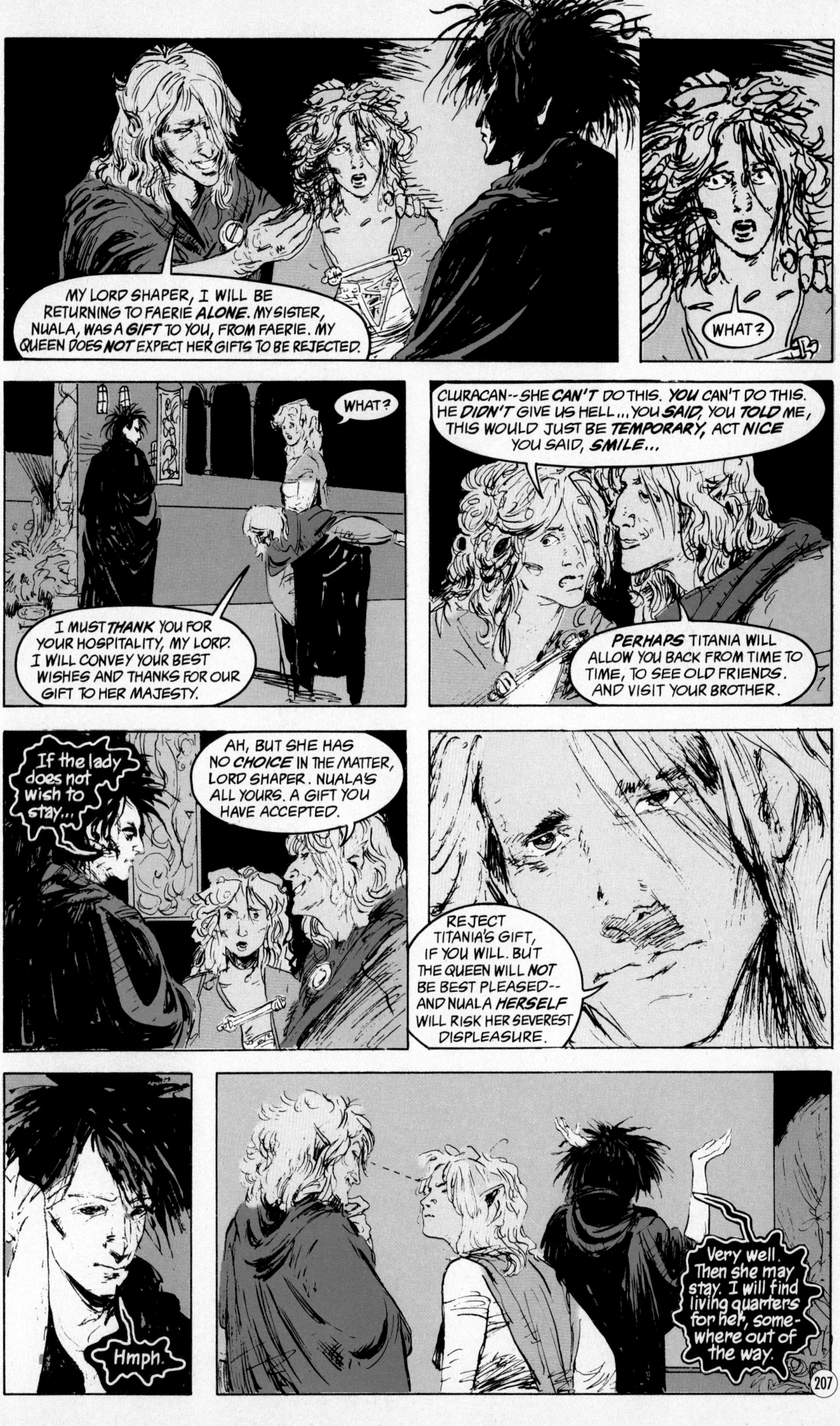

MY LORD SHAPER, I WILL BE RETURNING TO FAERIE ALONE. MY SISTER, NUALA, WAS A GIFT TO YOU, FROM FAERIE. MY QUEEN DOES NOT EXPECT HER GIFTS TO BE REJECTED.
WHAT?
WHAT?
I MUST THANK YOU FOR YOUR HOSPITALITY, MY LORD. I WILL CONVEY YOUR BEST WISHES AND THANKS FOR OUR GIFT TO HER MAJESTY.
CLURACAN--SHE CAN'T DO THIS. YOU CAN'T DO THIS. HE DIDN'T GIVE US HELL... YOU SAID, YOU TOLD ME, THIS WOULD JUST BE TEMPORARY, ACT NICE YOU SAID, SMILE...
PERHAPS TITANIA WILL ALLOW YOU BACK FROM TIME TO TIME, TO SEE OLD FRIENDS. AND VISIT YOUR BROTHER.
If the lady does not wish to stay...
AH, BUT SHE HAS NO CHOICE IN THE MATTER, LORD SHAPER. NUALA'S ALL YOURS. A GIFT YOU HAVE ACCEPTED.
REJECT TITANIA'S GIFT, IF YOU WILL. BUT THE QUEEN WILL NOT BE BEST PLEASED-- AND NUALA HERSELF WILL RISK HER SEVEREST DISPLEASURE.
Hmph.
Very well. Then she may stay. I will find living quarters for her, some-where out of the way.

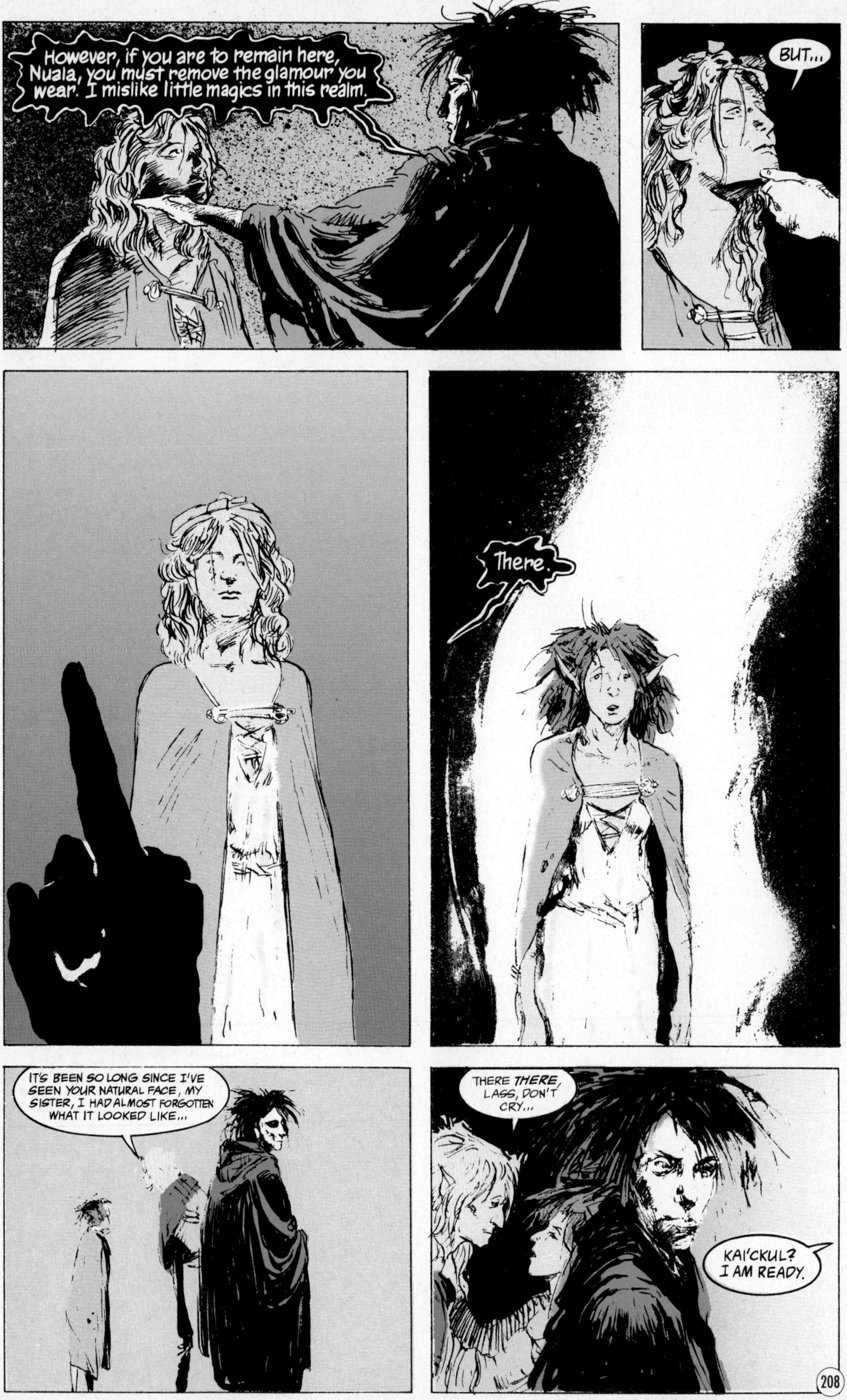
However, if you are to remain here, Nuala, you must remove the glamour you wear. I mislike little magics in this realm.
BUT...
There.
IT'S BEEN SO LONG SINCE I'VE SEEN YOUR NATURAL FACE, MY SISTER, I HAD ALMOST FORGOTTEN WHAT IT LOOKED LIKE...
THERE THERE, LASS, DON'T CRY...
KAI'CKUL? I AM READY.

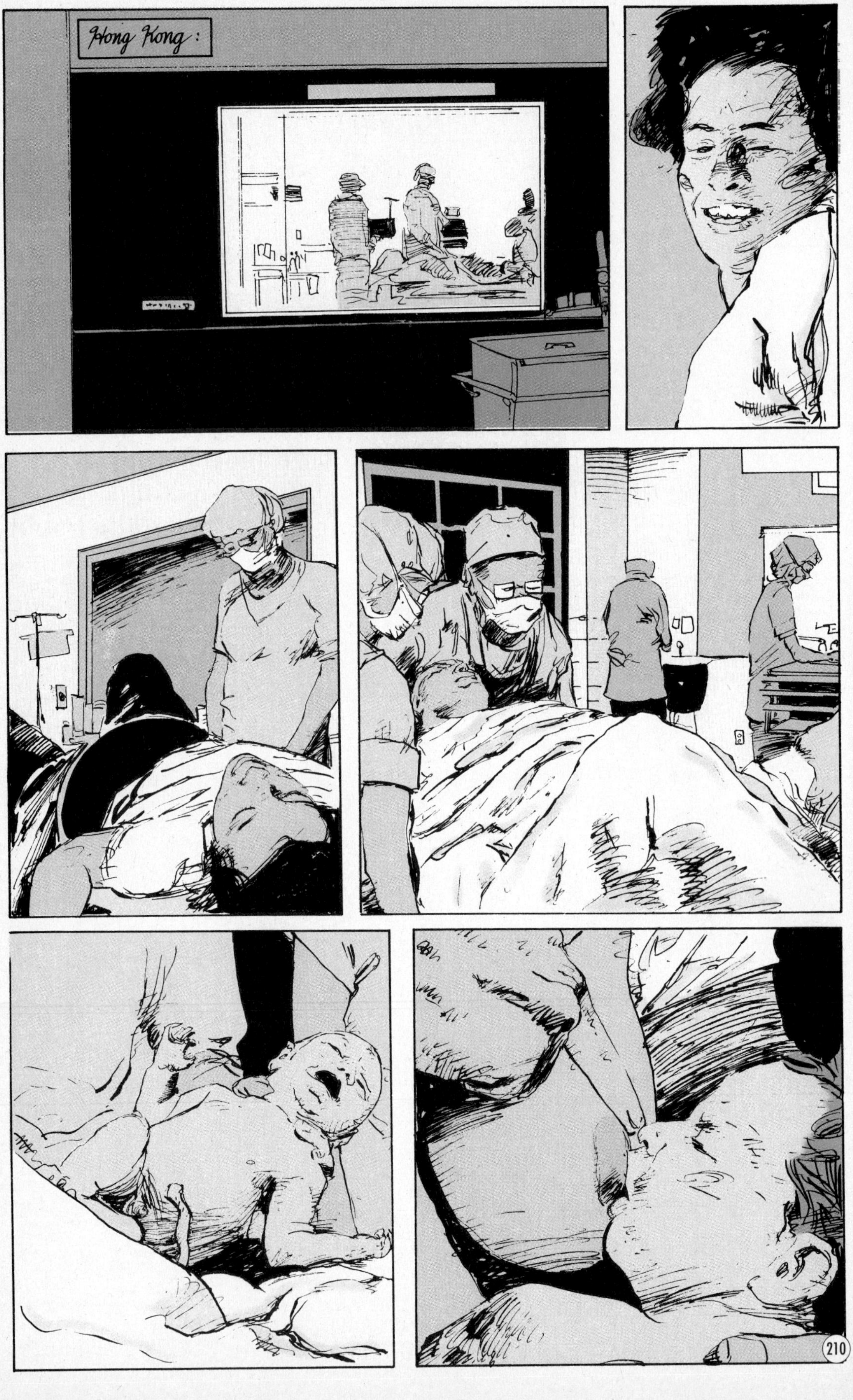
Hong Kong:

Perth, Western Australia:

Y'KNOW, I'VE SEEN YOU BEFORE, MATE. DOWN ON THE BEACH. SLEEPING *ROUGH*, ARE WE?

THERE ARE *WORSE* PLACES.

I'LL TELL YOU *THIS* FOR FREE, ANY KID WHO TRIED BATHING TOPLESS 'ROUND HERE TWENTY *YEARS* AGO, WELL, *WE'D'VE* SAID SHE WAS NO *BETTER* THAN SHE SHOULD BE.

I SUPPOSE THAT WE ARE.

IT CAN GETS A A BIT WARM IN THE DAYTIME, BUT CRACK A TUBE, OR GO FOR A DIP, AND YOU'RE RIGHT AS RAIN.

I DON'T COME DOWN HERE MUCH IN THE DAY, ME.

BEACHES ARE FOR THE *YOUNGSTERS,* IN THE DAYTIME. Y'KNOW, STARIN' AT ALL THE YOUNG SHEILAS WITH NOTHING TO COVER THEIR NEVER-YOU-MINDS.

REALLY. DO GO ON.

212

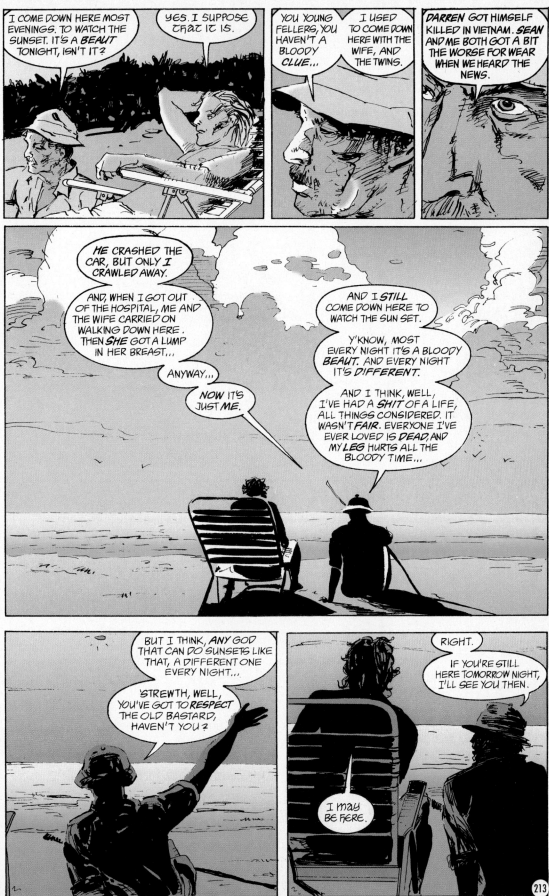

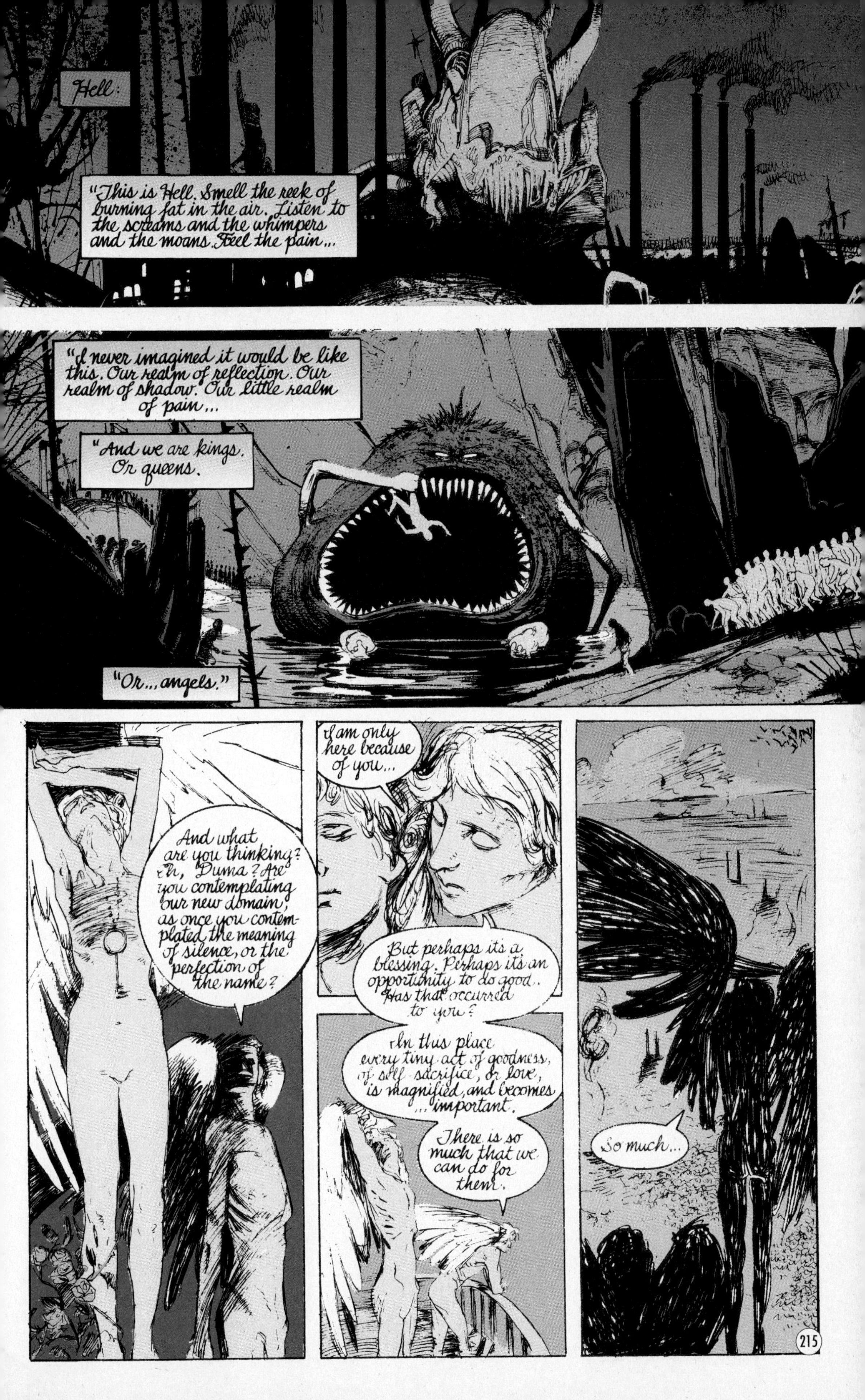
Hell:
"This is Hell. Smell the reek of burning fat in the air. Listen to the screams and the whimpers and the moans. Feel the pain...
"I never imagined it would be like this. Our realm of reflection. Our realm of shadow. Our little realm of pain...
"And we are kings. Or queens.
"Or... angels."
And what are you thinking? Eh, Duma? Are you contemplating our new domain, as once you contemplated the meaning of silence, or the perfection of the name?
I am only here because of you...
But perhaps its a blessing. Perhaps it's an opportunity to do good. Has that occurred to you?
In this place every tiny act of goodness, of self sacrifice, or love, is magnified, and becomes ... important.
There is so much that we can do for them.
So much...

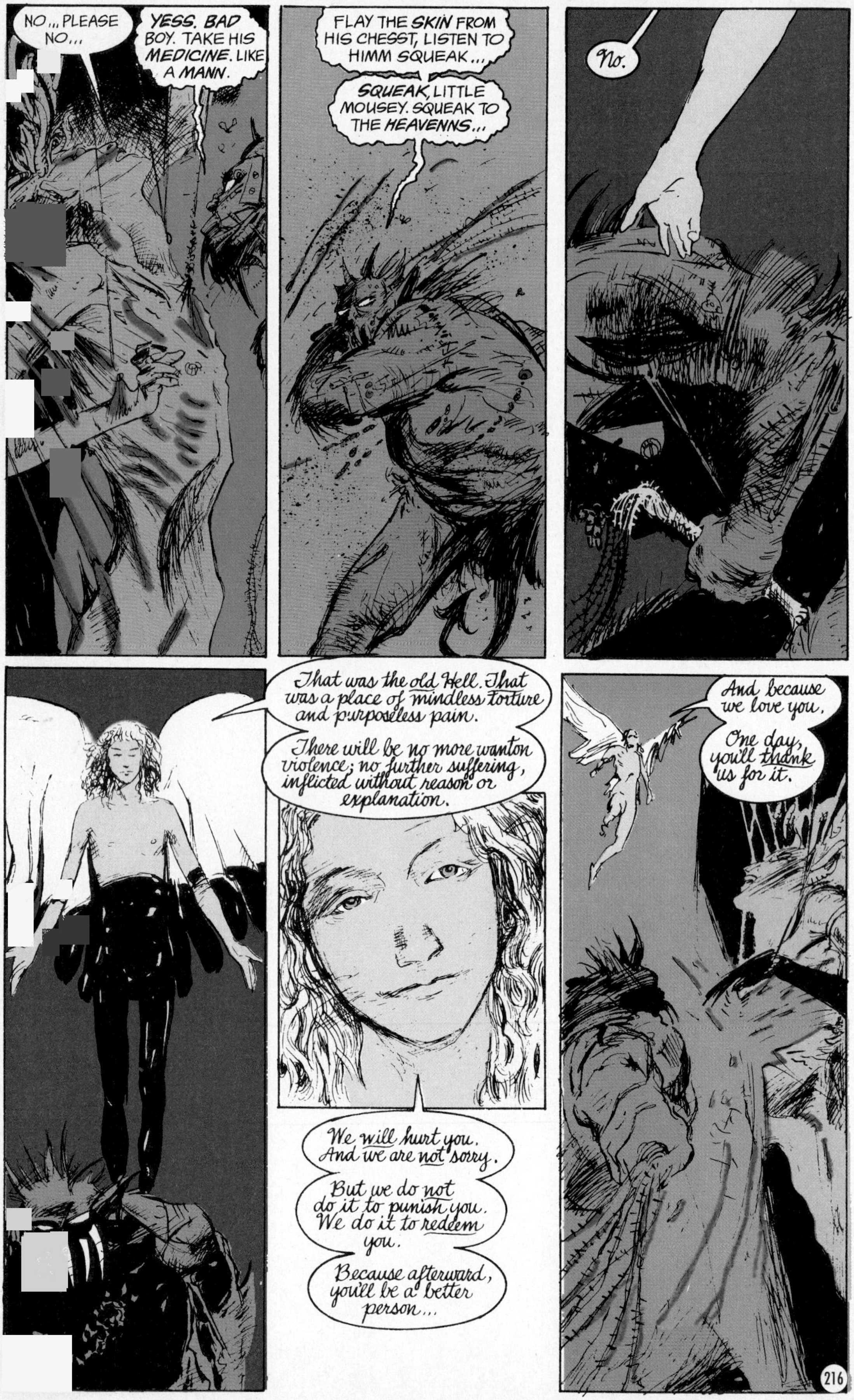
NO... PLEASE NO...
YESS. BAD BOY. TAKE HIS MEDICINE. LIKE A MANN.
FLAY THE SKIN FROM HIS CHESST, LISTEN TO HIMM SQUEAK...
SQUEAK, LITTLE MOUSEY. SQUEAK TO THE HEAVENNS...
No.
That was the old Hell. That was a place of mindless torture and purposeless pain.
There will be no more wanton violence; no further suffering inflicted without reason or explanation.
We will hurt you. And we are not sorry.
But we do not do it to punish you. We do it to redeem you.
Because afterward, you'll be a better person...
And because we love you.
One day, you'll thank us for it.

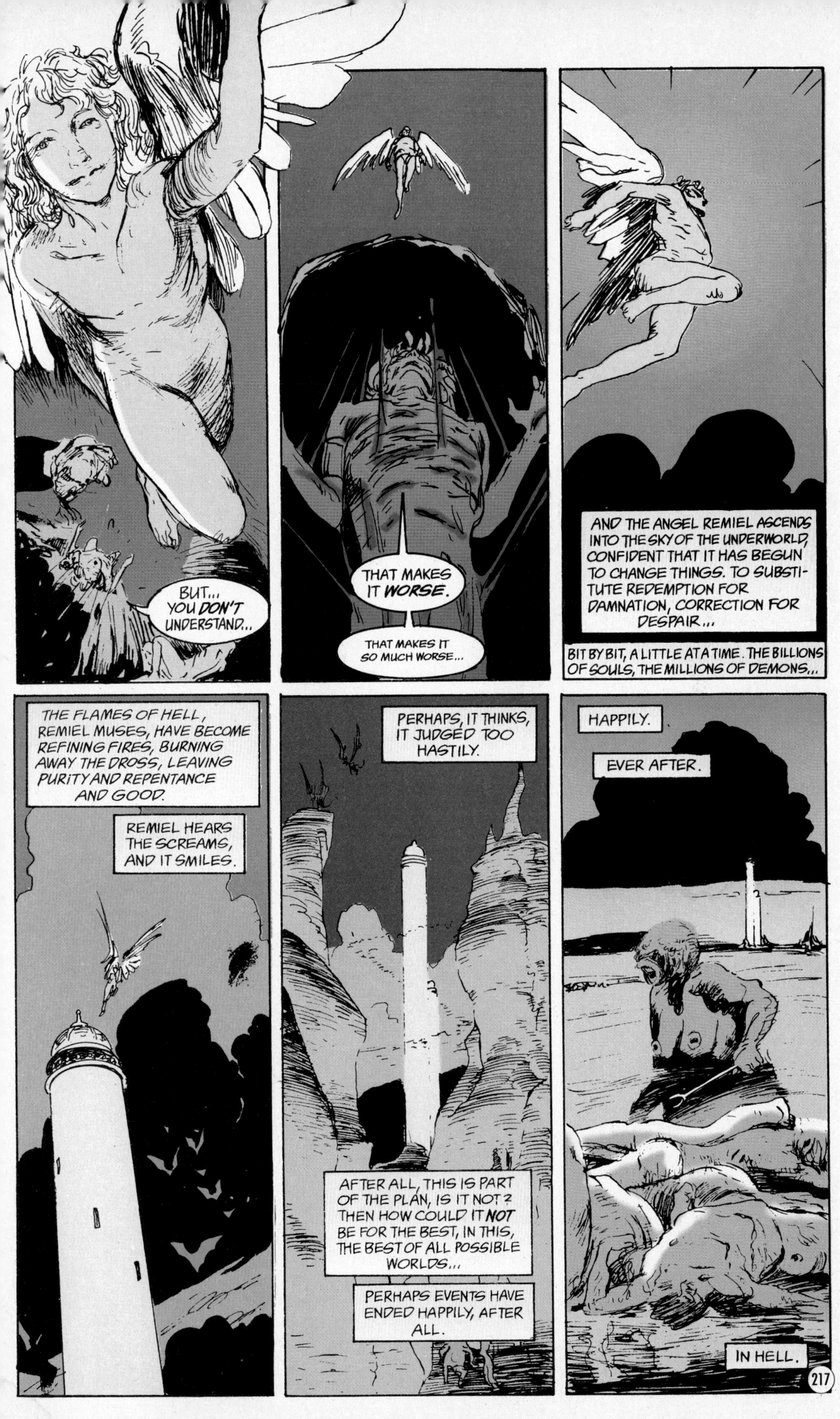
BUT... YOU DON'T UNDERSTAND...
THAT MAKES IT WORSE.
THAT MAKES IT SO MUCH WORSE...
AND THE ANGEL REMIEL ASCENDS INTO THE SKY OF THE UNDERWORLD, CONFIDENT THAT IT HAS BEGUN TO CHANGE THINGS. TO SUBSTITUTE REDEMPTION FOR DAMNATION, CORRECTION FOR DESPAIR...
BIT BY BIT, A LITTLE AT A TIME. THE BILLIONS OF SOULS, THE MILLIONS OF DEMONS...
THE FLAMES OF HELL, REMIEL MUSES, HAVE BECOME REFINING FIRES, BURNING AWAY THE DROSS, LEAVING PURITY AND REPENTANCE AND GOOD.
REMIEL HEARS THE SCREAMS, AND IT SMILES.
PERHAPS, IT THINKS, IT JUDGED TOO HASTILY.
AFTER ALL, THIS IS PART OF THE PLAN, IS IT NOT? THEN HOW COULD IT NOT BE FOR THE BEST, IN THIS, THE BEST OF ALL POSSIBLE WORLDS...
PERHAPS EVENTS HAVE ENDED HAPPILY, AFTER ALL.
HAPPILY.
EVER AFTER.
IN HELL.

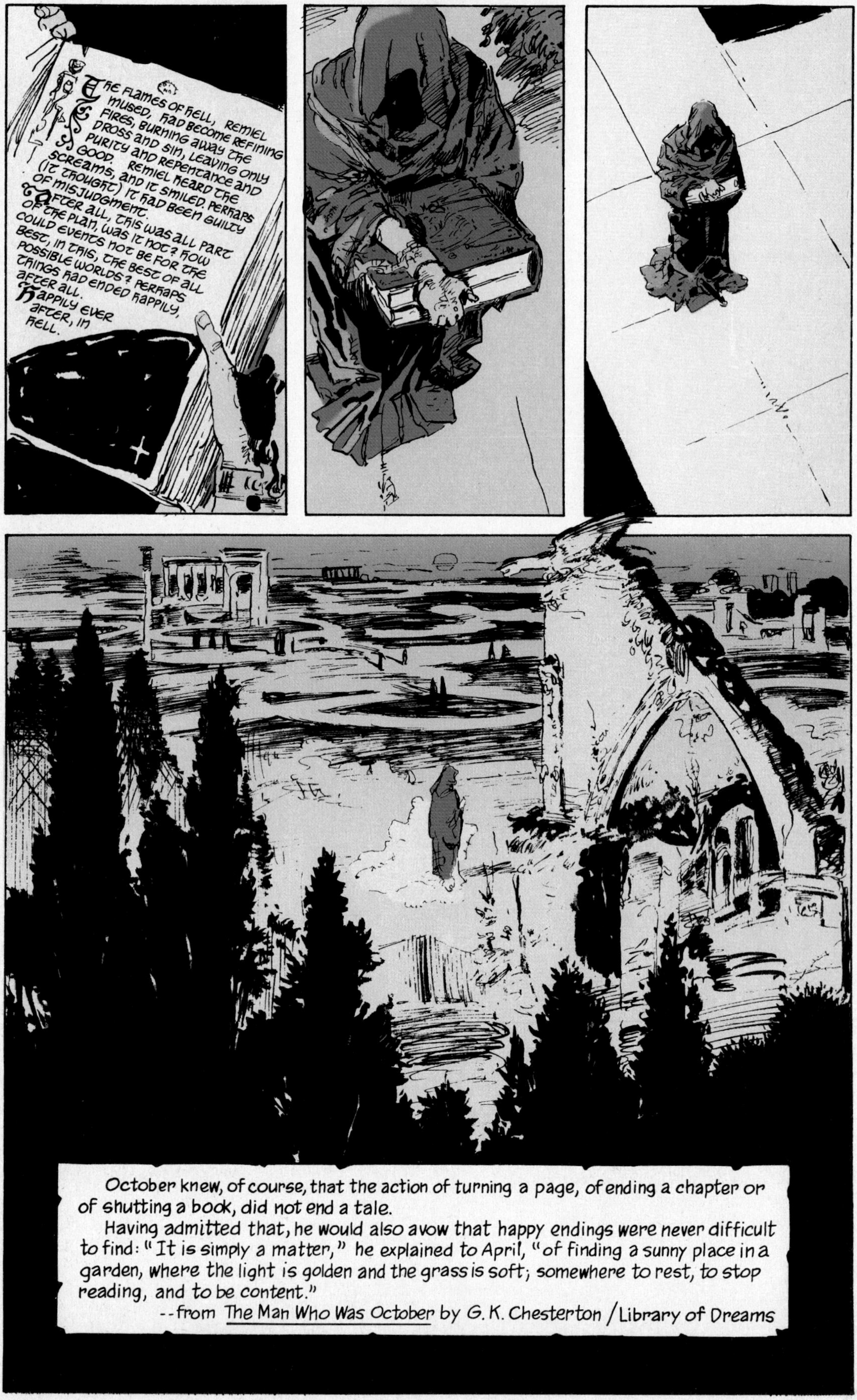
THE FLAMES OF HELL, REMIEL MUSED, HAD BECOME REFINING FIRES, BURNING AWAY THE DROSS AND SIN, LEAVING ONLY PURITY AND REPENTANCE AND GOOD. REMIEL HEARD THE SCREAMS, AND IT SMILED. PERHAPS (IT THOUGHT) IT HAD BEEN GUILTY OF MISJUDGMENT.
AFTER ALL, THIS WAS ALL PART OF THE PLAN, WAS IT NOT? HOW COULD EVENTS NOT BE FOR THE BEST, IN THIS, THE BEST OF ALL POSSIBLE WORLDS? PERHAPS THINGS HAD ENDED HAPPILY, AFTER ALL.
HAPPILY EVER AFTER, IN HELL.
October knew, of course, that the action of turning a page, of ending a chapter or of shutting a book, did not end a tale.
Having admitted that, he would also avow that happy endings were never difficult to find: "It is simply a matter," he explained to April, "of finding a sunny place in a garden, where the light is golden and the grass is soft; somewhere to rest, to stop reading, and to be content."
--from The Man Who Was October by G.K. Chesterton / Library of Dreams

b i o g r a p h i e s

NEIL GAIMAN
writer

To set certain popular misconceptions to rest once and for all:

1) He was not found wandering the sewers of London as a child during the winter of 1864, unable to say anything more than "Powerful big rats, gentlemen."

2) He was never exhibited in public houses to the curious; only briefly in July, 1865, to selected gentlemen of standing from the scientific and literary community.

3) He did not have a vestigial tail.

4) He did indeed have what most people would commonly understand as "eyes."

5) He was not actually the pilot of the Zeppelin, although he did disappear for good following the explosion.

6) There is quite obviously no "underground kingdom beneath London inhabited by huge, intelligent rodents." And even if there were, any suggestion of Neil's involvement in the mazy territorial negotiations between Londons Above and Below can be considered a joke, and in poor taste at that.

7) He was afraid of neither mirrors nor street conjurers.

8) There were no tooth-marks on the bones.

KELLEY JONES
penciller
episodes 1,2,3,5,6

When he was born, in 1802, Kelley Jones had every appearance of being in his mid-nineties. He astonished physicians by growing younger with each year that passed. This photograph, taken in his seventieth year, appears to be that of a man in his twenties. He died as an infant in 1888, killed in a nursery fire. A recording of his voice reciting Keats's '*To Autumn*' was discovered on the telephone answering machine of a taxi company in Toronto in 1979, but was erased by a temporary secretary who failed to understand its worth.

by NEIL GAIMAN

MIKE DRINGENBERG
penciller
episodes 0,∞

"... all of the people were coming and I said to them and I said, there's no hope for me here, none of them have faces, always walking, and I never saw any of them before, and they keep touching me in the night, always in the night, sometimes when the rain comes, and no-one sees them but me, grey eyes maybe screaming, and I said to them, and I said to them ..."

P. CRAIG RUSSELL
inker
episode 3

The details of his black life and dubious death are written in certain books, and the foolish and the curious may seek them out. Nothing could induce us to elaborate here: by comparison Gilles de Rais was an angel in human form, and de Sade a weak and simpering child. The world is well rid of him—if rid of him it truly is.

MATT WAGNER
penciller
episode 4

Matt Wagner was the only man to be elected posthumously to the United States Senate. He served three terms before being narrowly defeated by a living candidate in 1874, whereupon he retired from public life. Until recently his jawbone was on display in the Smithsonian Institution.

GEORGE PRATT
inker
episodes 5,∞

Documented cases of spontaneous human combustion are rare; however, in all the annals of this phenomenon, only George Pratt was able to combust on cue. As a thaumaturgic Music Hall 'turn,' Mister Pratt would ignite on stage, in front of a paying audience, whereupon Millicent Wirth, his lover and assistant, would extinguish the blaze with a patent liquid of Pratt's own invention. This photograph was taken of 'Combustible George' the afternoon before his final performance, in Boston, in 1901. 'Miss Millie's' subsequent trial and acquittal was a *cause célèbre* for many weeks. Fifty years later she filled a bathtub with gasoline and climbed into it, naked, holding a lighted taper.

MALCOLM JONES III
inker
episodes 0,1,2

This photograph of one of Malcolm Jones's three homunculi was originally published in the *Journal of the American Society for Psychical Knowledge*. Measuring no more than six inches in height, these tiny creatures were, it is said, capable of human speech, and were wholly subordinate to Jones's will. None of them survived Jones by more than a week, disintegrating to dried blood, rose petals and ashes.

DICK GIORDANO
inker
episode 6

Impresario, shipping magnate, oil baron, surgeon, and philanthropist. One Thursday morning in November, 1893, Giordano took his usual table at the Savoy Hotel and requested the waiter bring him 'a newspaper, a bootjack, the Bible, a pint of vinegar, a paper of pins, and some barley sugar.' Upon the waiter's refusal to comply with this extraordinary request, Giordano's face dissolved into silent tears. "Aye, me, sir," he said, "you have condemned an honest man to his doom." Thereupon he hailed a cab, and was heard to tell the driver to take him to his office, a journey of no more than fifteen minutes. He was, of course, never seen again, although his tiepin was cut from the stomach of a twenty-five pound sturgeon caught in the Black Sea on the first day of World War One.

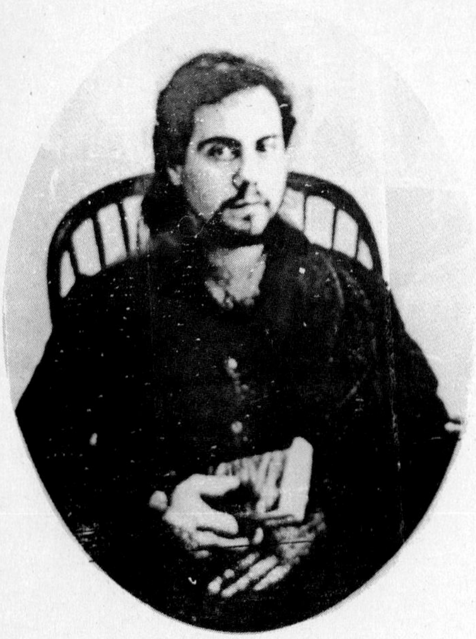

DANIEL VOZZO

colourist

episodes 2,3,4,5,6,∞

Professor Vozzo's handbook, *Ten Thousand Important Questions Resolved for the Modern Gentleman*, issued in monthly parts from October 1889 on, contained essays on such vital subjects as: *"Is dancing, as usually conducted, compatible with a high standard of morality?" "Was the purchase of Alaska by this government wise?" "Does the study of physical sciences militate against religious belief?" "Has our government a right to disfranchise the polygamists of Utah?"*

Not satisfied with resolving these questions, and many others of equal import, by 1894 he began to address such issues as: *"Is there a purpose to existence?"* and *"What is the composition of the Philosopher's Stone?"*

At this time Vozzo began to complain of being followed by women with the faces of animals. All copies of the latter installments of his handbook were bought up by an anonymous cartel, and destroyed, and shortly thereafter Vozzo was removed to a private asylum. He is still there, and he has not aged, although on the advice of a long-dead physician his tongue was surgically removed, and he is permitted no writing materials.

STEVE OLIFF

colourist

episodes 0,1

Best known for his revolutionary embalming techniques. Upon his death in 1897 his collection of perfectly preserved schoolchildren was donated to the Royal College of Surgeons. It may be inspected by prior appointment, although several of the older boys were damaged by falling masonry during the Blitz, and have been removed from the permanent exhibition.

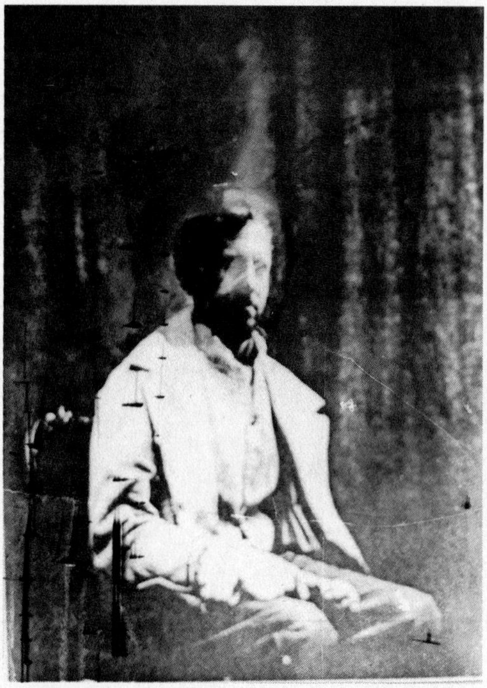

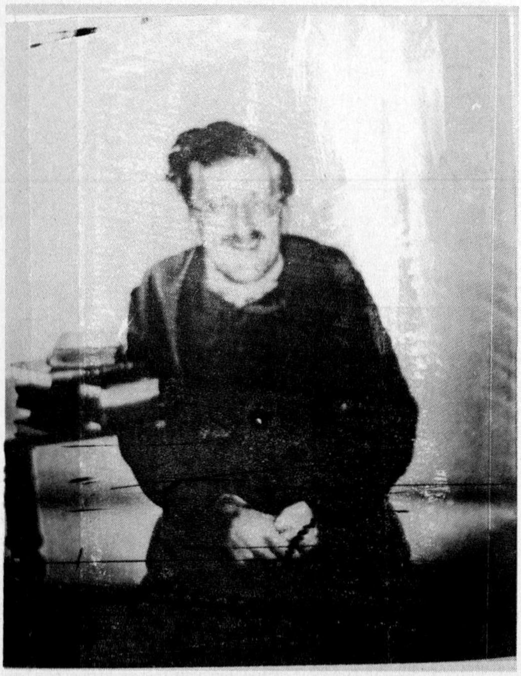

TODD KLEIN

letterer

Was never convicted of any capital crime, for reasons that still remain shrouded in mystery.

KAREN BERGER
editor

They say she done them all of them in. They say she done it with an axe.

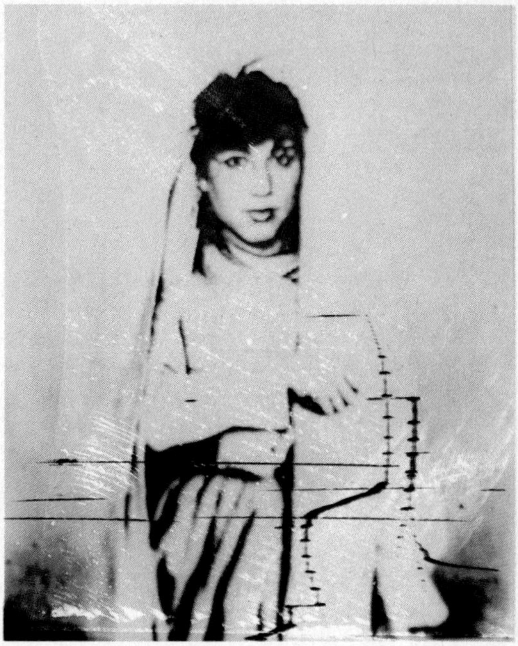

ALISA KWITNEY
assistant editor

According to an old New York folk-tale, Alisa Kwitney appears in a bathroom mirror to people in the final stages of *delirium tremens*, and pleads with them to mend their ways. In another version of the same story she can be induced (by threatening to break the mirror) to reveal winning lottery ticket numbers.

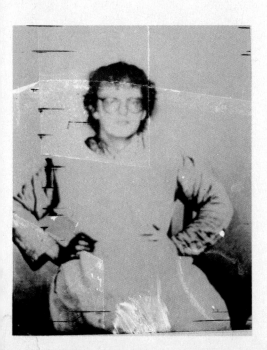

TOM PEYER
assistant editor

Notorious for his cross-dressing during a period when society frowned on such hobbies, Peyer (the illegitimate son of Francis Egerton, the Eighth Earl of Bridgewater and self-styled Prince of the Holy Roman Empire), was arrested at the outbreak of the Crimean War for singing an obscene ballad in a public place while dressed as a washerwoman. The ballad, in the *Parlarie* Argot, went as follows:

> *Nanti dinarly; the omee of the khazi*
> *Says due bionc peroney, manjaree on the cross.*
> *We'll all have to scarper the latty in the morning*
> *Before the bona omee of the khazi shakes his doss.*

DAVE McKEAN
covers and design

This photograph, found in the Hanussen collection, appears at a hasty first glance to be a portrait of a bearded man in a hat, his coat glittering with five brass buttons. A second, and more careful look reveals that this is simply an illusion: we are looking from above at a snowy landscape: the 'coat' is a river, the 'buttons' stepping stones, the 'face' an island, and a fallen tree, the 'hat' a small body of water in the distance. Photographic illusions of this kind were popular with our forefathers; to our more sophisticated eyes, however, the deception is transparent, and once we see it for what it is, we are unable to see the face that once we thought we saw. The seagull in the foreground is extremely blurred, due to the lengthy exposures Victorian photography demanded.

HARLAN ELLISON
introduction

Harlan Ellison is the author of fifty-eight books and is listed in the *Swedish National Encyclopedia*.